Writing Spaces:
Travel, Global Cities and
Landscapes

Eds. I-Chun Wang, Mary Theis, and Christopher Larkosh

Center for the Humanities
National Sun Yat-sen University

National Sun Yat-sen University
Humanities and Social Sciences Series and
the Sun Yat-sen Journal of Humanities Series

Published in 2013 by the Center for the Humanities
and the College of Liberal Arts, National Sun Yat-sen
University, 70 Lien-Hai Road, Kaohsiung 80424, Taiwan

Published with financial assistance by
National Sun Yat-sen University

Printed and bound in Taiwan by OKprint, Kaohsiung

Writing Spaces: Travel, Global Cities and Landscapes
Edited by   I-Chun Wang, Mary Theis,
and Christopher Larkosh
Editorial assistant: Chein-Hang Liu

書名(英文)：Writing Spaces: Travel, Global Cities
　　　　　　and Landscapes
發行人：國立中山大學
主編：I-Chun Wang (王儀君)、Mary Theis、
　　　Christopher Larkosh
出版者：國立中山大學人文研究中心
地址：80424 高雄市鼓山區蓮海路 70 號
電話：(07)5252000 轉 3241
傳真：(07)5250818
網址：http://humanitiescenter.nsysu.edu.tw/
發行日期：中華民國 102 年 8 月
定價：新台幣 280 元
展售處：國家書店
　　　　五南文化廣場
　　　　高雄復文書局
　　　　高雄市蓮海路 70 號/ (07)525-0930
版次：初版
印刷：六合打字行
ISBN: 978-986-03-7590-9
GPN: 1010201438

Writing Spaces: Travel, Global Cities and Landscapes
Editors: I-Chun Wang, Mary Theis, and Christopher Larkosh

Table of Contents

Spaces and Landscape Writing

Introduction: Writing Spaces: Travel, Cities and Spatial Writing

I-Chun Wang

Landscape description has been a significant element in travel literature. In the past ten years probably because of growing awareness of nature and environment, landscape writing has been a trend signifying the relationship between nature and the humans, the discrepancies between the civilized and the primitive, as well as the ways of interpreting lives of the past and the present. Landscape descriptions in tales of travelers are never exhaustive; some are informative and some are dramatic. Travelers may look into the past with nostalgic mood and some wayfarers tend to unveil the cultures of unknown lands. Robyn Davidson says, travel books may elaborate "home and abroad, occident and orient, center and periphery" but travel books can be "deceptive" because they "create the illusion that there is still an uncontaminated Elsewhere to discover" (6); namely, spatial writing in travel literature can be allegorical, symbolic and at the same time critical and descriptive. Sophisticated readers are always fascinated by the descriptions of *terra incognita* and alarmed by the comments on ruins and contaminated environment. However, we also notice spatial writing in different periods carries different meanings. As Emily C. Bartels said, in Renaissance England "the rise of cross-cultural interest and exchange was accompanied by an intensified production and reproduction of visions of "other" worlds" (433).

Morocco, geographically the most westerly among the North African countries, and a country lying across the Strait of Gibraltar, is a good example. Morocco was part of the Roman province of Mauritania and since the 8th century it has been influenced by the Arabs. The relationship between England and Africa can be referred to the reign of King John of England (1116-1216) when he dispatched a secret agent to secure Moroccan support to counter French power against England (Srhir 85). In the next two hundred years, European history witnessed King John of Portugal seized Ceuta, the French established trading post in St. Louis, the present Senegal of West Africa (year 1624) and the Dutch captured Goree, Elmina Castle and Luana on the west coast of Africa. The trades of gold, ivory, and pepper accelerated the demand of labor, reinforcing the development of slave trade. Although the British African Company of Merchants was founded in 1750s, Queen Elizabeth I and of England sent Edward Hogan to Morocco for saltpetre in 1577, and Austrian emperor sent Sir Anthony Sherley to Morocco in 1605 (Leo Africanus? Vol. II 369). The rivalry for African trades not only promotes mercantilism in Europe and stimulates local power to trade gold and slaves for muskets but also attracts European travelers to the multilayered culture of the Old World. Each one of them unveils trade opportunities and the landscapes of the imperial cities of Africa. William Lithgow of Lanark (1582–1645) visited Morocco, Algiers as well as Tunis and Tripoli. In his writings, he not only writes about trade relations between Levant and Tunis but also pirates and the wars and battles that happened in imperial cities. Richard Jobson talks about gold trades over the river of Gambra; Edmond Hogan, the first English Ambassador to the court of Morocco, promotes trades so that sugar and saltpeter were successfully imported by England.

This book, *Writing Spaces: Travel, Global Cities and Landscapes,* consists of three sections. The first section consists of three papers on travel literature. Claude Rawson's essay, "Gulliver, Travel and Empire," a keynote speech for 2011 International Conference held by the Center for the Humanities at National Sun Yat-sen University, discusses Gulliver's Travels as "a central document of European intellectual history, touching the most important debates about colonial exploration, conquest, and genocide" (1). Chia-Huan Chen explores the images of the Chinese as the Other in John Bell and George Anson, while Melissa Lee discusses the languages of hospitality found in Early Modern captivity narratives and how questions of acculturation and belonging. The second section focuses on the "Other" city. Borim's paper deals with aesthetics of architecture; Rajendra's paper represents South African Indian writings. Larkosh, by exploring a number of divergent narratives of colonization, displacement, imperial expansion and national consolidation, finds San Francisco as Urban "Other". Yokota-Murakam traces the reason why Osaka has become a city of carnivalesque hybridity.

The section of Spaces and Landscape Writing approaches landscapes through different perspectives. Shao finds in contemporary Taiwan literature topos of forgotten landscapes, while Barros-Grela and Bobadilla-Pérez discuss dystopian scenarios. Kocak explores the meaning of space in George Elliott Clarke's novel *George & Rue* via Michel Foucault's notion of heterotopia. Kim brings up the meanings of spaces in the cape as well as the sea. Mi's paper on homescape by discussing "jia" compares and contrasts spatial deterritorialization and cultural imagination of a new home in modern Chinese literature. Spatial imagination and travel narratives discussed in the papers mentioned above not only highlight geographical experience of the people but also question the relationship between the self and the other. I am grateful for the support from National Sun Yat-sen University and appreciate Professor Mary Theis and Professor Christopher Larkosh for their editorial work and suggestions. My thanks also extend to my assistant Chian-hang Liu for the production of this volume.

Works Cited

Bartels, Emily C. "Making More of the Moor: Aaron, Othello and the Renaissance Refashionings of Race." *Shakespeare Quarterly* 41.4 (1990): 433-54.

Davidson, Robyn. *The Picador book of Journeys*. London: Picador. 2002.

Rawson, Claude. "Gulliver, Travel and Empire." *Writing Spaces: Travel, Global Cities and Landscape*. Eds. I-Chun Wang, Mary Theis, and Christopher Larkosh. Kaohsiung: Center for the Humanities, 2013.

National Sun Yat-sen University, 2013

Gulliver, Travel and Empire

Claude Rawson

Gulliver's Travels is not a travel-book. Although it is formally a parody of travel-writings, a species of book Swift referred to as "abundance of Trash," but read for pleasure, travel-writing is hardly its main preoccupation.[1] The object of the parody, as often in Swift, is not the main target of the satire, but a vehicle for the expression of more central human concerns. This generic elusiveness or uncertainty contributes throughout to a certain unease in the reading experience, a product of a certain hostile edginess in Swift's relations with his readers. Nor does the work conform in a simple sense to the type of moral allegory common in travel fictions which criticise a society by submitting it to a foreign perspective, or else by describing foreign societies with disconcerting similarities or shaming differences. Such allegories are of course formally apparent throughout, but they are transcended in *Gulliver's Travels* by the fact that what is under scrutiny is not any particular society or group of societies, but all societies, and indeed the radical character of the human animal itself, independently of race, sex or geographical habitat.

From the beginning, *Gulliver's Travels* is a trap for innocent readers:

> My Father had a small Estate in *Nottinghamshire*; I was the Third of five Sons. He sent me to *Emanuel-College* in *Cambridge*, at Fourteen Years old, where I resided three Years, and applied my self close to my Studies: But the Charge of maintaining me (although I had a very scanty Allowance) being too great for a narrow Fortune; I was bound Apprentice to Mr. *James Bates*, an eminent Surgeon in *London*, with whom I continued four Years; and my Father now and then sending me small Sums of Money, I laid them out in learning Navigation, and other Parts of the Mathematicks, useful to those who intend to travel, as I always believed it would be some time or other my Fortune to do. When I left Mr. *Bates*, I went down to my Father; where, by the Assistance of him and my Uncle *John*, and some other Relations, I got Forty Pounds, and a Promise of Thirty Pounds a Year to maintain me at *Leyden*: There I studied Physick two Years and seven Months, knowing it would be useful in long Voyages. (I.I)[2]

This is how the narrative begins, and how, in the first edition of 1726, the reader gains the main impression of the character at the outset. He appears at first sight as a classic example of the ingenuously "normal" observer, unlikely to be encumbered with dissident or antisocial prejudices, and plain and matter of fact in his outlook and speech. We are going to be disabused before long. Even this first impression, to an alert or knowlegeable reader, is potentially open to vague suspicions. There is a small indefinable crackle of uncertainty in "The Publisher to the Reader," signed by Gulliver's cousin Richard Sympson, of whom we know nothing yet, which precedes the narrative, and which speaks without prior context of Gulliver's prolixity, and his addiction to sailors' jargon, of which the book has had to be pruned. Some references to Gulliver's reputation for "Veracity," and to his "good Esteem among his Neighbours," acquire their full piquancy in the light of later knowledge (and there is naturally no trace yet of later complaints about corruptions in the text of the first edition). The "Publisher" (here meaning "editor," i.e. Sympson himself) also refers to the family origins of the Gullivers in Banbury, home of the Banbury saints, a hotbed of Puritanism.[3]

These lead naturally to covertly intimated wrinkles in the bland surface of the opening narrative itself. A hint of anti-Puritan or anti-Dutch sentiment might be detected, by knowing readers, in the references to Emmanuel College or the University of Leyden. Some readers have latterly suspected that the Mr. in "Mr. Bates" might have been pronounced master, and Gulliver does refer to the death of "my good Master *Bates*," a pun that may or may not be accidental. It seems, on balance, doubtful to me, not because of its smuttiness, but because the sniggering has a quite unSwiftian lack of focus, as well as on linguistic grounds (the latter, however, both as to the pronunciation of "Mr." and of the extent of currency of the word "masturbate" in 1726, non-conclusive).[4] These potential crackles of disturbance might, to the very knowing, be further compounded by the fact that the frontispiece portrait of Gulliver in 1726 gave him the same age as Swift and some resemblance of feature.[5]

But the dominant initial impact of the opening narrative is to discourage rather than stimulate guardedness. The disconcerting subtexts are initially indefinite, and of secondary force, to be fully realised only at a later stage. The main satiric undeceptions unfold only when we discover that the plain narrative is leading us to highly disingenuous territory, not only lacking in factual credibility but charged with a morally disturbing content inconsistent with the blandness of the narrative voice. A well-known aspect of the work's early history is that a number of readers were nevertheless taken in, or thought they were expected to be, by the "realism" of the manner, an old gentleman looking for Lilliput on the map, a sea captain claiming that the author had mistaken

Gulliver's home address, and an Irish bishop who prided himself on not being deceived by this pack of "improbable lies."[6]

These comic misprisions are an early index of the frustrating and indeterminate generic character of the writing: travel book? parody of travel book? fictional travel narrative? otherworldly fantasy, story or satire? and if some or all of these, in what mixture or proportion from one sentence or paragraph to the next? The stylistic indicators are unstable, and an innocent reading is never properly allowed to gain a foothold. But no one is likely to escape the teasing invitation to such a reading contained in the opening. That some readers were fully taken in was a not entirely accidental victory of hoaxmanship. However, it would have been completely counterproductive of the work's whole satiric design if most readers fell into that trap.

Accordingly, Swift took measures in a subsequent set of revisions to ensure that innocent readers were more emphatically disabused from the start. The atmosphere of elusive and self-undermining uncertainty was reinforced in the finalised text, which was included in Faulkner's four-volume edition of Swift's *Works* in 1735, with changes to text and front matter which could only compound the effect of destabilising everything the book subsequently says, not only about travel or empire, but all human affairs. Whatever other purposes may have led to these changes, there is no doubting the determination to neutralise all possibility of a naïve untroubled reading of the kind apparently encouraged by the original opening narrative, which nevertheless still survives to tease us. To begin with, the frontispiece portrait, which once gave Gulliver's name and age, now stands over the rubric "Splendide Mendax," baldly announcing that the narrative is a lie. A resemblance to known portraits of Swift may still be detected by unusually informed readers, reinforced by comparison with the portrait of Swift himself in the first volume of the *Works*, 1735, of which the revised *Gulliver's Travels* occupies volume III, where it still appears nominally as the work of Gulliver, within a collected edition of Swift's writings.[7] An uneasy subtextual traffic between "real" author and fictional narrator is continued even as the unreliable mendacity of the latter is being advertised.

Secondly, inserted among the paratexts between the frontispiece and the narrative, is the cantankerous letter to Gulliver's Cousin Sympson, first published in the 1735 edition, but fictively dated "*April* 2, 1727," i.e. six months or so after the first publication of the work on 28 October 1726, in which Gulliver expresses exasperation that the world hasn't mended "after above six Months Warning," despite the fact that his book has drawn attention to its many failings:

Behold, after above six Months Warning, I cannot learn that my Book hath produced one single Effect according to mine Intentions: I desired you would let me know by a Letter, when Party and Faction were extinguished; Judges learned and upright; Pleaders honest and modest, with some small Tincture of common Sense; and *Smithfield* blazing with Pyramids of Law-Books; the young Nobility's Education entirely changed; the Physicians banished; the female *Yahoos* abounding in Virtue, Honour, Truth and good Sense: Courts and Levees of great Ministers thoroughly weeded and swept; Wit, Merit and Learning rewarded; all Disgracers of the Press in Prose and Verse, condemned to eat nothing but their own Cotten, and quench their Thirst with their own Ink. These, and a Thousand other Reformations, I firmly counted upon by your Encouragement; as indeed they were plainly deducible from the Precepts delivered in my Book. And, it must be owned, that seven Months were a sufficient Time to correct every Vice and Folly to which *Yahoos* are subject; if their Natures had been capable of the least Disposition to Virtue or Wisdom: Yet so far have you been from answering mine Expectation in any of your Letters; that on the contrary, you are loading our Carrier every Week with Libels, and Keys, and Reflections, and Memoirs, and Second Parts; wherein I see myself accused of reflecting upon great States-Folk; of degrading Human Nature, (for so they have still the Confidence to stile it) and of abusing the Female Sex. I find likewise, that the Writers of those Bundles are not agreed among themselves; for some of them will not allow me to be Author of mine own Travels; and others make me an Author of Books to which I am wholly a Stranger.

("A Letter from Capt. Gulliver to his Cousin Sympson")

The list of complaints goes on to quarrel with the factual accuracy (including times and dates) and textual integrity of the work as published. It makes shrill professions of veracity, in contrast with the sober confidence of the opening narrative itself. It offers an initially opaque intimation of his preference for the company of his horses over that of his family after his final return. Finally, after having indignantly noted the book's failure, after six months, to bring any halt "to all Abuses and Corruptions, at least in this little Island, as I had Reason to expect," it concludes with a disavowal of any hope of mending the human race, though at the same time speaking of "some Corrections, which you may insert, if ever there should be a second Edition":

> I find likewise, that your Printer hath been so careless as to confound the Times, and mistake the Dates of my several Voyages and Returns; neither assigning the true Year, or the true Month, or Day of the Month: And I hear the original Manuscript is all destroyed, since the Publication of my Book. Neither have I any Copy left; however, I have sent you some Corrections, which you may insert, if ever there should be a second Edition . . .
>
> Indeed I must confess, that as to the People of *Lilliput, Brobdingrag*, (for so the Word should have been spelt, and not erroneously *Brobdingnag*) and *Laputa*; I have never yet heard of any *Yahoo* so presumptuous as to dispute their Being, or the Facts I have related concerning them; because the Truth immediately strikes every Reader with Conviction. And, is there less Probability in my Account of the *Houyhnhnms* or *Yahoos*, when it is manifest as to the latter, there are so many Thousands in this City, who only differ from their Brother Brutes in *Houyhnhnmland*, because they use a sort of *Jabber*, and do not go naked. I wrote for their Amendment, and not their Approbation. The united Praise of the whole Race would be of less Consequence to me, than the neighing of those two degenerate *Houyhnhnms* I keep in my Stable; because, from these, degenerate as they are, I still improve in some Virtues, without any Mixture of Vice.
>
> Do these miserable Animals presume to think that I am so far degenerated as to defend my Veracity . . .
>
> I have other Complaints to make upon this vexatious Occasion; but I forbear troubling myself or you any further. I must freely confess, that since my last Return, some corruptions of my *Yahoo* Nature have revived in me by Conversing with a few of your Species, and particularly those of mine own Family, by an unavoidable Necessity; else I should never have attempted so absurd a Project as that of reforming the *Yahoo* Race in this Kingdom; but, I have now done with all such visionary Schemes for ever.
>
> *April* 2, 1727.

The Letter to Sympson runs to six pages in the edition of 1735 (I have quoted less than half). It is intended to be lingered on, in all its disconcerting and not always self-explanatory bad temper. After a brief "Advertisement," addressing the matter of textual corruptions and adding mystifications of its own, and which itself draws attention to the ensuing Letter, the Letter to Sympson is, in the final version of 1735, the reader's first introduction to Lemuel Gulliver's *Travels into Several Remote Nations of the World*. The angry and irrational outburst is itself unsettling to encounter at the beginning of any work of fiction (or fact). Its effect on a reading of the narrative proper, when we reach its opening paragraph in I. i, is to enforce a discordant adjustment whose exact nature, in advance of the various undeceptions which unfold in the course of the narrative, cannot be satisfactorily stabilised. The voice of the Letter to Sympson is that of the disenchanted and misanthropic Gulliver whom we do not meet until the later chapters of Book IV, a fact of which we become aware only in hindsight, or on a subsequent reading.

In this sense, *Gulliver's Travels* resembles modern novels with dislocated chronologies, whose time-sequences are functions of a character's or narrator's knowledge or memory, not of linear succession, and whose full local flavour can only be apprehended after a full exposure to the fiction as a whole. [8] The effect of such intimate fictive immediacies, of the kind we encounter in Joseph Conrad, Ford Madox Ford, or William Faulkner, is foreign to the whole conception of Swift's work, which has no more interest in, or awareness of, such sophisticated forms of fictional illusion than it has with the simpler forms of verism we have seen Swift seeking to guard against, and which the Letter to Sympson was in fact an effort to counteract. The Letter is an afterthought brought in to regulate an unexpected side effect of the species of rudimentary narratorial perspective, which resembles the "historic present" in grammar, in which Gulliver recounts his voyages in the style of the person he was at the various times of the given experience, rather than as the *ex post facto* coordinator of the composition as a whole. The Letter's bewilderingly angry accents generate defenses against the fiction, not collaborative sympathy, and as the work develops we can see them as part of a continuing quarrelsome intimacy. This note comes fully into its own in the opening paragraph of the final chapter:

> Thus, gentle Reader, I have given thee a faithful History of my Travels for Sixteen Years, and above Seven Months; wherein I have not been so studious of Ornament as of Truth. I could perhaps like others have astonished thee with strange improbable Tales; but I rather chose to relate

> plain Matter of Fact in the simplest Manner and Style;
> because my principal Design was to inform, and not to
> amuse thee. (IV. xii)

This brings full circle a relationship with the reader that has in reality existed under the surface throughout, and which the revised opening including the Letter to Sympson formalised in 1735 with a revived and explicit aggressiveness. Formally too, this opening of the last chapter of the last book is a mirror of the first chapter of the first, both in their way mimicking the "plain Matter of Fact in the simplest Manner and Style" of travel-writers, and of expressing a dim view of the pretension. The mock-disavowal of "strange improbable Tales" anticipates the bishop who preened himself on finding the book "full of improbable lies." It comes in the teeth of stories of six-inch and twelve-foot human societies, flying islands, otherworldly communities, senile immortals, bestial humanoids and rational horses. The "Trash" of travel-writers, the "diverting Books" we know Swift to have been using for entertainment in 1722, is an immediate object of parody. But it comes over with far less force than the crackle of aggression against the "gentle Reader," that directly addressed a second person singular, as used here for inferiors and familiars, towards whom familiarity has bred contempt.

"My principal Design was to inform, and not to amuse thee" is a stinging variation on the Letter to Sympson's remark that "I wrote for their Amendment, and not their Approbation," which, since the Letter is a prefatory afterthought, and written for a later edition, is actually, in this as in other ways, an echo of the final chapter, and not the other way round. It is, moreover, unlikely to be an accident that, whichever was written first, the sentence from the final chapter echoes, or is echoed by, the remark to Pope on 29 September 1725, just when Swift had finished and was amending and transcribing his "Travells, in four Parts Compleat," that his intention was "to vex the world rather th[a]n divert it."[9] The variation has a peculiar sting, "vex" expressing authorial purpose outside the text, while "inform" is a poker-faced affirmation of something the reader cannot possibly take at face value, but whose factual impossibility is transcended by the moral truth of the allegory contained within it, which Gulliver's Letter to Sympson referred to as his defeated call for the world's "Amendment." If parody of mere travel-writings becomes a wholly subsidiary object of interest, it is the carrier for intense charges of inculpation against the "Remote Nations" portrayed, as these come to encompass the whole of humankind, including "thee," its hapless representative, the "gentle Reader," who, as far as the work can reveal, has committed no particular offense, only the absolute offense of being Yahoo, which implies all others, and which, in a characteristic Swiftian turn, equally encompasses the author.

So the travel, truthful or mendacious, which describes foreign lands, is not what it appears to be, an exposure of how other races behave, or even of the shortcomings of such exposures. Alien groups traduced by European invaders remain as despicable as the despisers claim, but also no different from anyone else. Humanity's despised subgroups, Indians, Irish, women, beggars, are correctly seen for what they are by people who, when the truth is known, are precisely as despicable for the same reasons. It is thus that the Yahoos, that stereotype of "all savage Nations" (IV. ii), embodying generic features of outlandish "Indians," and widely understood to refer specifically to the Irish "natives," are revealed to be biologically identical with the rest of us, ostensibly rather worse than we are, though, as is sometimes hinted, actually not quite so bad. The idea, sometimes entertained in the Ph.D. era in whose twilight we are now living, that the identity of Yahoo with Gulliver and ourselves is a crazed emanation of Gulliver's addled brain, is neutralised by the graphic episode in IV. viii in which a young Yahoo female demonstrates biological kinship by desiring to mate with him.

The process of widening inculpation, from despised subgroup to the rest of the human race, is replicated with almost schematic emphasis three years later, in *A Modest Proposal*, whose fictional argument is based on a traditional notion among European (not just English) writers that the Irish were by nature cannibal, like American Indians, to whom they were commonly assimilated.[10] Contrary to traditional misapprehensions, *A Modest Proposal* is neither a Dickensian protest at the conditions of the poor, nor a diatribe against English exploitation of Ireland, but an "economic" tract by a profiteering do-gooder who thinks the economy might be improved by exploiting the anthropophagous proclivities of the Irish natives. Swift is not friendly to these natives. He portrays them as a beggarly, thieving, adulterous riff-raff, who, if they could be taught that their bastard offspring were a cashable asset, might take better care to preserve and nourish them in infancy, and also refrain from beating their wives when they are pregnant for fear of a miscarriage. [11] As soon as the proposer has established that such a harnessing of natural cannibal propensities can be expected to result in a profitable commerce, however, it becomes unexpectedly evident that the likely consumers of the meat product will not be the native producers of the babies, but the affluent ruling groups of the settler community, the administrators, clergy and merchants with whom Swift himself is demographically and socially aligned, and who are precisely the group most inclined to refer to the natives as cannibals.

The target of the satire is the failure of these settler groups to manage their own economic interest. The proposer, like Swift himself, had once advocated curbing the ruinous behaviour of absentee landlords or the wasteful preference for fashionable English clothes over goods of Irish manufacture, and hoped in general to encourage commercial probity and patriotic good sense in his fellow citizens. As in *Gulliver's Travels*, an unstable symbiosis exists between an unSwiftian (and in this case especially outlandish) speaker, and an authorial Swift, who, in the proposer's list of virtuous but unimplemented "other Expedients" (*PW*, XII. 116-7), is placing on record his own polemical activism, from the *Proposal for the Universal Use of Irish Manufacture* (1720) to the *Drapier's Letters* (1724) and the *Short View of the State of Ireland* (1728). Swift's own pamphleteering continued indeed beyond *A Modest Proposal*, culminating in the non-ironic (and, unusually, signed) *Proposal for Giving Badges to the Beggars* (1737), which establishes Swift's attitude to Irish beggars with an explicitness which will seem unsettling to those modern readers who may detect a frisson of analogy with Nazi practices (though "badging" has a long history).[12] As in *Gulliver's Travels* again, the speaker in *A Modest Proposal* can neither be identified with Swift nor safely uncoupled from him, and many misreadings of both works are caused by critics who attempt one or the other.

Badging, incidentally, is not the only Nazi "analogy" that returns to haunt us, in either *Gulliver's Travels* or *A Modest Proposal*. Sails, clothes and other objects are manufactured from the skins of Yahoos (IV. x) or of Irish infants (*PW*, XII. 112).[13] These too have a long ancestry in the annals of human behaviour. Swift's sources would have included Herodotus and Strabo on Scythians, often described as ancestors of the Irish as well as of Amerindians.[14] Needless to say, Swift knew nothing about Nazis. Nor was he proposing a revival of atavistic technologies. He was, as André Breton understood in 1939, contemplating a species of human "cruelty" in a spirit of macabre fantasy.[15] Its disturbing playfulness does not imply approval of any possible enactment, but it does explore territory not unknown to human behaviour, as the Nazi example was to demonstrate. Swift would certainly have regarded that example as among the lowest depths to which Yahoos might sink. As Breton perceived, it is in some ways idle to ascribe approval or disapproval to a macabre jokerie designed to disturb and to shock rather than to engage moral responses. At the same time, moral concerns are inevitably activated at some level of cruel play and, in so far as punitive cruelties are the issue, the joke disparages victims and castigators alike.

Since, in *A Modest Proposal*, it is evident that the society cannot be expected to behave in its own rational interest by adopting the "other

Expedients" Swift himself had advocated, the proposer concludes that the only economically workable alternative is the cannibal-scheme, in which the natives ostensibly revert to type by producing the home-grown commodity, while it is the rulers who will actually consume it. In this unexpected displacement, the eating is done not by the presumed cannibal group, but, as I have mentioned, by those most likely to call the cannibals cannibals. The cannibal slur has tacitly widened to a commonplace political *tu quoque*, in which the colonist behaves as badly as the colonised are accused of doing (or worse). The English oppressors (i.e. the remote rulers from London who are the ultimate enemy) are for once largely unimplicated in the equation, until, in a final twist, the proposer acknowledges that he knows "*a Country which would be glad to eat up our whole Nation, without [Salt]*" (*PW*, XII. 117).

The scenario is a variation on an ancient idea in which tyranny is compared to cannibalism, as in the "people-devouring king" (*demoboros basileus*) of the *Iliad* (I. 231), an analogy developed by Plato, Aristotle, Thomas More, Erasmus and others.[16] Though often a figure of speech, this formula has variously flirted with literal connotations. Early forms of the "postcolonial" argument that European invaders are more cannibal than the cannibal "natives," as in Montaigne's famous essays "Of Cannibals" and "Of Coaches" (I. xxxi, III. vi) and *A Modest Proposal* itself, hint teasingly at literal meanings while simultaneously shrinking from them, a matter I have discussed more fully elsewhere.[17] The *Modest Proposal*'s extension of the cannibal imputation to the English oppressor is metaphorical, and one supposes that the cannibalistic local purchasers of the Irish infants, while purported to be "literal" consumers in the terms of the fiction, are intended as an allegorical figuration of Ireland's self-destructive condition, seen as self-consuming, like Stephen Dedalus's "old sow that eats her farrow," a phrase mindful of Swift's pamphlet.[18] Since the joke relies on the traditional imputation that Irish natives *are* literally cannibal, the fact that they don't themselves eat their babies acquires an additional piquancy, leaving them with the disrepute without the guilt of the deed.

This figurative fantasy, however, builds on a literal mythology, backed by recorded incidents of famine-cannibalism, concerning Irish natives. The irony is redirected, in something like Montaigne's way, to the Anglo-Irish settlers, though its further extension to the English themselves is secondary to Swift's attack on the intermediate or settler caste, which is the pamphlet's principal political target. This attack by no means exculpates the "natives," who are no more "harmless" than those of *Gulliver's Travels*, a beggarly riff-raff whose fitness for a biblical extermination from "the Face of the Earth" is the subject of a "non-ironic" outburst in *A Proposal for Giving Badges to the*

Beggars, a work which provides an essential background to the earlier ironic pamphlet (*PW*, XIII. 139). The English of London, whose menace to eat "*our whole Nation*" hovers on the perimeter, appear as an incremental afterthought to the prior surprise that it is not the natives but the settlers who are supposedly to perform the act. If they are not for once the main villains, they play their part in a widening satirical embrace, whose implication is that no one, as in *Gulliver's Travels*, escapes whipping. Their inclusion parallels the Gulliverian demography in which an inculpation, initially attached to the despised group, spreads in widening circles to all others, including the despisers and exploiters, without ever disavowing the initial inculpation. *A Modest Proposal* is a variation of the Gulliverian formula, in which what begins as a satire on Irish Yahoos, encompasses not only "all savage Nations," but their conquerors, and all intermediate groups as well, except that in the pamphlet the intermediate group is the main culprit.

This pattern of universalising inculpation underlies all aspects of *Gulliver's Travels* itself, including the topics of travel and empire. This is apprehended not primarily as a matter of doctrine or theme, but as a pervasive atmosphere of the narrative, its turns and ironies, its interplay between competing voices of satirist and narrator, and its peculiar way of inducing and sustaining a readerly discomfort bordering on disorientated panic. Much heat has been expended on the question of whether Swift is an anti-imperialist or a supporter of colonial oppression, but the issue as posed is transcended by larger perspectives. He is no friend of the Irish "natives," but denounces the English tyranny over Ireland, allegorised in the balance of terror of the Flying Island of Book III and in various other ways. Nor is he a promoter of final solutions by genocidal extermination of the kind contemplated by the Houyhnhnm Assembly in IV. ix, which he nevertheless does not disavow: "The Question to be debated was, Whether the *Yahoos* should be exterminated from the Face of the Earth." This detail has been used to align the Houyhnhnms with Nazi totalitarianism, with the implication either that Swift is in sympathy with such things, or that Swift is signalling his antipathy for the Houyhnhnms. The Houyhnhnms' language, however, echoes God's declaration, on the eve of the Flood, that "I will destroy man whom I have created from the face of the earth" (Genesis, 6.7). Swift is conscious of the allusion (Book IV, without being a religious allegory, has many allusions to Genesis). It would be difficult to argue that the book of Genesis intends God to appear as a genocidal maniac, and one must assume that the implication there, as presumably in Swift, is that humankind deserves the punishment. That the Nazis invoked the same phrase, apparently in Luther's translation, in their own extermination plans may tell us various things about our relation to killspeak (including that of Genesis).[19]

The issue resists schematic solutions of the sort that appeal to interpreters, especially those who like to portray Swift as a politically correct university chaplain. But Yahoo equals human, and if the suggestion that humans deserve the punishment has Biblical authority, the idea of exterminating the human race, as a matter of secular advocacy in a modern fiction, remains starkly shocking. On the other hand, in the terms of that fiction, the Yahoos are, in Houyhnhnm society, not fellow creatures but a species of noxious brute, like rats or insects, whom human societies exterminate for health and security reasons without traditionally raising the spectre of culpable genocide. And yet, to the "reader," Yahoos remain human or humanoid (that is indeed the main point of the fiction), and uneasiness is generated even as the allegorical terms of the fiction are allowed for. The shock remains, and the idea of human punishability is never unsaid. At the same time, the plan, while never disavowed, is never executed, and remains in an indefinite limbo in which the discredit of culpability coexists with a shrinking from the discredit of enforcing punishment, while the Houyhnhnms continue to enact unsettling analogues of future Nazi scenarios: they even consider whether they should sterilise the Yahoos instead of exterminating them, achieving the same result in a "humanely" gradualist way while benefiting from the Yahoos' labour for a generation.[20]

Swift did not know these analogues, but they are potentials of the human imagination, at the level of what Breton called "black humour," a cruel play with forbidden concepts, unrestrained, as Breton puts it, by the restrictions of morality and satire.[21] Breton saw Swift as the "véritable initiateur" of such black humour. It cannot literally be dissociated from morality or satire, certainly not in Swift's case. But it exists in a penumbral zone of inculpation and elusiveness, in which dangerous moral points are intimated in a mode of partial non-commitment, disturbing to the reader without implicating the author in unacceptable allegiances. An either-way-you-lose irony holds on to Yahoo culpability without permitting the shocking enactment of a punishment nevertheless conceded to be due.

It is one of the resources of the novel-resembling yet non-novelistic fiction of *Gulliver's Travels* to release such charged indeterminacies, which have less to do with the impersonal caprices of a post-structuralist verbal sign than with the highly focused and personal quarrel which Swift conducts with his readers through a style of uniquely intimate and slippery aggressiveness. When the narrative revisits empire for the last time, in that final chapter in which Gulliver reminds the gentle reader that his "principal Design was to inform, and not to amuse thee," this aggressiveness is filtered through an elaborate orchestration of narrative voices, in which the character Gulliver and the controlling voice of the satirist, while pointedly and necessarily distinct, interpenetrate one another unremittingly.

A few paragraphs later, in a fit of citizenly responsibility, Gulliver considers his obligation "as a Subject of *England*, to have given in a Memorial to a Secretary of State, at my first coming over; because, whatever Lands are discovered by a Subject, belong to the Crown" (IV. xii). The reader is evidently being set up for an anti-imperialist diatribe, and will not be disappointed. But the payoff is characteristically not quite what we expect, though it is not in every way unexpected either. In his principled way, Gullliver will not perform this particular "Duty." The Lilliputians are hardly worth the expense, while conquest of the other nations would not "be as easy as those of *Ferdinando Cortez* over the naked *Americans*." Gulliver doubts "whether an *English* Army would be much at their Ease with the Flying Island over their Heads," which gains piquancy from the fact that this Island is itself the instrument of English tyranny over Ireland. As to the Brobdingnagians and Houyhnhnms, we would stand no chance. Even the peace-loving Houyhnhnms, for all their incomprehension of war, would inflict a crushing defeat on any invader:

> Imagine twenty Thousand of them breaking into the Midst of an *European* Army, confounding the Ranks, overturning the Carriages, battering the Warriors Faces into Mummy, by terrible Yerks from their hinder Hoofs. (IV. xii)

The gloating of the detail is very unHouyhnhnm-like. It has something of that "great Diversion of all the Spectators" which Gulliver identified as a nasty feature of the European conduct of war in his description to the Master Houyhnhnm (IV. v). There, and in his parallel rhapsody on gunpowder to the King of Brobdingnag (II. vii), Gulliver himself is gloating too, but to his discredit rather than (as we clearly sense in IV. xii) with some complicit participation from his author, one of many signs of Swift's overt participation in the things he satirises.

The anti-imperial irony remains broadly on message throughout these local wrinkles and disturbances. The gloating at the warriors' faces battered into mummy may be put down to Gulliver's misanthropy, by now a bit unhinged, but it crackles with a serves-them-right satisfaction that is consistent with the words about destroying the Yahoos from the face of the earth, and there is a clear sense that Swift is adjusting the distance between himself and his speaker to take account of this. An even more significant disturbance occurs within, and just after, Gulliver's most eloquent and impassioned diatribe against colonial conquest, as he concludes his reasons for not reporting his discovered territories to the government:

> To say the Truth, I had conceived a few Scruples with relation to the distributive Justice of Princes upon those Occasions. For Instance, A Crew of Pyrates are driven by a Storm they know not whither; at length a Boy discovers Land from the Top-mast; they go on Shore to rob and plunder; they see an harmless People, are entertained with Kindness, they give the Country a new Name, they take formal Possession of it for the King, they set up a rotten Plank or a Stone for a Memorial, they murder two or three Dozen of the Natives, bring away a Couple more by Force for a Sample, return home, and get their Pardon. Here commences a new Dominion acquired with a Title by *Divine Right*. Ships are sent with the first Opportunity; the Natives driven out or destroyed, their Princes tortured to discover their Gold; a free Licence given to all Acts of Inhumanity and Lust; the Earth reeking with the Blood of its Inhabitants: And this execrable Crew of Butchers employed in so pious an Expedition, is a *modern Colony* sent to convert and civilize an idolatrous and barbarous People. (IV. xii)

This is one of the great denunciations of imperial conquest, in the tradition of Las Casas and Montaigne.[22] It may be commensurate with Gulliver's anger, but seems wholly outside his normal powers of eloquence, which clearly derive from authorial endorsement, except that that endorsement is itself undermined by the description of the conquered natives as "an harmless People." This is consistent with nothing that we have been shown in the rest of the work, and is stridently at odds both with the Yahoos, the representatives of "all savage Nations," and the real-life savages of New Holland who had recently harassed Gulliver on his expulsion from Houyhnhnmland. The phrase corresponds to no reality offered anywhere in the text, and seems to exist solely to highlight the even greater barbarity of the European conquerors. The whole passage, far from being an expression either of Gulliver's character, or some Swiftian compassion for oppressed peoples, exists in a twilight zone between both, without being either. It may not be an exaggeration to say that the "harmless People" no more invite compassion than the beggarly rabble of *A Modest Proposal*, and that the satire is telling us mainly that while the rabble we despise is no better than it should be, "our" own conduct is no better and probably worse.

Which brings us to a further turn in the irony, when, in the immediately succeeding paragraph, Gulliver voices another disconcerting redirection:

> But this Description, I confess, doth by no means affect the *British* Nation, who may be an Example to the whole World for their Wisdom, Care, and Justice in planting Colonies; their liberal Endowments for the Advancement of Religion and Learning; their Choice of devout and able Pastors to propagate *Christianity*; their Caution in stocking their Provinces with People of sober Lives and Conversations from this the Mother Kingdom; their strict Regard to the Distribution of Justice, in supplying the Civil Administration through all their Colonies with Officers of the greatest Abilities, utter Strangers to Corruption: And to crown all, by sending the most vigilant and virtuous Governors, who have no other Views than the Happiness of the People over whom they preside, and the Honour of the King their Master. (IV. xii)

The passage also belongs to a long line of self-approving compliments to British imperial prowess, superior in its Protestant probity and civic decency to the inhumane doings of the Spanish Black Legend and the murderous extortions of the other Catholic powers. Such celebrations go back at least as far as Hakluyt and continue, long after Swift, not only in jingoist effusions but from the undemagogically fastidious pens of Edward Gibbon and Joseph Conrad, with his "red" places on the map, where "real work is done."[23] One can imagine circumstances in which Swift, in a mood to preserve law and order among Irish natives or a Dissenting mob, might have spoken to similar effect. But he here treats the words with stinging irony, as a fatuous complacency which only a Gulliver might be expected to express. And yet, whatever we may say about Gulliver at the present moment in the story, he is anything but fatuously complacent. It seems inconceivable from all his surrounding utterances that he would now speak in such accents, though in the work's earlier sections, including the opening chapter of Book I, the speech would be quite in character with his loyal affection for his own dear country.

The example brings up once again the difficulty of reading Gulliver as a "character." Just as it seems unlikely that he would be capable of the fervid eloquence of denunciation in the preceding paragraph, so the "Swiftian" irony of his praise of British doings would seem outside the range either of his outlook or his verbal skills. If the ascription of both passages to "Swift" is not without complications, it is from Swift, not Gulliver, that they emanate, though their formal processing through Gulliver's narrative voice is part of their elusive force.

The unbalanced and anti-social behaviour of Gulliver at the end of Book IV is sometimes taken as a change of "character" suggestive of a new distance between him and his author. One inference from this is sometimes alleged to be that Swift is disowning Gulliver's misanthropy, and, like a good modern community leader, insinuating a more tolerant and less rejectionist perspective. The truth seems to be that the distance is not "new," and that Gulliver has no "character" to change anyway. Swift is just as separate from the early naïve Gulliver as he is from the late disenchanted one. The rhetorical eloquence of Gulliver's late alienation contains the traditional satirist's irony that the world is so incurably wicked that it will drive people of ordinary decency to madness. The satirist virtuously crazed by an unmendable world becomes open to derision not in a way that neutralises his perceptions, but as a means for the author to concede the excessive reaction without denying the facts which provoked it. Gulliver's madness is not a psychological study of mental disintegration, but a means for Swift to say that while Gulliver is mad but not wrong, Swift can endorse his rightness without being mad. The situation is the product of a continuous elusive interplay between narrative and authorial voices, not of a character's point of view or an explicit authorial statement of doctrine.

Gulliver's view of humanity is presented as unhinged but not untrue. It is, indeed, unhinged by the truth inherent in it. Gulliver's treatment of the Portuguese Captain, or his predilection for the company of his horses rather than his family, are comically insulting reminders that even good, or more or less "harmless," Yahoos are nevertheless Yahoos, as the biologically objective fact of the Yahoo girl's sexual passion for Gulliver also reminds us, independently of Gulliver's state of mind or point of view.

The unfolding structure of the work is a process of progressive inculpation, from the ironic escalations of Books I and II to the absolute categorisation of human depravities in Book IV. The first three books offer the traditional satirical castigation of specific vices and follies, personal, social and political. The culprits are blamed for what they do. In Book IV, they are blamed for what they are. The transition to this absolute perspective occurs towards the end of Book III, in the episode of the Struldbruggs:

> When they came to Fourscore Years, which is reckoned the Extremity of living in this Country, they had not only all the Follies and Infirmities of other old Men, but many more which arose from the dreadful Prospect of never dying. They were not only opinionative, peevish, covetous, morose, vain, talkative; but uncapable of Friendship, and dead to all natural Affection, which never descended below their Grand-children. Envy and impotent Desires, are their prevailing Passions. . . .
>
> At Ninety they lose their Teeth and Hair; they have at that Age no Distinction of Taste, but eat and drink whatever they can get, without Relish or Appetite. The Diseases they were subject to, still continue without encreasing or diminishing. In talking, they forget the common Appellation of Things, and the Names of Persons, even of those who are their nearest Friends and Relations. . . .
>
> They were the most mortifying Sight I ever beheld; and the Women more horrible than the Men. Besides the usual Deformities in extreme old Age, they acquired an additional Ghastliness in Proportion to their Number of Years, which is not to be described. (III. x)

The place of this episode in the overall rhythm of the work is not that of a mere *fait divers* in the apparently episodic miscellany of Book III. Its placing changes the tone to one which expresses disgust and contempt not for behaviours that can or should be changed, but for behaviours that are inescapable to the nature of the creatures in question. It is after this that the reader's experience has to adjust itself to the more absolute definitional realities of Book IV, to which all human activity, not least travel and imperial dominion, ineluctably conform.

Notes

1. Jonathan Swift to Charles Ford, 22 July 1722; a few days earlier, on 13 July, he told his woman friend Esther Vanhomrigh (Vanessa) that he had been reading "I know not how many diverting Books of History and Travells," *Correspondence of Jonathan Swift*, ed. David Woolley, Frankfurt, Peter Lang, 5 vols., 1999 — , II. 428, 424.

2. Quotations, unless otherwise indicated, are from *The Prose Writings of Jonathan Swift*, ed. Herbert Davis *et al.*, 16 vols., Oxford, Blackwell, 1939-1974 (*PW*). *Gulliver's Travels* occupies volume XI.

3. For Swift on Banbury Saints, see "A Discourse Concerning the Mechanical Operation of the Spirit" (1704), *PW*, I. 184.

4. OED, s.v. "Mr, n." (Etymology) reports that the word was "often written in the full form *master*" until the latter half of the seventeenth century, but that at the beginning of the eighteenth century "Master" and "Mr" ("mister") were already regarded as distinct words. The pronunciation "Mister" or "Myster" prefixed to names is recorded in OED, s.v. "Mister, n. 2," as early as 1523. The earliest OED recording for the verb "masturbate" (1839) is unreliably late. The Latin verb *masturbor* and noun *masturbator* occur in Martial (IX. 41.7, XI. 104.13, XIV. 203.2). This fact, and the seventeenth-century currency of "mastuprate," suggest that the alleged pun would not be unintelligible in 1726, though the usage would seem to have had limited currency. For information on the Latin forms of this and related terms, see Thomas W. Laqueur, *Solitary Sex: A Cultural History of Masturbation*, New York, Zone Books, 2003, pp. 96-110, 442-5 nn. From Burton's use of the alternative term "mastupration" in 1621, recorded by OED, which Laqueur oddly refers to as "the first English use of 'masturbation'" (169), the English vocabulary of "self-pollution" in the seventeenth and eighteenth centuries provides little evidence for wide usage or familiarity of the term "masturbate" and its derivatives (see Laqueur, pp. 168 ff.).

5. For a fuller discussion of the frontispiece portraits, see the Introduction to *Gulliver's Travels*, ed. Claude Rawson and Ian Higgins, Oxford, Oxford University Press, 2005 (hereafter *GT*), pp. xi-xii, xvi-xvii, xliv-xlvi.

6. John Arbuthnot to Swift, 5 November, and Swift to Pope, 17 November 1726, *Correspondence*, ed. Woolley, III. 45, 56.

7. See *GT*, "Introduction," xvi-xviii. The portraits are reproduced at pp. xliv-xlvi.

8. The technique and some of its aspirations are described by Ford Madox Ford in *Joseph Conrad: A Personal Remembrance*, 1924, pp. 129-30, and discussed in Claude Rawson, "Swift's 'I' Narrators," *The Essential Writings of Jonathan Swift*, ed.. Claude Rawson and Ian Higgins, New York, W. W. Norton, 2010, pp. 874-89.

9. Swift to Pope, 29 September 1725, *Correspondence*, II. 606.

10. Claude Rawson, *God, Gulliver, and Genocide: Barbarism and the European Imagination, 1492-1945*, Oxford University Press, 2001, pp. 79-91, 324-8 nn. (hereafter *GGG*).

11. *A Modest Proposal for Preventing the Children of Poor People in Ireland, from being a Burden to their Parents or Country; and for Making them Beneficial to the Publick*, 1729, *PW* XII. 107-18, esp. 110, 115.
12. On medieval and earlier badging, see *Encyclopaedia Judaica*, ed. Michael Berenbaum and Fred Slotnik, 2nd edn., Detroit, Macmillan Reference, 2007, 22 vols., III. 45-8 (s.v "Badge, Jewish").
13. See *GGG*, pp. 275-87.
14. Herodotus, IV. lxiv, lxx; Strabo, VII. iii. 6-7. For Amerindian analogues, see *GGG*, p. 326, n. 157. On the Scythian-Irish connection, see *GGG*, pp. 79, 324 n. 137-8.
15. André Breton, *Anthologie de l'humour noir* (1939), rev. edn., Paris, 1966, pp. 13-14, 19-21.
16. Plato, *Republic*, 571 A-D; Aristotle, *Nicomachean Ethics*, 1148B-1149A. For More, Erasmus and others, see Rawson, *Satire and Sentiment 1660-1830*, Cambridge, Cambridge University Press, 1994, pp. 192-3 n. 201.
17. *GGG*, pp. 24-33, 69-91.
18. James Joyce, *Portrait of the Artist as a Young Man*, New York, Viking, 1978, p. 203.
19. On the Nazi use of the Biblical phrase, see Heinrich Himmler, speech of 6 October 1943, cited *GGG*, pp. 287, 372 n. 82.
20. For fuller discussion, see *GGG*, pp. 256-66, 287-98.
21. Breton, *Anthologie de l'humour noir*, pp. 9-21, esp. 13-14, 19-21.
22. Bartolomé de las Casas, *A Short Account of the Destruction of the Indies* (1552), trs. Nigel Griffin, London, Penguin, 1992, *passim*; and especially *Historia de las Indias* (1561, but unpublished until 1875-6), Prologue, section 4, in *Obras completas*, ed. Miguel Angel Medina et al., Madrid, Allianza, 1994, III. 338; Montaigne, *Complete Essays*, III. vi, trs. Donald M. Frame, Stanford, Stanford University Press, 1965, p. 695.
23. For documentation, see *GGG*, pp. 22-3, 312-3 n. 13; Joseph Conrad, *Heart of Darkness*, ed. Robert Kimbrough, New York, W. W. Norton, 3rd edn., 1988, p. 13.

Works Cited

Bartolomé de las Casas. *A Short Account of the Destruction of the Indies (1552)*. Trans. Nigel Giffin. London: Penguin, 1992.

Breton, André . *Anthologie de l'humour noir* (1939). rev. edn. Paris: Pauvert, 1966.

Conrad, Joseph. *Heart of Darkness*. Ed. Robert Kimbrough. New York: W. W. Norton, 3rd edn, 1988.

Joyce, James. *Portrait of the Artist as a Young Man*. New York: Viking, 1978.

Laqueur, Thomas W. *Solitary Sex: A Cultural History of Masturbation*. New York: Zone Books, 2003.

Michael Berenbaum and Fred Slotniks, eds. *Encyclopaedia Judaica*. 2nd edn. Detroit: Macmillan Reference, 2007.

Montaigne, Michel de. *Complete Essays*, III. vi, trs. Donald M. Frame. Stanford: Stanford UP, 1965.

Rawson, Claude. *Gulliver and the Gentle Reader: Studies in Swift and Our Time*. London: Humanity Books, 1991.

---. *God, Gulliver and Genocide: Barbarism and the European Imagination, 1492-1945*. Oxford: Oxford UP, 2001.

---. "Introduction." *Gulliver's Travels*. Eds. Claude Rawson and Ian Higgins. Oxford: Oxford UP, 2005. ix-xliii.

---. *Satire and Sentiment, 1660-1830: Stress Points in the English Augustan Tradition*. New Haven: Yale UP, 2000.

---. "Swift's 'I' Narrators." *The Essential Writings of Jonathan Swift*. Eds. Claude Rawson and Ian Higgins. New York: Norton, 2010. 874-89.

Strabo. *Geography*. Trans, Horace Leonard Jones. London: Harvard UP, 1988.

Swift, Jonathan. *Essential Writings*. Eds. Claude Rawson and Ian Higgins. New York: Norton, 2010.

---. *The Prose Writings of Jonathan Swift*. Ed. Herbert Davis. et al. 16 vols. Oxford: Blackwell, 1939-1974.

---. *Correspondence of Jonathan Swift*. Ed. David Woolley. 5 vols. Frankfurt: Peter Lang, 1999.

A Kaleidoscopic View of China: A Comparative Study of Two Travelogues by George Anson and John Bell

Eric Chia-Hwan Chen

Introduction

Ever since the sea routes from Europe to China were discovered by the Portuguese and the Spanish explorers in the late fifteenth century and the early sixteenth century,[1] more and more European explorers and merchants flooded to this vast oriental country. In 1514, a Portuguese ship reached Canton and the people onboard successfully traded with the local people. She is now generally believed to be the first European ship to have visited China in history (Pratt 14). Around two hundred years later, the fast-growing British East India Company, following the footsteps of the Portuguese, the Spanish and the Dutch, also extended its reach to China and successfully established a factory in Canton in 1715 (Pratt 15). Thanks to a number of original or translated travelogues about China left by the early European visitors, many famous British writers, such as Daniel Defoe, Samuel Johnson, Horace Walpole, Oliver Goldsmith, Thomas Percy, and Samuel Taylor Coleridge, were able to derive inspiration from these works to create their personal images of China and her people.

From the 1750s to the 1840s, around twenty travelogues or memoirs related to China were written by British hands (Qiu Ye, "Yingguo"). Before the Macartney embassy left for China in 1792, the most favored authentic English travelogues about China were very likely George Anson's *A Voyage round the World in the Years M DCC XL, I, II, III, IV, by George Anson* (1748) and John Bell's *Travels from St Petersburg in Russia to Divers Parts of Asia* (1763) as both works include extensive descriptions about the daily life of the Chinese.

In his *La littérature comparée* (1989) Yves Chevrel suggests that traveling has been the best way to meet foreigners since ancient times (Meng 15). Meng Hua also indicates that the study of travelogues is a traditional field of comparative literature and suggests:

> The authors of travelogues often play double roles: they are constructors and promoters of *imaginaire social*, but they are also conditioned by it to a certain degree. Their images of foreign lands are usually reflections of the *imaginaire social*. Hence, in conducting an magological research of travelogues,

> one often has to approach the texts via the intellectual history
> and mental history of the narrators' nation. (16)

Both Chevrel and Meng stress the importance of studying travelogues to analyze the images of foreign lands or foreign peoples in a national discourse as those authentic and popular travelogues usually serve the following functions. First, they can be used as coordinates which determine whether an image of "the Other" depicted in a fictional text is supporting or subverting the stereotypical image of "the Other" in question. This is based upon the observation that a travelogue tends to reflect the author/observer's will to reproduce an immediate reality as faithfully as possible. Hence, the nature of travelogue is similar to that of historical account because both are believed to be faithful records of human activities. If an image of "the Other" in a literary text is similar to that of a genuine travelogue, it is less likely to change people's image of "the Other." On the contrary, if an image of "the Other" is different from that of a genuine travelogue, it is more likely to challenge people's well-established knowledge about "the Other." Second, as I am about to illustrate later, the identity and mentality of the traveler, the destination, the motivation and result of the journey as well as the people the travelers encounter may all contribute to the perspective of the narration and the tone of the travelogue. It is therefore interesting to see how China could be so differently represented by two visitors from the same country and the same epoch.

Motivations and Results of John Bell and George Anson's Journeys to China

In 1719, a Scottish doctor named John Bell joined a Russian embassy to China soon after he completed a three-year service as a physician in the Russian embassy to Persia. This journey to China lasted for about two years and Bell came back to Moscow in January 1722.

Bell and the Russian embassy, sent by Peter the Great and led by Ambassador Leoff Vassilovich Ismayloff, entered the Chinese territories on 22 September 1720 and left China on 6 April 1721. Being a core member of a foreign embassy and thus treated as a guest by the Chinese celestial government, Bell was able to know many officials of the imperial court while he visited China. During his six-month stay in China, mostly in the capital Peking [Pekin in Bell's work], he wrote numerous notes and these notes became the raw materials for his book decades later.

Around twenty years after Bell's journey to China, another famous British visitor arrived on the southeastern territory of China but had a completely different experience. On 18 September 1740, Commodore George Anson and his squadron, which was comprised of six warships, two storeships and 1,955 men, left Portsmouth and sailed westward to the Pacific, where the squadron was due to meet its foes, the Spaniards. Three years and nine months later, the only surviving ship of the whole squadron, the *Centurion*, finally came back to England on 15 June 1744. This expedition claimed more than 1,300 souls and only 145 men of the original squadron were able to see England again (Rodger).[2]

As Anson's squadron had successfully captured eight Spanish ships[3] as prizes and made a handsome profit in the expeditions, his legendary voyage was esteemed by the contemporary British public, noted N. A. M. Rodger, as "a classic tale of endurance and leadership in the face of fearful disasters. . . which did something to restore national self-esteem battered by an unsuccessful war." Except for being compared to Sir Francis Drake, who circumnavigated the world from 1577 to 1580 and was involved in the defeat of the Spanish Armanda in 1588, Anson has also often classed with Christopher Columbus and James Cook for his tremendous achievements on the sea (Houston 262). Soon after he came back to London, Anson was promoted to rear-admiral in April 1745 and then vice-admiral in July 1746.

Without any permission from the Chinese authority, Anson's huge, yet damaged *Centurion* visited Macao and Canton to replenish her stores and provisions when she was on her way back to England. This 60-gun warship first appeared in the waters of Macao on 13 November 1742 and eventually left Canton on 7 December 1743. When Anson visited China with his gigantic *Centurion*, he hoped the Chinese would receive him with respect. Yet, to his disappointment, the local Chinese officials seemed to be completely ignorant of the great military power of England and thus showed little respect to Anson and his crew. For instance, he had great difficulty in getting his warship repaired and obtaining enough provision. He even found some local merchants tricked him by selling him stone-crammed fowl and water-injected hogs (Anson 524-25). Due to several unpleasant experiences in negotiating with the local Chinese officials and merchants, Anson left China with a very unfavorable impression.

Popularity of Anson and Bell's Travelogues

In 1748, four years after Anson came back to England, a book entitled *A Voyage round the World in the Years MDCCXL, I, II, III, IV, by George Anson* was finished and published by Richard Walter,[4] the chaplain of the *Centurion*. Being recognized as the only official report of Anson's journey, this book immediately became a best-seller and was reprinted in its full or abridged form in numerous editions. Furthermore, it was soon translated into several other European languages, creating a widespread interest among foreign readers.[5]

As for Bell, he did not publish his China travelogue until 1763, nearly a quarter of a century after he finished his last diplomatic mission in Russia in 1738. In his book, *Travels from St Petersburg in Russia to Divers Parts of Asia*, Bell publicized his China travelogue with three other travelogues,[6] but the account of his visit to China was generally considered the most complete and interesting part of the whole book (Carter and Harrison, Stevenson 2). This book was highly regarded by its readers and had considerable success in the late eighteenth and early nineteenth centuries (Stevenson i). For instance, Sir George Staunton, the first British Ambassador to China, praises it "(t)he veracity of Mr Bell's narrative may perhaps be considered to be too well established to need at present any further confirmation," while the *Quarterly Review* in 1817 claimed it "the best model perhaps for travel-writing in the English language" (Stevenson i).

When Bell's book first came out in 1763, it was printed in two handsome quarto volumes and sold by subscription (Stevenson 25). Its high demand by readers of various backgrounds is confirmed by its long list of nearly 510 subscribers and sales of more than 610 sets.[7]

Images of China and the Chinese in Bell and Anson's Travelogues

As the naval force of a country was usually considered an important index of her strength after the late sixteenth century, many European countries spent a lot of money to build powerful fleets and Britain was no exception. After the British fleet defeated the Spanish Armada in 1588, Britain became one of the most powerful countries in the world. Hence, when Anson and his shipmates visited the southeast coast of China, they paid close attention to the local naval force of Canton and Macao and concluded that the Chinese navy was by no means a match for the *Centurion*, even though she was not in her best shape.

In addition, when the British government used its powerful naval force to secure sea routes to the major ports of other countries, British colonizers also followed their national flag and settle in various less developed parts of the world. As the military powers of the local inhabitants were usually much inferior to that of the British troops, many British intellectuals gradually formed a contemptuous attitude towards the peoples of the overseas settlements and their cultures. As a result, a number of biases of the "the Other" were generated from and supported by the military superiority of the British government after she took the leading role in exploring the unindustrialized parts of the world.

As mentioned earlier, Anson had few pleasing experiences in China. His impressions of China and her inhabitants were therefore mostly negative. In his travelogue, Anson gave many examples to discredit the characteristics of the Chinese and complained that China, in comparison to England, was an autocratic and stagnant country, whose poor military force suggested she could be an easy prey for any well-equipped European force.

In terms of his image of China, Anson confidently suggested that "the *Centurion* alone was capable of destroying the whole navigation of the port of *Canton*, or of any other port in *China*, without running the least risqué from all the force the *Chinese* could collect" (479-80). He even proudly declared that the British sailors had behaved with great "modesty and reserve" not to have attacked the indefensible Chinese (480). Elsewhere the chaplain of *Centurion* also challenged the "boundless panegyric" found in many early Jesuits' accounts of the Chinese government and claimed:

> [T]he favourable accounts often given of their prudent regulations for the administration of their domestic affairs, are sufficiently confuted by their transactions with Mr. *Anson*: For we have seen that their Magistrates are corrupt, their people thievish, and their tribunals crafty and venal. Nor is the constitution of the Empire, or the general orders of the State less liable to exception: Since that form of Government, which does not in the first place provide for the security of the public against the enterprises of foreign powers, is certainly a most defective institution. (544-45)

Therefore, the much-praised Chinese government sketched by the Jesuits, in the eyes of Anson, was nothing but an inefficient, inflexible, unhelpful and vulnerable administration, which was run by a group of crafty, corrupt, greedy, immoral, and venal officials.

Anson and his fellow travelers were fiercely critical of the Chinese people's characteristics. For instance, the Chinese merchants were described by Anson as "dastardly." In addition, he claimed that the Chinese were "extremely defective in all military skills" (512). As for their collective ethnical nature, Anson suggested:

> [I]t may perhaps be impossible for an (sic) *European*, ignorant of the customs and manners of that nation, to be fully apprized of the real incitements to this behaviour. Indeed, thus

> much may undoubtedly be asserted, that in artifice, falsehood,
> and an attachment to all kinds of lucre, many of the *Chinese*
> are difficult to be paralleled by any other people; but then the
> combination of these talents and the manners in which they are
> applied in particular emergencies, are often beyond the reach
> of a Foreigner's penetration. .... (518-19)

Suggesting that the "talent" of the Chinese for artifice and falsehood was unable to be surpassed by other peoples and even beyond the imagination of foreigners, the narrator therefore degraded the ethnic characteristics of the Chinese. To further illustrate his antipathy for the Chinese as a whole, he added that the Chinese were mostly "fraudulent and selfish" (519) and they were a very unhygienic people because some Chinese fishermen had followed the *Centurion* and picked up the carrion dumped by the British sailors (525). As for the mechanical skills of the Chinese, Anson condescendingly suggested that they might outdo others only by their capacity for imitation. Therefore, the Chinese were unable to challenge the British or any other Europeans in the design and manufacture of the more complex weapons of war, such as cannons and warships (541). In terms of the literature and the language of the Chinese, the author, without any knowledge, repudiated the former as "obstinacy" and "absurdity" (542), the latter as "rude and inartificial (sic)," thus what was full of "infinite obscurity and confusion" (542).[8] He concluded his remarks in an authoritative tone that "the history and inventions of past ages, recorded by these perplexed symbols, must frequently prove unintelligible; and consequently the learning and boasted antiquity of the Nation must, in numerous instances, be extremely problematical" (543).

Therefore, though some individual Chinese were once praised as frank and honest when they showed good will to Anson or his shipmates,[9] overall the images of the Chinese in Anson's travelogue are represented negatively: arrogant, backward, greedy, hypocritical, selfish, timid, unhygienic and unintelligent.

On the purpose of representing the foreigners in a specific way, Jean-Marc Moura suggests:

> The images of foreigners belong to a network of a basic
> description of a society and any group of people confirm their
> own identities by either identifying with or rejecting these
> images. Therefore, any reference to foreigners or a description
> of them will reflect a social system. In other words, one people
> begins to take shape when they differentiate themselves from
> the others.[10] (230)

Applying this concept to interpret the Chinese images in Anson's travelogue, whenever the author assigns a negative image to the Chinese as a cultural "the Other," he also simultaneously attributes a positive auto-image to "the Self" in either a direct or an indirect way. By contrasting, yet interdependent, relationships between "the Self" and "the Other," one can effectively differentiate oneself from "the Other" and establish one's own identity. Hence, the negative images attributed to the Chinese by Anson and his fellow travelers have actually refracted a series of positive images of the British and their country: their own government was a more efficient, powerful, progressive, warlike, wealthy and well-governed administrative body, and the British a brave, civilized, disciplined, dutiful, honest, humane, hygienic, industrious, ingenious, intelligent, righteous, talented, and unselfish people. To a certain degree, Anson's account of the Chinese perfectly fits into the traditional heroic discourse of western literature, in which many a time a national or tribal hero fights against a foreign villain and eventually survives. Being depicted as the vicious "the Other," the Chinese serve as a foil to highlight the heroic and noble traits of Anson and his surviving English crew.

In 1763 John Bell published his *Travels from St Petersburg in Russia to Divers Parts of Asia*, in which he included four detailed accounts of his early travels to several Asian and European countries as a physician in Russian embassies, plus an English translation of a journal written by a Russian consul named Lorenz de Lange, who recounted his seventeen-month residence in Peking.[11]

The significance of Bell's book in studying British images of the Chinese can be illustrated by highlighting the following facts. To begin with, Bell was the first British traveler to visit the capital of China in person and leave an account of his visit.[12] Second, he was the first British visitor who had an audience with the Chinese emperor and his council members. Third, as Bell claimed that he only wrote about what he personally saw or heard about on his journey[13] and his work shows no distinctive evidence of whimsicality,[14] his account of China and her people is a work of great value as one contrasts it with other eighteenth century English literary works of imagination, such as Horace Walpole's *A Letter from Xo Ho* (1757) and Oliver Goldsmith's *The Citizen of the World* (1762).

There is one important feature which makes Bell's account of China different from other authentic travelogues left by other British or European visitors. Other writers tended to use "the Chinese" as a collective term to refer to all people living in China, whereas Bell has clearly distinguished the ruling Tartars from the subjected Han Chinese in his writing. Therefore, when he uses the term "the Chinese," he refers to the Han Chinese who are subjected by the Mantzur [Manchu] Tartars after 1664, rather than all the people of the Qing Empire. Bearing this feature in mind will help us to see the fact that Bell's images of the people in China actually comprise both his images of the Han Chinese and his images of the Tartars.

Bell's account of his life in China covers many aspects of the daily life of the Han Chinese and the ruling Tartars, such as the imperial ceremony of receiving foreign delegates, the hunting sport of Emperor Kanghsi [Kamhi in Bell's text], the royal banquets given by Kanghsi, the duties of foreign missions at the Chinese imperial court, the structure and size of the Great Wall, the natural resources of China, the history of military conflicts between the Tartars and the Han Chinese, the religions of the Chinese, the Chinese New Year festivals, the diplomatic relationships between China and her neighbouring states, as well as Chinese fairy tales.[15]

Bell describes the Chinese as follows: "[t]he Chinese are generally of a middle size, and slender make; but very active" (184). As for the Chinese ladies, Bell elaborates a little bit more:

> I shall now make a few remarks upon the ladies, who have many good qualities besides their beauty. They are very cleanly, and modest in their dress. Their eyes are black, so little, that, when they laugh, you can scarce see them. Their hair is black as jet, and neatly tied up, in a knot, on the crown of the head, adorned with artificial flowers of their own making; which are very becoming. The better sort, who are seldom exposed to the air, have good complexions. Those who are inclined to the olive, take care to add a touch of white and red paint, which they apply very nicely. (183)

He then finished the description by indicating the Chinese ladies of distinction were seldom seen outside. When they went out to visit their close relations, they always travelled in closed chairs and were attended by servants (183-84). In addition, Bell also highlighted the fashion of binding feet at an early age, a practice popular only among Chinese ladies and seldom found among ladies of Tartar origin. What is of interest here is that Bell does not condemn the practice of foot-binding as his other European predecessors did. Instead, he gives a full account of it, which includes a folktale about the origin of foot-binding, and leaves the moral judgment to his readers.

In contrast to Anson, Bell obviously has a much higher regard for the Chinese. He says:

> The Chinese are a civilized and hospitable people; complaisant to strangers, and to one another; very regular in their manners and behaviour, and respectful to their superiors; but, above all, their regard for their parents, and decent treatment of their women of all ranks, ought to be imitated, and deserve great praise. There good qualities are a natural consequence of the sobriety, and uniformity of life, to which they have been long accustomed.
>
> The general regularity, and decency of manners, among the Chinese, is obvious to all who see and observe them with the least attention. (182)

This short passage reveals Bell's belief that the Chinese people have many positive qualities and are by no means less civilized than his fellow countrymen in terms of their manners and temperament. In fact, he even implies that the Europeans should follow the example of the Chinese in practicing filial piety and respecting women of all ranks. In addition to those good qualities listed above, in other passages Bell also points out many other positive characteristics of the Chinese: such as being honest,[16] ingenious, thoughtful, parsimonious, patient, and peaceable (176, 181-84).

Like many early European visitors to China, Bell also pays close attention to the religions of the Chinese. However, unlike most of his European predecessors, he does not condemn the idolatry practiced by the Han Chinese and the Tartars. He simply describes the ritual practice and then objectively distinguishes the idol worshippers from people of other religious beliefs, such as the theists, Christians, Muslims and atheists. Here is an example of his close and unbiased observation:

> As to the religion of the Chinese, I cannot pretend to give a distinct account of it. According to the best information I could procure, they are divided into several sects; among which, that of the Theists is the most rational and respectable. They worship one God, whom they call Tien, the Heaven or the highest Lord, and pay no religious homage to the images of their countrymen. This sect has subsisted for many ages longer than Christianity, and is still most in vogue; being embraced by the Emperor himself and most of the grandees, and men of learning. The common people are generally idolaters. The   few Jews and Mahometans, residing here, are supposed to have entered China about six or seven hundred years ago, in company with the western Tartars. There is a

> very inconsiderable sect, called Cross-worshippers. They
> worship the holy cross; but have lost all other marks of
> Christianity; which makes it probable the gospel was preached
> in this country before the arrival of the missionaries; but by
> whom is uncertain. The Christians, at present, are computed to
> amount to one hundred thousand, of both sexes. I have been
> told, the Chinese have also some Atheists among them. (184-
> 85)

This cautious observation reflects Bell's open-mindedness to the various religious beliefs of the Chinese. Being a Christian himself, he describes Chinese theists as "rational" and "respectful" and even claims the history of Chinese theism longer than that of Christianity, a fact not many of his European contemporaries were willing to admit. [17] Elsewhere, except for suggesting some features of the pagan idols as monstrous and the history of some mythological idols and saints as too absurd to be mentioned, he does not repudiate the Chinese for practicing idolatry. Instead, he thinks "[t]hese priests were not at all superstitious, as appeared sufficiently from the little reverence they paid to their idols, and statues of reputed saints" (123). Thus, though some Chinese monks have shown inadequate respect for their idols and statues, which they worshiped as emblems of deities or spirits, Bell does not reprimand them as superstitious people at all.

As a whole, Bell does not particularly find any fault with the Chinese, although he was strongly appalled by two practices: the inhumane act of abandoning newborn babies in the streets, which is often practiced by the poor Chinese families who cannot afford many kids, and the unhygienic conduct of eating lice, which is commonly found among the Chinese beggars. [18] With regard to the practice of abandoning newborn babies, Bell reflects:

> I must, however, take notice of one shocking and
> unnatural practice; which appears more extraordinary in a
> country so well regulated and governed as China. I mean, that
> of exposing so many new-born infants in the streets. This,
> indeed, is only done by the poor, who have more wives than
> they can maintain. [19] (183)

This description of an merciless deed often found among the poor Chinese families is one of the few negative accounts that blemishes Bell's overall positive image of the Chinese.

Due to the nature of Bell's mission to China, he had many chances to observe the Chinese officials and the emperor at a close distance. His accounts of the Chinese ruling classes, in comparison to those left by early British explorers and sailors who visited only the southeastern coast of China for business or military purposes and whose acquaintances were either local officials or citizens, seem to reveal a rather different picture of the Chinese ruling classes.

As an official member of a Russian embassy, Bell made the acquaintance of several Chinese officials, presumably men of distinction, and declared himself well received by them on many private occasions during his stay in Peking. In his account he praises the Chinese Master of Ceremonies as "a person of great politeness" and "a good friend to the Christians" (127); the Prime Minister as "a great sportsman" and "an honest man" (141). As for his image of Emperor Kanghsi, the Chinese monarch is praised as a man of humanity, good nature, affability, self-discipline, generous disposition and more than once referred to as a philosopher.[20] In some passages Bell even refers to him as "the good old Emperor" to show his favorable impression of this oriental monarch. In addition to these positive characteristics, Bell was also impressed how Kanghsi dealt with the disputes between the Jesuits and the Dominicans over the "rites controversy."[21] In the dispute between the Jesuits and the Dominicans,

> The Emperor himself tried to make the parties compromise matters; but, finding his endeavours ineffectual, he left them to agree or dispute according to their pleasure. He inclined, indeed, to favour the opinion of the Jesuits, which he thought most reasonable. At any rate, it must be acknowledged an instance of uncommon condescension, for an heathen Emperor to interest himself so much in the peace of a Christian church.[22] (150)

Lacking a substantial understanding of the moral and political significance embedded in the rites controversy, Bell naively assumed that Kanghsi was willing to let the Jesuits and the Dominicans settle their own disputes over the issue of paying tributes to ancestors open-mindedly and therefore applauded the Emperor's "uncommon condescension." This misunderstanding, or possibly an intentional misinterpretation, of Kanghsi's magnanimity to Christianity might probably mirror Bell's hope of seeing an oriental heathen monarch favouring Christianity. In another episode, Bell noted Kanghsi's open-mindedness to music of various origins. He reflected that "[t]he Emperor told the [the Russian] ambassador, that he knew well their musick [music] would not please a European ear; but that every nation liked their own best" (163). Elsewhere Bell also remarked that China, under the dominance of Kanghsi, was an empire run by a "prudent management and mild government" (177). So, if we summarize Bell's positive accounts of Kanghsi's temperaments and his achievements, we may say that Bell's image of Kanghsi is probably not far from Plate's image of a philosopher king.[23]

It is interesting to note that when Bell notes down those characteristics and practices of the Chinese and the Tartars, he often compares them to those of his fellow countrymen or even his contemporary Europeans. Hence, as he reflects on the similarities and differences between the Chinese and the British, his work somehow simultaneously mirrors the auto-images of his fellow countrymen or even the contemporary Europeans in general. For instance, in one passage in which Bell notes a grand royal banquet hosted by Kanghsi, he comments that the Chinese in many ways act differently from the Europeans. He said "[i]n this,[24] as in many other things, the behaviour of the Chinese is quite contrary to that of the Europeans" (136).[25]

As for the similarities between the people of Britain and China, Bell noticed that the British people's fondness of cock-fighting was as strong as the Chinese's fondness for quail-fighting, though this sport was usually found only among the vulgar in England.[26] Elsewhere he also mentioned "[t]hese people [the Chinese] expose their gold and silver, and other goods of value, with as much freedom and security, as the merchants do in London or Amsterdam" (152). Hence, given the fact that the cultures of the Europeans and the Chinese are so different from each other's, there is remarkably small difference in the humanity of them.

Conclusion

This study shows that one's motive and background are likely the most important key factors to influence one's interpretation of a foreign culture and to shape one's image of the people who create that culture. Here motive includes one's motive of visiting a foreign land and one's motive of writing down his or her experience in a foreign land; while background includes people encountered at a foreign land, reception received at a foreign land, one's preconceived ideas about the foreign people, as well as one's attitude toward the foreign people and their culture.

In conclusion, as Anson and Bell depict various characteristics and practices of the Chinese in their individual travelogue, they always have their fellow countrymen in mind and keep reminding their readers from time to time how differently or similarly the Chinese have behaved and thought as the

British or the Europeans in general. Comparatively speaking, Anson's auto-images of the British repeatedly suggest that the British are a much more civilized, friendly, honest, hygienic, knowledgeable, rational and self-disciplined people than the Chinese, whereas Bell's auto-images of his own fellow countrymen tend to imply the British and the Chinese are very much the same in terms of their characteristics and humanity and in some specific aspects the Chinese can even serve as a role model for the British to follow.

Notes

1. The Portuguese Vasco da Gama (1460-1524) found a sea route from Europe to Asia via the Cape of Good Hope in 1498, while his fellow countryman Fernando de Magallanes (1480-1521), working for the Spanish government, sailed west and found another sea route to Asia via South America in 1522. After that, more Europeans came to Asia via these sea routes. See Xin Jianfei, *Shijie de zhongguo guan* [China in World View] (Taipei: Boyuan, 1993) 123.

2. Regarding the death toll of Anson's squadron, only four crew members died in battle, most of the others from scurvy. See Alan Frost and Glyndwr Williams, "The Beginnings of Britain's Exploration of the Pacific Ocean in the Eighteenth Century," *The Mariner's Mirror* 83.4 (1997): 410.

3. None of these Spanish ships was brought back to England as Anson's squadron was seriously short of people to man them. Yet, all the gold and silver of these ships were moved to *Centurion* before the ships were sunk. See Staffordshire County Education Department, *George and Thomas Anson*, 16-19. 1977.

4. Walter's authorship of the book was soon questioned in 1761 when James Wilson, the editor of *Mathematical Tracts* of Benjamin Robins, claimed that Robins was the real author of the book and Walter only provided his notes for Robins to use when composing the book. Walter did not repudiate the accusation immediately and it was probably because he was too ill to respond. For more discussion about the authorship debate, see Elizabeth Baigent, "Walter, Richard (1717–1785)." *Oxford DNB*, Ed. H. C. G. Matthew and Brian Harrison. Oxford: OUP, 2004. 15 June. 2011 and Brett D. Steele, "Robins, Benjamin (1707–1751)." *Oxford DNB*, ed. H. C. G. Matthew and Brian Harrison. Oxford: OUP, 2004. 15 June 2011 <http://www.oxforddnb.com>.

5.   The first German translation appeared in 1749, French and Russian in 1751.
6.   These three travelogues include two trips to Persia (1715-18, 1722) as well as one trip to Constantinople (1737-38). The text of Bell's journey to China quoted here is from J. L. Stevenson's *A Journey from St Petersburg to Pekin, 1719-22* (1965). Stevenson extracts Bell's itinerary to Peking from the 1763 edition and gives it a comprehensive introduction and extensive notes.
7.   For a complete list of subscribers of the 1763 edition, see Bell 225-31. Up to 1811 the whole set was reprinted 5 times, including one pirate edition released in Ireland. The French translation appeared in 1766 and the Russian translation in 1776. See Stevenson 25.
8.   It is interesting to note that Anson knew nothing about the Chinese language, let alone Chinese literature, but he criticized both like he was an expert.
9.   It is only when the Chinese individuals show kind intention toward the British or when they comply with the request of the British that they are given positive comments.
10. This English translation is mine.
11. De Lange's diplomatic status as a Russian consul residing in Peking was not fully recognized by the court of China and he was given no chance to present his credentials from Peter the Great (1672-1725) to the imperial court of China. This was because his presence in Peking as a permanent diplomatic agent would violate the Qing court's tradition of receiving foreign representatives. Therefore, even though the emperor had granted permission to allow de Lange to stay in Peking, the Chinese officials skillfully dodged the recognition of his diplomatic identity by not receiving his credentials. See Stevenson 19. In fact, a similar request to appoint a diplomatic agent to reside in Peking permanently was proposed to the throne of China again by George III (1738-1820). It was rejected by Emperor Qianlong because it fundamentally infringed upon "the Celestial Empire's ceremonial system." For more discussion on this issue see Alain Peyrefitte, *The Collision of Two Civilisations* (London: Harvill, 1993) 198, 290 and James L. Hevia, *Cherishing Men from Afar: Qing Guest Ritual and the Macartney Embassy of 1793* (Durham: Duke UP, 1995) 187-89.
12. In fact, another British physician named Thomas Garvan visited the capital of China five years earlier than Bell. Garvan used to work for the

Russian Czar as well before he was invited by Emperor Kanghsi to work at his court in Peking. Nevertheless, Garvan did not leave any writing about his life in China. This consequently made Bell the first British writer who ever wrote about his life there. See Qin Ye's "Yingguoren guanyu Beijing de soubu zhenshi youji" [The First Authentic Traveling Account about Beijing Written by an Englishman]. 19 Nov. 2003 <http://www/china.org.cn/chinese/HIAW/445207.htm>. In addition, British citizens' first presence in China could be dated as early as 1637, when John Weddell (1583-1639/40) visited Macao and Canton. Weddell even fought several skirmishes with local Chinese militia when he forced his way up to a port in Anunghoy. These skirmishes were noted by diarist Peter Mundy, who joined Weddell's journey to China in 1637. However, for unknown reasons, Mundy's manuscript was not published until the early twentieth century by the Hakluyt Society in 1907, entitled *The Travels of Peter Mundy in Europe and Asia, 1608-1667*. After Weddell's visit, British ships were more frequently seen in the waters of China and four British commercial centres were established in China between 1672 and 1700. See Qin Quojing and Gao Huanting, *Qianlong huangdi yu Magaerni* [Emperor Qianlong and Sir George Macartney] (Beijing: Zijincheng, 1998) 22-23. There are two authentic travel accounts mentioning the Chinese written by Englishmen and published before Bell's book. They are William Dampier's *A New Voyage round the World: Describing Particularly, the Isthmus of America, Several Coasts and Islands in the West Indies, the Isles of Cape Verd, the Passage by Terra del Fuego, the South Sea Coasts of Chili, Peru, and Mexico; the Isle of Guam one of the Ladrones, Mindanao, and Other Philippine and East-India Islands near Cambodia, China, Formosa, Luconia, Celebes, &c. New Holland, Sumatra, Nicobar Isles; the Cape of Good Hope, and Santa Hellena. Their Soil, Rivers, Harbours, Plants, Fruits, Animals, and Inhabitants. Their Customs, Religion, Government, Trade, & c.* [also known as A New Voyage round the World] (1697) and Alexander Hamilton's *A New Account of the East Indies: Being the Observations and Remarks of Capt. Alexander Hamilton, Who Spent His Time There from the Year 1688 to 1723* [also known as *A New Account of the East Indies*] (1727). However, neither Dampier nor Hamilton had ever visited the capital of China during their short visits to the country.

13. Bell's principle of writing his itinerary is "[i]t is the business of a traveller to describe places and things without prejudice or partiality; and exhibit

them fairly, as they really appear. This principle it shall be my study to keep always in view." See Stevenson 25.

14. Stevenson justifies the reliability of Bell's work by saying "[t]here is another background which needs only the briefest of mentions, so little influence does it have on the book, and that is the vision of 'Cathay', that perfect land ruled by philosophy, which remained a powerful literary convention throughout most of the eighteenth century, though the convention outlasted the belief that such a place existed. John Bell takes no account whatever of it, carefully setting down only what he saw, and recording, sometimes with qualification, only what he believed to be true of the things he was told, and with no sideways glances at the nonsense—often, it is true, engaging nonsense—that was still in his day being written about China by those who had never been there." See Stevenson 21.

15. The sections dedicated to China and her people run from chapter VII to chapter XIII in the 1965 edition.

16. Of the honesty of the Chinese, Bell seemed to praise it with a slight reservation. He said "[t]hey are honest, and observe the strictest honour and justice in their dealings. It must, however, be acknowledged, that not a few of them are much addicted to knavery, and well skilled in the arts of cheating. They have, indeed, found many Europeans as great proficients in that art as themselves. And if you once cheat them, they are sure to retaliate on the first opportunity." See Bell 184.

17. Seventeenth and eighteenth-century British writers with distinctive Christian backgrounds, such as William Nichols (1655-1716), a Church of England clergyman, and George Berkeley (1685-1753), a Church of Ireland bishop, often question the authenticity of Chinese multi-millennial history as claimed by Chinese historians and propagated by the Jesuits. They attacked the Chinese, whose reliance on Jesuits for calendrical modification is well-known in European academia, for their poor astrological knowledge and dismiss the longstanding history of China as unreliable. See Ge Guilu, *Wuwai de yuanyin—yingguo zuojia yu zhongguo wenhua* [*Distant Voices beyond London: English Writers and Chinese Culture*] (Yinchuan: Ningxia renmin, 2002) 118-19, 121.

18. Bell notes his experience of seeing a Chinese beggar eating lice as follows: "while walking through the street, I observed an old beggar picking vermin from his tattered cloaths, and putting them into his mouth; a practice, which, it seems, is very common among this class of people. When a Chinese and Tartar are angry at one another, the Tartar, in

reproach, calls the Chinese louse-eater; and the latter, in return, calls the other fish-skin coat; because the Mantzur Tartars, who live near the river Amoor, subsist by fishing, and, in summer, wear coats made of the skins of fishes. But this habit is used only in summer; for, in winter, they wear furs." This description of Chinese beggars eating lice is probably the earliest reference that can be found in English literary history. In his work, Staunton also noted that "[p]ersons not so opulent as to be delicate, are sometimes found to ransack every department of nature to satisfy their appetites. And even the vermin that prey upon uncleanly persons, have been known to serve as a prey in their turn to them." See Staunton, vol. 2, 159. On consuming vermin among the Chinese poor, Ye Duyi, the Chinese translator of Staunton's itinerary, regarded Staunton's story groundless as there was no Chinese record or hearsay of Chinese eating lice. See Ye's *Yingshi yejian qianlong jishi* (Hongkong: Joint, 1994) 381. It is likely that Ye did not read Bell's work when he translated Staunton's itinerary into Chinese. Bell's account therefore becomes an important reference to verify the reliability of Staunton's observation.

19.   19. In his itinerary Staunton provided a detailed account regarding why the Chinese poor abandoned newborn babies, mostly female ones, in the streets and explained why foreign missionaries adopt them and convert them to Christianity. See Staunton, vol. 1, 39-40.

20.   See Bell 138, 150, 155, 162-63 and 179 for specific descriptions.

21.   This "rites controversy" was started by Pope Clement XI's Bull *Ex Illa Die* of March 1715, in which he repudiated the Jesuits' tolerance of Chinese converts' practice of paying tribute to their deceased parents or relations, a practice he considered next to idolatry. On hearing Clement XI's bull in 1717, Kanghsi was so upset as to issue a prohibition of Christianity throughout his empire. Another bull of a similar nature was issued by Clement XI in 1720 which made Kanghsi decide to ban Christianity again in 1721, though he still allowed a number of missionaries to work in his court. Thereafter missionaries were not allowed to disseminate Christianity in public for more than one hundred years, until Emperor Tongzhi rescinded the prohibition in 1862. For more information about the Rites Controversy, see Stevenson's note on 150-51; Guo Fuxiang and Zuo Yuanpo, *Zhongguo huangdi yu yangren* [Chinese Emperors and Foreigners] (Bejing: Shishi, 2001), 195-208; Zhang Guogang, *Cong zhongxi chushi dao liyizhizheng—mingqing chuanjiaoshi yu zhongxi wenhua jiaoliu* [From China's First Encounter with Europe to

Rites Controversy—Missionaries of Ming and Qing Dynasty and the Cultural Exchange between China and Europe] (Beijing: Renmin, 2003), 413-502.

22. In fact, the reason for Kanghsi to favor the Jesuits was because paying tribute to ancestors was considered by the Chinese a practice of filial piety, a moral conduct which was much emphasized by the Confucianists. Being a follower and a defender of Confucian dogma himself as well as a monarch with ultimate authority, Kanghsi therefore could not stand Clement XI's provocative Bulls, which endangered the Chinese sense of morality and challenged his authority. It is rather the peaceful life of his subjects than the peace of the church that concerned Kanghsi. Bell seemed unable to see through the implication involved in the rites controversy, but willing to believe Kanghsi was interested in maintaining harmony between different Christian sects.

23. In his *Sept Discours en Vers sur l'Homme* (1738, translated into English in 1759 by Thomas Nugent under the title *An Essay on Universal History*), Voltaire also mentions that philosophical characteristics were often found on Chinese emperors. He says "The emperor has been high pontif[f] time immemorial, it is he who sacrifices to *Tien*, the supreme ruler of heaven and earth: he is considered also as the first philosopher in the empire; and his edicts are generally instructions and lessons of morality." See Voltaire, *An Essay on Universal History*, vol. 1 (London, 1759) 22.

24. Bell is referring to the Chinese habit of serving dessert before the main dishes, see Bell 136.

25. In another instance Bell recalls the contrary ideas about places of honor at an imperial audience held by the Chinese and the Europeans. He said "[a]s the customs of the Chinese are, in many instances, quite contrary to those of the Europeans; so, I have been informed, that, among them, the left hand is the place of greatest honour." See Bell 161.

26. Bell highlights that the sport of quail-fighting was conducted at a Mandarin's house, while cock-fighting was generally considered a vulgar sport in England and therefore not to be found among the British gentry. See Bell 122.

Works Cited

Anson, George. *A Voyage round the World, in the Year MDCCXL, I, II, III, IV*. Comp. Richard Walter. London, 1748. *Eighteenth Century Collections Online*. 15 June 2011 <http://galenet.galegroup.com/servlet/ECCO>.

Baigent, Elizabeth. "Walter, Richard (1717–1785)." *Oxford DNB*. Ed. H. C. G. Matthew and Brian Harrison. Oxford: OUP, 2004. 15 June 2011 <http://www.oxforddnb.com>.

Bell, John. *A Journey from St. Petersburg to Pekin, 1719-22*. Ed. and Introd. J. L. Stevenson. Edinburgh: Edinburgh UP, 1965.

Carter, Philip and Robert Harrison. "Bell, John (1691–1780)." *Oxford DNB*. Ed. H. C. G. Matthew and Brian Harrison, 2004. 2 June 2011 <http://www.oxforddnb.com>.

Frost, Alan and Glyndwr Williams. "The Beginnings of Britain's Exploration of the Pacific Ocean in the Eighteenth Century." *The Mariner's Mirror* 83.4 (1997): 410-18.

Ge, Guilu. *Wu Wai De Yuan Yin—Yingguo Zuojia Yu Zhongguo Wenhua* [Distant Voices beyond London: English Writers and Chinese Culture]. Yinchuan: Ningxia renmin, 2002.

Guo, Fuxiang and Zuo Yuanpo. *Zhongguo Huangdi Yu Yangren* [Chinese Emperors and Foreigners]. Bejing: Shishi, 2001.

Hevia, James L. *Cherishing Men from Afar: Qing Guest Ritual and the Macartney Embassy of 1793*. Durham: Duke UP, 1995.

Houston, R. A.. "New Light on Anson's Voyage, 1740-4: A Mad Sailor on Land and Sea." *The Mariner's Mirror* 88.3 (2002): 260-70.

Meng, Hua. "Bijiaowenxue Xingxiangxue Lunwen Fanyi Yanjiu Zhaji" [Translations of Comparative Imagology: Papers and Research Notes]. *Bijiawenxue Xingxiangxue* [Imagologie en literature comparée]. Ed. Meng Hua. Beijing: Beijing UP, 2001. 1-16.

Moura, Jean-Marc. "Imagologie littéraire et mythocritique: rencontres et divergences de deux recherches comparatistes." *Mythes et Littérature*. Ed. Pierre Brunel. Paris: Presses de L'Université de Paris-Sorbonne, 1994. 129-41.

Peyrefitte, Alain. *The Collision of Two Civilisations: The British Expedition to China in 1792-4*. Trans. Jon Rothschild. London: Harvill, 1993.

Pratt, John T. *China and Britain*. London: Collins, 1927.

Qin, Quojing and Gao Huanting. *Qianlong huangdi yu Magaerni* [Emperor Qianlong and Sir George Macartney]. Beijing: Zijincheng, 1998.

Qiu, Ye. "Yingguo zaoqi youji de zhongguo xingxiang kaocha: zong shu" [A Comprehensive Review of the Chinese Images in Early English

Travelogues], *Zhonghua Dushu Bao* 8 Oct. 2003. <http://www.gmw.cn/01ds/2003-10/08/10-24dbe7998352b9e48256db90005d265.htm>.

---. "Yingguoren guanyu Beijing de soubu zhenshi youji" [The First Authentic Traveling Account about Beijing Written by an Englishman]. *Zhonghua Dushu Bao* 19 Nov. 2003 <http://www.china.org.cn/chinese/HIAW/445207.htm>.

Rodger, N. A. M. "Anson, George, Baron Anson (1697–1762)." *Oxford DNB*. Ed. H. C. G. Matthew and Brian Harrison. Oxford: OUP, 2004. 7 June 2011 <http://www.oxforddnb.com>.

Staffordshire County Education Department. *George and Thomas Anson*. Stafford: Staffordshire Country Education Department, 1977.

Staunton, George. *An Authentic Account of an Embassy from the King of Great Britain to the Emperor of China*. 2 vols. Philadelphia, 1799.

Steele, Brett D. "Robins, Benjamin (1707–1751)." *Oxford DNB*. Ed. H. C. G. Matthew and Brian Harrison. Oxford: OUP, 2004. 15 June 2011 <http://www.oxforddnb.com>.

Stevenson, John Lynn. "Introduction." *A Journey from St Petersburg to Pekin, 1719-22*. By John Bell. Edinburgh: Edinburgh UP, 1965. 1-27.

Voltaire. *An Essay on Universal History*. Trans. Thomas Nugent. London, 1759. *Eighteenth Century Collections Online*. 25 June 2011 <http://galenet.galegroup.com/servlet/ECCO>.

Xin, Jianfei. *Shijie De Zhongguo Guan* [China in World View]. Taipei: Bo yuan, 1993.

Ye, Duyi. *Yingshi Yejian Qianlong Jishi* [An Authentic Account of an Embassy from the King of Great Britain to the Emperor of China]. Hongkong: Joint, 1994.

Zhang, Guogang. *Cong Zhongxi Chushi Dao Liyizhizheng—Mingqing Chuanjiaoshi Yu Zhongxi Wenhua Jiaoliu* [From China First Encounter with Europe to Rites Controversy—Missionaries of Ming and Qing Dynasty and the Cultural Exchange between China and Europe]. Beijing: Renmin, 2003.

Travel, Immigration and Hospitality in the Americas

Melissa Lee

> "An Act of Hospitality, can only be poetic."
> -Jacques Derrida

What does a politics of travel and immigration mean in a new transnational society? The Early Modern period in the Americas consisted of distinct groups that travelled to the New World, forged of fragmented communities living uneasily within uncertain and indistinct geographical borders. Heidrun Friese's description of 'a politics of hospitality' and a wide-reaching cosmopolitanism aptly applies to this New World burgeoning community of multi-cultural ethnicities and transatlantic settlers (74). Of particular interest are the Anglo-European settlers distinguished as a Transatlantic travelling culture that negotiated their in between ness, complying with the traditions of England and their new-found knowledge of Amerindian culture.

This article explores the languages of hospitality used in issues of diplomacy and state, particularly through the use of 17th and 18th century captivity narratives. In Immanuel Kant's 1798 treatise on 'Perpetual Peace and Hospitality,' he explores the relationship between hospitality and diplomacy. Kant's conclusions are: that every stranger has the right to be treated not with hostility, but extended the right of shelter, or the right that is extended to all men that have a right to 'the common possession of the surface of this earth' (78). Derrida further extrapolates from this statement the following analysis that 'In order to extend hospitality, one needs to have a firm representation of what one calls home or a clear definition of one's nation. The concept of home and ownership, the role of 'host' has to be established before the extension of hospitality' (56). Several aspects of my research on the following colonial captivity narratives will resonate with postcolonial theory: reading captivity narratives within the subtext of contradictions, deconstructing binary oppositions between colonizer and colonized, deconstructing imperialist notions, and destabilizing dominant discourse. Following scholars such as Frederic Cooper, Laura Ann Stoler and Lisa Voigt, I have found that many colonial writings from this period have been organized around specific imperialist powers too literally, and should, instead be re-examined, much like postcolonial texts as a circle of exchange, hybridity, a fluid back and forth of exchange between communities. One particular example of this case study includes the examined captivity narrative of Scottish born Mary Jemison (who gave birth to children registered as members of the Seneca tribe). Through the lens of hospitality, I aim to raise issues of transnationalism and border crossings, relevant in discussing early ideas of citizenship and the emerging nation. I hope to reveal that the act of hospitality in relation to nation states is both paradoxically welcoming and violent, involved in the conquering of land and power in the New World. I hope to reveal the construction of home and hospitality in order to draw boundary lines, and outline differences between the Amerindians, Puritan and Spanish settlers, and later, the American Revolutionaries and the Creoles. These boundary lines are both artificially imagined and sanctioned in order to demarcate and create illusory territories used as a form of control, ownership, and command in the New World.

Empire expansion in the late seventeenth to early eighteenth century have involved languages of home, and travel, resulting in an early conception of the Americas related to entitlement, acting on an outlining of territory, and the building of a national identity. The conceptual and geographical borders of home are threatened not only by the trespass of physical boundaries, and the subsequent violent hostility of the host and trespasser, but by the nature of acculturation in acquiring the identity and duties of the host. The earliest meaning of hospitality according to the OED is 'herboringe of pore men' or 'the harbouring of poor men.' Taken from a thirteenth century edition of the Bible, the implication is that hospitality is the sheltering of those impoverished that are 'in need' ('poor') (474). 'Harbouring,' or used as a noun as harbour connotes implications of safety, shelter or asylum. In contemporary English usage, hospitality is often referred to as 'receiving with goodwill or liberally entertaining guests, visitors, or strangers.' In today's contemporary definition, hospitality, which was originally used to denote sheltering, or entertaining visitors, guests, those in need, has been expanded to include implications of humanitarianism, or strength in character. In the latter definition, 'harbouring' or safehousing is replaced with the more general and congenial word 'entertaining,' liberally used to extend to not only poor men but also guests and strangers. Implied in this action is the idea that to receive or entertain a guest or a visitor, is to stake ownership of a residence and establish territorial rights as host in one's home and to place the other party as 'visitor' or 'guest.'

Another simple etymological correlation is the word 'Guest,' derived from the Latin 'hostis,' synonym for 'enemy' when compounded with the word 'hosti-pot.' (*OED*, 470, 472, 534). One can ascertain quite paradoxically that 'hostis' (hostile) and 'hospes' (hospitable) deriving from the same root suggests a close integral relationship between the two seemingly vastly different actions. The Latin *hostem* (*hostis*) stranger, enemy, was used in medieval warfare to refer to enemies in a military expedition (*OED* 470).

Derrida explains this word phenomenon as a relationship that harbors a 'self-contradiction' in its own body (8). One particular example of self-contradiction is the very limits of hospitality that are imposed upon the guest and host. The temporary nature of hospitality itself imposes a violent contradiction (Derrida 4).

The threatening nature of the alien wilderness and the hostile outsider is controlled by the domestic parameters of the private home household. The rules of hospitality are compromised when the outsider (whom is forbidden to enter) crosses the private domestic threshold. When this violation occurs, the host's right to home and ownership is placed into. Thus, this idea of "home" can imply violence and a potential hostility even when it paradoxically comforts with the evocation of a domestic private space.

By waging cultural and physical warfare against those hostile to their newfound residence, the transatlantic European settlers claimed ownership by reinventing themselves from 'travelers' and 'guests' to 'host.' Using such cultural warfare tactics as publishing promotional tracts and best-selling captivity narratives, the European settlers turned a travel narrative into a proprietary ownership tale. Once hospitality is contextualized in the language of ownership, it becomes a politicized and highly strategic tactical maneuver in the larger struggle to claim a homeland. Drawing from these definitions, my paper explores hospitality as a means of cultural interchange and mutual historical navigation.

The travel and acculturation themes of the first Captivity Narratives represent a cultural shift in Western literature that gestures towards a newfound communities heading towards multiplicity and hybridity. The documented exchanges and interactions of Puritan, Chicano, and Spanish settlers reveal reciprocal relationships founded that relent to each civilization's cultural differences and are thus changed and altered in return. These situations reveal the political side of hospitality, a courtship of cultural custom and domestic duty, as well as a process of acculturation. The visitor, upon entering the host's domain follows the prescribed customs of the host, is given a gracious welcome, and thus the laws of hospitality are followed. If, by chance the rules of hospitality are broken (for example if the visit turns into a trespass), aggressive tactics by the trespasser are anticipated. In *A Narrative of the Life of Mrs. Mary Jemison*, Jemison describes the details of her original capture of her parents along with herself as a young child from their home by six Shawnee Amerindians and four Frenchmen Jemison's tale is of an enforced march through the wilderness, 'without a mouthful of food or a drop of water, even though we had not eaten the night before.' The retelling of the narrative is particularly focused on the giving and sharing of provisions, an aspect related to the theme of hospitality. Jemison describes their first night of captivity lying on the ground 'supperless,' 'without a drop of water to satisfy the craving of our appetites.' Finally the next day, the captives are given a full breakfast, but Jemison describes in sorrowful outrage, that the provisions that were used to make their meal were taken from their own home. Jemison's father is in such sorrow over this breach of custom that he is unable to eat, 'so overcome with the situation.' In this scenario, Jemison's outrage is peculiarly focused on the detail that the breakfast used to feed the captives was forcibly taken from their own home a couple of days prior. Here, part of the overturn in roles is the Amerindians, now acting as host in feeding the captives, but using the own food taken from their homes, in their previous role as trespassers.

Having spent four years living with the Shawnee Amerindians, Jemison no longer feels like an outsider or a captive prisoner. Instead, she details that 'with them was my home; my family was there, and there I had many friends to whom I was warmly attached in consideration of the favors, affection and friendship with which they had uniformly treated me, from the time of my adoption" (58). Jemison's role is transformed from captive and visitor, to a respected and beloved member of their society. This transformation aligns with Hilary Wyss' description of the Amerindian definition of community being dependent upon a cultural system of belonging (Wyss 65).

Jemison's identification with her captors and her disinterest in returning to the European colonies show a resistance in the archetype of the captured sentimental heroine. Having been captured at 17 years old, she spends the majority of her life with the Seneca tribe (she is already quite elderly when she publishes her captivity narrative), orally dictated to Seaver in interviews. Seaver's preface reveals that Jemison's naturalization and strong familial bonds with the Amerindian community is one of unnaturalness, as it relates to her direct association and embrace with the Other. One particular example is Jemison's tale of being forcibly asked to leave her Amerindian family by a European Dutch settler, John Van Sice. Sice's determination to forcibly redeem Jemison to the Anglo-European community for personal and lucrative gain is sharply contrasted with the giving and welcoming nature of the Amerindian homes that house Jemison selflessly. Here, the white stranger is the outsider that threatens the Amerindian community of which Jemison is a part of. When she flees from the community, she flees from the Anglo-White settler Sice, as well as to protect her Amerindian family (592). Jemison's strong preference for her new way of live with the Amerindian community is clearly expressed by her joy at escaping Sice's grasp. Derrida writes that the very peak of hospitality includes 'folding the foreign other into the internal law of the host (wirt)' (7). This is relevant to Jemison's situation in which she is no longer a traveler, captive or guest, but as a cultural host and member of society. Jemison's excellent knowledge of Cree, her refusal to return to the Anglo-European community and calling her Amerindian hosts her 'family' demonstrates her identification with the Amerindian community. Wyss champions Jemison as a particular figure in American history that disrupts our previous stereotypes about the founders of our nation and instead reveals the racial and multi-cultural hybridity that the new Americas were comprised of consisting of differing individuals and mixed communities (18).

Jemison decides not to go back to the colonies and acquires land as an Amerindian. She relays in detail the tale of her Amerindian brother Kau-jises-tau-ge-au offering her liberty to leave the Amerindian community and return to the Anglo-European settlers. However, the condition of her going included that she would have to leave her son behind, whom she had conceived with an Amerindian in the community. Because of her inability to leave her children, and her knowledge that if she 'should be so fortunate to find [her] relatives,' they would not be understanding and instead 'they would despise them, if not myself; and treat us as enemies; or, at least with a degree of cold indifference, which I thought I could not endure' (80). Jemison's decision to stay within the Amerindian community results in her Amerindian brother eventually granting her 'a piece of land that [she] could call [her own.' Jemison's original position as a captive guest is overturned when she decides to stay of her own volition; the land given to her confirms her new role as host. Jemison becomes quite well-known for the reputable quality of her hospitality. The opening preface of Seaver's introduction is that Jemison's 'house was the stranger's home' (15). Jemison's generosity as host speaks to the high level of comfort that she felt as owner and proprietor of the land, helping the hungry, naked and the homeless (10). In Jemison's home, 'the weary wanderer was always made comfortable.'

Though Jemison's narrative is always included in the captivity narrative genre, it is distinct from the moralistic religious tales of Mary Rowlandson, Susannah Johnson, or the captured heroine of the Panther Narrative. Jemison's tale has a happy ending in which she culturally adapts to the Amerindian way of life, lives a long and healthy life bearing several children within the community. The only disapproval that is expressed is by her biographer Seaver in the introduction, stating that 'although her bosom companion was an ancient Indian warrior, and notwithstanding her children and associates were all Indians, yet it was found that she possessed an uncommon share of hospitality' (5). Here, Seaver shows the prejudice of the biographer, particularly in his belief that the civilized action of hospitality is only limited to the Anglo European community.

Jemison's eventual acculturation and identification with the Amerindians allows her to later negotiated on behalf of the Seneca tribe during the 'Treaty of Big Tree,' her mixed son with another Amerindian, also appointed and given an important ranking position in the Amerindian community. Seaver's opening introduction of her appearance describes her as neatly caught between the Anglo-European and Amerindian world. Jemison is small with a 'white complexion,' speaks English 'plainly and distinctly, with a little of the Irish emphasis,' but 'has acquired the habit of peeping from under eye-brows' which is a characterstic that Seaver claims is 'from her long residence with the Indians' and is able to cross a stream on a log or pole with consistent steadiness. These mix of characteristics both Amerindian and European illuminate Jemison's in-between-ness resulting in a cross-fertilization of cultures that enrich our understanding of the multicultural and Early Modern history.

The mixed hybridity and fractured identities making up of the people of the early Americas is further exemplified in the captivity narratives of Chilean soldier and writer Francisco Nunez de Pineda y Bascunan. Pineda published a memoirs about his own captivity among the Araucanians in *Cautiverio feiz y razon individual de las guerras dilatadas del reino de Chile* [Happy Captivity and Individual Reason for the Prolonged Wars of Chile] (1663) as a positive cultural experience, exemplified by the adjective 'Happy' in the title of his narrative. In a different stylistic tradition from the Puritan sentimental female distress fiction, the majority of Creole captivity writers portrayed their captivity as an educational experience, using their situations to learn valuable cultural habitable tools as well as insider knowledge of the geography and environment of the New World. According to Pineda, his exposure to the Amerindians resulted in two positive changes in his life: 1.) Learning and adopting many of the cultural indigenous customs and 2) using the rare inside experience and knowledge production in order to further the Spanish imperialist empire (Voigt 23). After his captivity, Pineda was appointed Maestro de Campo in 1656 by the Governor of Chile Pedro Porter Casanate and had an important role in the Spanish victory in Conuco and the relief of the fort of Boroa (Voigt 23) Pineda makes the argument in his text that the captivity allows for a 'transformation' from the native cultures that is beneficial to understanding and working from a position of authority and knowledge on the environment (Voight 23). As early as the Fifteenth century, countries such as Portugal recognized the unique anthropological knowledge that captives possessed once returning to their home community.

The early Indian captivity narratives reveal the limitations in the ethics of hospitality in particularly illuminating ownership, cultural assimilation and land themes that are all a larger part of hospitality narratives. Questions of hospitality in the creation of the nation state are judicial as well as proprietary. The citizen or settler as owner or host exercises hospitality narratives that border upon judicial as well as proprietary themes. Cultural acculturation also plays a large part in the legitimate claiming of host ownership as exemplified by Mary Jemison's integration into the Seneca Indian host culture. These discussions privilege a further exploration of themes of belonging, ethnicity and nationhood. In the renowned 1786 Abraham Panther narrative, the female narrator conquers the wilderness making it belong to herself as home while simultaneously holding on to her cultural values. Similarly, Mary Rowlandson's captivity narrative has shown particular anxiety in establishing her immutableness of character in her emphasis on her preserved chastity during the duration of her captivity, as well as blind religious faith. In contrast, Jemison's intermarriage with an Amerindian and the bearing of several children in her adopted community reveals an acculturation process that is celebrated (176).

Though the Indian Captivity Narrative is generally regarded by scholars as one of the few distinctively socially performative American genres, captivity writing encompasses a range of ethnicities from Spanish, French, and Chicano to Puritan English. Imperialist cultural origins have resulted in a mixed legacy of the Americas to a succeeding generation of writers. Female captivity narratives were encouraged as spiritual and moralistic tracts in order to uphold societal order, as well as promotional material to lure Europeans to the new world. These popular narratives fostered a transatlantic fiction that introduced a subject of acculturation into the other. The 'other' is not only referred to as the foreign element and a marker of difference from the European settlers but it also refers to foreign invasion; women that were captured and in danger of succumbing to the foreign culture, to becoming part of the cultural other. Female captivity narratives in particular had an emphasis on reinforcing imperialist oppositions and settlers living in a 'savage' environment as opposed to the transformative identification behind a mixing of cultures between captor and captive. The 'foreign' is a term commonly used to distinguish from 'domestic' when referring to a community or a country's policies and affairs. Captivity narratives problematize this relationship between domestic and foreign. The role of Puritan captivity narratives were published on themes of religious morality, hoping to benefit those in distress, benefit the afflicted, as well as promote the Americas as a new European home. An individual such as Mary Jemison, caught between the Anglo-European and Amerindian world became historical figures that celebrated the hybrid and multi-ethnic history of the new Americas.

Works Cited

Armstrong, Nancy and Leonard Tennenhouse. "The American Origins of the English Novel." *American Literary History* 4.3 (Autumn, 1992): 368-410.

Buell, Lawrence. *The New England Literary Culture from the Revolution through to Renaissance*. Cambridge University Press, 1989.

Derrida, Jacques. *Of Hospitality: Cultural Memory in the Present*. California: Stanford University Press, 2000.

Friese, Heidrun. "The Limits of Hospitality." *Paragraph* 32 (2009): 51-68.

"Guest" *The Oxford English Dictionary*. 2nd ed. 1989. www.oed.com. Oxford University Press, April 30th 2012.

"Hospitality." *The Oxford English Dictionary*. 2nd ed. 1989. www.oed.com. Oxford University Press, April 30th 2012.

Kant, Immanuel. *Perpetual Peace: A Philosophical Sketch*. Philadelphia: Slought Foundation Press, 2010.

Núñez de Pineda y Bascuñan, Francisco. *Happy Captivity and the Reason for the Prolonged Wars of the Kingdom of Chile*. London: The Folio Society, 1977.

Round, Phillip. *By Nature and Custom Cursed: Transatlantic Civil Discourse and New England Cultural Production 1620-1660*. Boston: University Press of New England, 2000.

Rowlandson, Mary. *The Narrative of the Captivity and Removes of Mrs. Mary Rowlandson* (1682). Lancaster: Cairns Collection of American Women Writers, Carter, Andrews and Co. 1828.

Seaver, James. *A Narrative of the Life of Mary Jemison*. Radford: Wilder Publications, 2011.

Voigt, Lisa. *Writing Captivity in the Early Modern Atlantic: Circulations of Knowledge and Authority in the Iberian and English Imperial Worlds*. North Carolina: University of North Carolina Press, 1996.

Wyss, Hilary E. "'Things That Do Accompany Salvation': Colonialism, Conversion, and Cultural Exchange in Experience Mayhew's *Indian Converts*." *Early American Literature* 33.1 (1998): 39-61.

On Belo Horizonte's Utopia

Dário Borim Jr.

Belo Horizonte's greatest architectural landmark, Pampulha Complex, built in the early 1940s, does not stand alone within the city's history of urban development and ideological pursuit, neither does lie it outside the grand narrative of world architecture's history. Oscar Niemeyer,[1] who designed it as a young architect, was already making his name abroad. In 1943, Philip Goodwin organized the exhibit *Brazil Builds* for New York's Museum of Modern Art, and a new concept was then affirmed, the Brazilian Style. Quoting Goodwin, Zilah Dekker summarizes it: sun-breakers, supporting pillars, Portuguese-style titles and the tropical landscape became the icons of a new style, and according to most contemporary interpretations, that "'Brazilian Style' expressed a stage forward in the maturity of the Modern Movement" (Dekker 160-161).

For most historians, and Niemeyer himself, the Pampulha Complex starts and sets the tone of a period within his long and fruitful career, which will end with his vast and much better known works in Brasília, informs us the Mineiro architect Danilo Macedo (22). In a comprehensive and authoritative article examining all of Niemeyer's prolific work in Belo Horizonte, Macedo[2] asserts that Niemeyer's first works, right after graduation, already revealed a "skillful, though restricted," reading of the Swiss master Le Corbusier (22-23). In reality, adds Macedo, the European was who suggested him the use of Portuguese-styled *azulejos* and granite (23).

More importantly, however, Macedo shows how Niemeyer's architectural production in Belo Horizonte always was—directly or indirectly—linked to the political figure of Jucelino Kubitschek, who served as mayor of that city (1940-1945) and governor of the state of Minas Gerais (1951-1955) before orchestrating the construction of Brasília on his first and only term as President of Brazil (1956-1961). If one divides that Belo Horizonte production into two periods, they will coincide exactly with Kubitschek's terms in office in that state (Macedo 23).

Early in 1940 the new mayor told Niemeyer he wanted to impress the nation with the young city's modernity while creating "a new leisure district in Pampulha, a pretty *bairro* like no other in the entire country—with a casino, a club, a church and a restaurant" (Niemeyer 93; Macedo 23). In plain language, that architectural project was a "caressing stroke of generosity to the state's elite" (Macedo 27). At the same time, it was a symbol of the country's real economic growth and one more substantial case of the patronizing bond between modern architecture and state-funded development for political propaganda and maintenance of a patriarchal order (Macedo 27).

Resembling the relationship between the nation's elite's quest for rapid economic improvement and the ultra-modern design for the new capital of Brazil, the curves, colors and setting of Belo Horizonte's Casa de Baile, Iatch Club, and São Francisco de Assis Church, among dozens of other iconic buildings, resulted from the imagination of a conceptual artist in tune with the penchant for modernity and utopia which had characterized the birth and growth of the city planned in the late 1800s to replace Ouro Preto as capital of Minas Gerais.

Inspired by such architectural nuances and based on historical and journalistic evidence, as well as anthropological and literary views, on Brazil's first city planned and executed from scratch, two questions will orient this discussion. First, what may Belo Horizonte's birth and growth narratives reveal about the ideologies of the times? Second, how is it that such a relatively young city (113 years old) has not only risen to become Brazil's third-largest metropolitan area, of nearly 5 million people, but also affirmed itself as a distinct cultural hub, despite its relative proximity to the two greatest power-houses of the largest and most populous South American nation, Rio de Janeiro and São Paulo, respectively located at 274 and 364 miles from Minas Gerais' capital? All and all, Belo Horizonte's overall impression of is that of a relatively successful experiment in urban utopia—but how so?

What's in a name?

Reflecting on the meaning of the name Belo Horizonte (Beautiful Horizon), which was officially assigned on December 12, 1897 to a new city "born" and inaugurated as the new capital of the Brazilian state of Minas Gerais, poet and journalist Laís Corrêa de Araújo argues that there are no limits to the depths of any horizon, except for the restrictions of the human gaze (14). Our eyes, she adds, do not have the power "to capture the utopia of countless distances" (14). Furthermore, the word horizon seems to disturb us as it interferes with an imaginary line between our world and our perception of the celestial sphere (15). In the middle 1890s, Brazil's most celebrated author, Machado de Assis, was not impressed, though. He discredited that name's choice and justified his rejection by contending that such a name was not a city's name but simply *"uma exclamação,"* that is, "an expletive" (Assis 23).

While the renowned writer from Rio de Janeiro would have allegedly preferred if Minas' new capital honored a patriot or another historic figure (Assis 23), he apparently failed to understand how Belo Horizonte's project planners and supporters did not want to look back into Brazil's past, which the old state capital, Ouro Preto, preserved and stood for. From its blueprint and ideological impulse, the city was proposed to leave behind the image of the state associated with the narrow streets and the decay of the monarchic legacy. Ironically, the village of approximately 25 humble brick houses, one single street, one single square and one single church, which was located at the center of that drawing (therefore, doomed to be destroyed and turned into the new state capital), was called Curral del-Rei, The King's Curral.

In reality, a village even smaller than Curral del-Rei had existed by the name of Belo Horizonte in the same area since 1701, when João Leite da Silva Ortiz, a *bandeirante,* that is, a member of the colonial gold-seeking expeditions, first saw the beauty of the horizon and the prospects of finding large quantities of the precious metal there. It was the beginning of Brazil's first gold rush after the mineral was found in that region in 1693 (Oliveira, *Belos* 15-16; Oliveira, *No tempo* 17).

Much later, with the optimism of the new political regime established in 1889, the republic, and with the ambitions of the prevailing positivist spirit of the Belle Époque in the tropics, Belo Horizonte was created to tap into the possibilities of the ongoing economic forces, especially coffee farming, ranching, iron ore, and precious stones. Furthermore, it was built for the future development and modernity of the region, which still could not be precisely foreseen. For historian Roberta de Souza Oliveira, the construction of a brand new capital for Minas Gerais faced significant opposition. Indeed, Oliveira describes the official vote on the transference of the state capital as "tense" (*Belos* 23). It constituted a very controversial matter,[3] but it also conveyed the strongest expression of the "ideal for renovation" on the republicans' part (23). They lacked of any other clearly defined political agenda, adds Oliveira (*Belos* 23).

On December 17, 1893 the state's Legislative Assembly approved Bello Horizonte (spelled with double "l" until 1943) by decree as the capital. One of the engineers who played the most important role in the selection and approval of the physical site for the new capital was Aarão Reis, who vehemently defended its central position within the state's vast area (as large as France) and its climatic appropriateness (particularly its mild temperatures). Reis described that site in both technical and poetic terms:

> To its advantageous position within the state and its geographical location at 19.55.22 degrees South Latitude and 1.10.05 degrees off Rio de Janeiro's Meridian, and more than 800 meters above sea level, we must add the circumstances

of its setting on the Arrudas River basin and the fact that its main topographic lineament crafts the admirable shape of an amphitheater: opening to the East, as if to receive early in the day the benefits of the sunlight; lying back, to the South, on the Curral mountain, which protects it from the cold and humid airstreams which cross over in that direction through the White Gold and Moeda mountains; and overlooking the North, where the Contagem mountain softens the effects of the frigid winds that traverse the less than salubrious São Francisco river waters (...). It is also completely unlocked to the East's winds (breezes, actually) that constantly whiff; and to the West's currents that sometimes puff from Paraopeba river valley, a river that runs at a higher altitude than the Velhas river and remains sheltered by an extensive woodland vastly irrigated by abundant tributaries and streams. (Oliveira, *Belos* 25)

Early Growth

Even if such a depiction by Reis verges on landscape romanticism, the chosen site itself undoubtedly had—and continues to have—its appeal. Off multiple mountain tops and around gentle, rolling hills, there remains the horizon where the new city was erected. Despite the intense industrial growth its vicinity and the mining exploits behind its natural rocky walls, Belo Horizonte has managed to keep most of the charm of its early physical geography intact. The transformations envisioned and their fruition, though, expose the mentality of the times in Brazil, the underpinning topic of this study's section. As Jeffrey Needell's *A Tropical* Belle Époque, an impressive investigation on the turn-of-the-century Rio de Janeiro reforms, proves it, that was a time of Paris' urban models' huge impact upon "Brazil's claims to Civilization and Progress" (44). The so-called Wonder City's engineer Francisco Pereira Passos's 1870s plans and early 1900s executions, for example, carried out the demolition of hundreds of colonial homes and other buildings in order to widen avenues and build new, long avenues and boulevards (Needell 36-38).

Back in the 1890s, poet Olavo Bilac was also writing for Rio de Janeiro's *Gazeta*, the same newspaper in which Machado de Assis published his objection to the new city's name. Bilac visited Curral del-Rei in 1894 and soon wrote a report on the remote grounds of the future capital. In 1903 he returned to the heart of the so-called *pacata e conservadora* (calm and conservative)

Minas and filed a second report, which extolled Belo Horizonte in nearly mystical proportions:

> Nine years only! And in these nine years, as if by miracle, in the midst of a *rude sertão* (or rustic hinterland), a beautiful modern city, with enormous avenues, with splendorous palaces, with admirable parks! Through wide and arborous streets, electric streetcars keep rolling; electric lights shine between elegant and hygienic buildings; electric engines support the works of huge machines at factories whose continuous thump-thump attune hymns of labor and peace. (Bilac 26)

Growth really came to town on a fast pace. By 1921, Belo Horizonte had surpassed the mark of 100,000 inhabitants. By 1937, when visited by another famous writer, São Paulo's Monteiro Lobato, the city had approximately half a million people. Lobato starts his essay "Belo Horizonte, a bela" (Belo Horizonte, the beautiful) with a plain statement on the impact which the city had imparted to him: "Belo Horizonte was the greatest surprise of my life" (Lobato 35). Comparing Belo Horizonte as a planned city to another one, Washington, DC, the Paulista writer contends that the North American capital's beauty does not surprise us, since it has emerged in the world's richest country (Lobato 40). According to Journalist and historian Jader de Oliveira, it was actually Washington's construction that inspired the erection and 1882 foundation of the city of La Plata, in Argentina, a model which, in turn, inspired Belo Horizonte's blueprint (27). Impressed by Belo Horizonte's architecture, landscaping, and general urban structure, Lobato thinks that Minas' capital's charm stuns anyone as "the greatest miracle of our poverty" (40).

In his characterization of the Mineiros' young capital, the Paulista novelist also alludes to Rio de Janeiro's and São Paulo's narrow, jammed, curvy and over-crowded streets in pitiful opposition to the modern, fluid, straight and parallel streets of Belo Horizonte. To him, Rio is picturesque, not "marvelous" (Lobato 38), and São Paulo's downtown area encapsulates all the urban awkwardness that requires juggling and acrobatic skills from those who walk through it (37). Belo Horizonte, on the other hand, offers the architectural refinement of "public buildings sharing a kinship of sobriety, elegance and distinction" (40).

It is evident, however, that even a city planned to stand for modernity and modernization may succumb to the dilapidating powers of unchartered urban growth. The balance and harmony between aesthetics and practicality can be put aside as business-oriented goals dictate structural changes that bring about, for instance, new but unwanted bridges and overpasses; or those changes that cut down trees by the hundreds, as it happened to Afonso Pena Ave, the main thoroughfare in downtown Belo Horizonte. The city actually used to boast such an impressive amount of trees until the end of the 1950s that, according to novelist Marques Rebello, it even became known as the garden city of magnolias (Rebello 46).

Much has changed, some of it for better, and some of it for worse, in the name of economic progress, though, including the landscaping issue. It is not difficult to understand how a city like Belo Horizonte has grown so fast, either, if we take into account its central position within the enormous geographical extension, population, economic output, and natural resources of the state of Minas Gerais (the second most populous and third most affluent member of the union). So, Belo Horizonte has gradually become the key element in a circuit of production and sales of industrial and agricultural goods from within the state.

By only a few years the construction of the new capital followed the abolition of slavery (1888) and the proclamation of the republic regime (1889). Prompting developments such as the reforms in Rio de Janeiro and the construction of Goiânia (a city planned from scratch and inaugurated in 1935), ideologies of economic growth, technological progress and rational urban development were some of the most common public concerns (Oliveira, *Belos* 22).

The middle of the 20th century certainly provided Brazil with a real chance to become an industrialized nation. When World War II crippled Europe from its purchase and manufacturing powers, Getulio Vargas' administration and the Brazilian elites in general seized the moment and invested heavily in both industrial and agricultural businesses. On that incipient wave of optimism of the early 1940s Jucelino Kubitschek, a remarkable political leader and an outstanding man of economic vision, became mayor of Belo Horizonte and immediately commissioned the works of Oscar Niemeyer, as previously discussed. The new style of architecture was clearly meant to represent a gateway to progress and modernity, but concrete, steel and tropical gardens did not suffice: human capital was in demand.

As the 20th century rolled on, a vast diversity of people migrated and became Belo-Horizontinos (the Portuguese word for the inhabitants of the capital city). To fulfill that population demand, a substantial human capital came to new city from different European and Middle-Eastern countries. Jader de Oliveira highlights the Italians' contribution in the medical field, for instance (46-47). As expected, a huge contingent came in from all corners of Minas, which today comprises of 857 municipalities. They also migrated from other areas of the nation (especially the Northeast and Central regions).

That vibrant human highway has increased the crime rate over the decades and added awkward infrastructure, inadequate public transportation, noise, poverty, plus visual and air pollution, to the city. All of such turmoil has been subject to critical discourses, including those of poets, like Carlos Drummond de Andrade, who resents the mining on the outskirts of Belo Horizonte, or lyricists and novelists, like Jorge Fernando Santos, who pens dramatic, humorous or romantic songs in a compact disk[4] wholly dedicated to the Mineiro's capital. It is the phenomenon of the "unplanned city" following the consecration of the "planned" one, as seminal works by James Holston, *The Modernist City* (particularly pp. 118-127), and James Scott, *Seeing Like a State* (especially pp. 125-132), explain in regards to Brasilia and other similar urban projects around the globe.

Rather than seeing Belo Horizonte's case as a failure, though, this study highlights the empowerment that resulted from that influx of people, despite the problems typically caused by a rapid growth in population anywhere on earth. In Belo Horizonte, something else happened. Planners sought it and newcomers did their part because it was their most natural pattern of behavior where they came from: they together created a large urban center where people have preserved values and life-styles of the small towns they had left behind. People find time and place to stop and chat in parks, streets, and squares, for example, as suggested by Jader de Oliveira: "Belo Horizonte combined the ambition of becoming a city model of harmonious urban lineage with that of preserving the bucolic contours of a small town" (28). The amenities and nuisance of a metropolitan development do co-exist there, but they have turned the old Curral del-Rei not only into the country's third most populous city but also into a very rich cultural hub, of eminently artistic and celebrated bohemian exploits.

The Cultural Hub

Money generates money, of course, and abundance of natural resources, such as iron ore, good soil, and water, boosts any economy where there is investment in industry and agro-business. When it comes to cultural output, though, it is understandable how one center may interfere in the development or stagnation of culture in other sites, which brings back the quandary presented in the beginning of this essay. How could Belo Horizonte have asserted itself culturally despite its proximity to Brazil's two giants of cultural production, Rio de Janeiro and São Paulo?

We all know that in the 19th century people did not travel as often or as easily as they progressively they did in the 20th century, and that literature and the printed media were arguably, then, the most influential among the exportable forms of the artistic representation of regional cultures. In Brazil the printing business was prohibited by the colonial power, Portugal, until the early 1800s. Until then, books that circulated in Brazil were exclusively published in Europe. Lisbon and Coimbra held at that time the loudest voice over what should or should not be shared in writing throughout the South American colony.

When people in Rio de Janeiro and the rest of the country were finally freed to disseminate culture by printing their own books and newspapers locally, writers from that city started to exert a type of symbolic power over the other parts of Brazil in a way that had never been possible. In addition, small institutions of higher education were finally founded and started to attract students from different regions of Brazil. Those young people of affluent families would have gone to Europe to pursue a career in law or medicine, for example. That movement inward made Rio de Janeiro a mighty disseminator of scientific and political thoughts as well as cultural models and trends that knew no rival until São Paulo's coffee riches and industrial developments allowed for a power shift in its favor.

Minas Gerais, which had staged the remarkable 18th century period of gigantic gold production and extra rich output of baroque painting, music, poetry and sculpture, was very decadent in the 19th century. Artists and intellectuals had been attached to the world of Lisbon's intelligentsia, or, to a lesser extent, to those of London and Paris. Now, the cheapest and easiest way to fame was moving to the nation's capital or building other strong forms of connection with the court by the sea. The flow of brains and talents from the mountains to the coast continued into the 20th century, but it also swerved to São Paulo as this city started to undergo extremely fast growth in various fields, including the performing arts and other types of media, of which radio and television were (and still are) the most influential in Brazilian society.

Since the 1970s, though, Belo Horizonte has gradually become a powerful center of cultural production as well. If Minas still sends artists and intellectuals to Rio de Janeiro, São Paulo and abroad, it's probably less because of the capital's lack of opportunities than because of the state's population's large, vibrant and adventurous nature. A portion of them will always keep an interest in leaving any way, no matter how much is at stake locally.

Despite that continuing export of brains and talents, Belo Horizonte exhibits an envious quality and number of art venues, musical developments, and cultural events. It is not a city that attracts a sizeable number of international tourists, as the *New York Times* writer Seth Kugel has declared, but that—this study will argue—has been changing. The city's anonymity outside Brazil, he contends, "was born of no coastline and thus no beaches, no famous Carnival and thus no February madness, and no big attractions save a few buildings designed by Oscar Niemeyer that pale next to his famous works in Brasília" (Kugel). The *New York Times* writer realizes, though, that Belo Horizonte does have a claim to fame: it is the bar capital of Brazil. With more than 12,000 bars, it brags about the greatest number of them per capita in the country. He will explain it better: "Not bars as in slick hotel lounges or boozy meat markets, but bars as in *botecos*, informal sit-down spots where multiple generations socialize, drink beer and often have an informal meal" (Kugel).

One can hardly dispute this informal aspect of life in Belo Horizonte. Neither can one question the value of Belo Horizonte's cuisine, which aggregates traits and traditions from various regions of the state. Several years ago, the city managed to combine those two sides of Belo Horizonte's leisure life—food and drinking—into one annual major event spread out all over town: Festival Comida de Boteco (Bar's Appetizers Festival). In April of every year, "some 40 of the top bars square off in categories like hygiene, beer frigidity, service and most importantly, best *tira-gosto*—or appetizer" (Kugel). Since winners are decided but by public ballot, Belo-Horizontinos, then, have "a flimsy excuse to go out every night for a month," adds Kugel. The commercial success of this initiative from the most-esteemed cachaça-making region of Brazil has been so overwhelming that in spite of that alleged lack of tourists, Comida de Boteco is now being organized in Rio de Janeiro, São Paulo, Brasília. Maybe other cities will soon follow suit.

Regardless of the way visitors see Belo-Horizonte's passion for gregarious hours at bars, that life style is arguably conducive to greater socialization, live music enjoyment, story-telling, and writing. The leisure choice of sitting for countless hours at the humbly cozy and highly informal Mercado Central (the exotic and legendary central market), or at the open-air cafes and bookstore tables on the sidewalks of town sectors like Savassi, for example, can afford those pleasures of human interaction and creative processes.

It is not surprising, then, that Minas Gerais has provided Brazil and the world with an array of outstanding authors since the 1700s. Even if they move to other states, and a significant number of them have done it, they carry Minas, the land of unequivocal Pão de Queijo (cheese bread), within themselves, and they never let go of its mystified ethos, tales, geographies and sensibilities. That's the case of Carlos Drummond de Andrade, Maria Clara Machado, and João Guimarães Rosa. Other Mineiro authors, though, have opted to live most of their lives in their home state, such as Adélia Prado, Murilo Rubião, and Roberto Drummond.

One can hardly dispute that the nightlife of Belo Horizonte (and that of other Minas cities and towns) is profoundly strung together by musical traditions, widespread opportunities for live performances, and cutting-edge contributions to Brazilian and world music. From the baroque richness of the chamber and religious music produced in Vila Rica (an artistic highlight in the bonanza years of intense gold extraction), to the foundational and prominent popular music movement called Clube da Esquina (championed by Milton Nascimento, Beto Guedes, Lô Borges and others at Belo Horizonte's Santa Tereza district street corners of Divinópolis and Paraisópolis, in the 1960s), to the contemporary world-class achievements of the experimental music group Uakti, Minas Gerais has had much to offer to this ancient art form. The capital, in particular, organizes at least three major annual jazz festivals, which bring to town an amazing number of outstanding musicians from various countries. Their gigs at bars, bookshops, coffee shops, theaters, or squares and street corners are often free of charge.

Plastic art exhibits as well as dance, film, and theater festivals abound, too. The astonishing Inhotim Cultural Institute, for instance, is a museum complex in the middle of a 45-acre botanical garden. Located in Brumadinho, a town that lies only 37 miles southwest from downtown Belo Horizonte, the institute is surrounded by 600 hectares of natural reserve forests. Opened in 2005, Inhotim's nine pavilions are nestled in a dazzling tropical landscape designed by Burle Marx. They carry art works from all over the world. As Latin America's largest outdoor art center, this complex receives as many as 4,000 visitors on a typical Sunday, according to the museum's administration. Inhotim's Artistic Director, Jochen Volz, contends that the institute "offers a reference, a place to return to time and again to study art, and a very special encounter with art, different from that provided by urban museums or galleries. The institute sets new standards for how to present art, within Brazil and worldwide" (Milliard). According to Volz, this is one of the various unique assets of that museum as a radical innovative project:

> Botany and art are two complementary and equally important activities at Inhotim. Neither is the garden merely a backdrop for the art, nor does the art simply furnish the park, as often appears to be the case in classical sculpture gardens. The

artists are directly involved in the botanical context in which their works are inserted. If successful, there is no clear distinction between where botany ends and art starts. (Milliard)

Belo Horizonte's reputation as an art hub also becomes stronger as Grupo Corpo does remarkable presentations, all over the world, of their prominent, sophisticated, and ground-breaking modern and post-modern dance choreographies. On a similar pattern of world visibility and distinguished reputation is the street theater group called Galpão, whose works excel in dramatic research and experimentation. They have been on the road for 28 years through the entire Brazil and 17 countries in four continents.

Conclusions, by Minas' Poetic Sea

Belo Horizonte's history undeniably bears elements of a utopian tale. If *Utopia,* Thomas More's 1516 fictional and historical narrative, underscores the notion of a sublime and yet non-existent paradise on earth, what perhaps matters the most is the search itself, not the discovery or thorough construction of that paradise per se. Renaissance expert Dominic Baker-Smith elaborates on the historical facts according to which *Utopia* was possibly inspired by an island near Cabo Frio, on the south coast of Rio de Janeiro state, which Amerigo Vespucci visited on his fourth voyage to the Americas, from May 1503 to June 1504 (Baker-Smith 76). Belo Horizonte, of course, is not an island or even a coastal town, but its inland location, natural resources and celebrated horizon were powerful enough to sustain the political ideology of progress and civilization that engendered its foundation. Its swift urban development has had its flaws, but the city has kept its profile as a humane and inviting place to live by the muscle of tradition and the dexterity for innovation.

In a direct response to the first question proposed at the onset of this study, one may conclude that two key moments of change and optimism in the history of Brazil have also shaped the horizons of Belo Horizonte's leaders and planners. The first was historical watershed was when the nation strived to redeem its human rights record, promote democracy, and reshape its socio-economic and political structures by initially abolishing slavery and subsequently proclaiming the republican regime. The second key moment was the window of opportunity created by world capitalism when massive destruction and genocide paralyzed the import and export of goods between Europe and the new world power, the United States. Suddenly Uncle Sam was interested in Latin America and the largest and richest nation south of the

Equator stepped up to the plate. The greatest political leader whom Brazil has ever seen after the 1930 rise of Getúlio Vargas was Jucelino Kubitschek, the one who invested his ambitious plans for growth and modernity as mayor the city of Belo Horizonte and governor of the state of Minas Gerais. Hope and materialization of dreams marked his tenure there, which allowed him to be democratically elected as the new president of a new nation ascending into the industrialized world. In that sense Belo Horizonte constituted the only and unequivocal ascending ramp in the trajectory of the legendary man who first promised and then built Brasília in five years, the nation's greatest symbol of determination and pride in self-transformation and modernity.

While replying to the second question posed in the beginning of this essay, one must realize that the immense creative powers and distinguished position of Belo Horizonte (and Minas Gerais at large) within Brazilian art and culture are undisputable. Less clear, though, are the precise forces that allow the city to stand so strong and so vociferous within a region that includes the cities of Rio de Janeiro and São Paulo. From what has been noted in this discussion, one may suspect Belo Horizonte is what is because an entire state of huge geographical extension, diverse cultural profile, and matchless character supports it. Because of its size and location, Minas shares artistic, demographic and economic attributes with six other states and even a small portion of the Distrito Federal, around Brasília. More significantly, perhaps, Belo Horizonte is a microcosm of that Minas' dual spirit: one of love for both tradition and innovation, one of concern for both reality and dreams.

The concept of a Beautiful Horizon, which names the capital, has become a hallmark of the city's brilliance across the celestial sphere of the nation. As Araújo puts it, "horizon" is a "poetic, seductive and occult" word (15). She wonders: does its meaning go beyond the very concept it suggests, an orthographic attempt, perhaps, at the representation of the relationship between humans and the world they cannot understand, between what is visible and regarded as truth and what is imagined and gracefully questioned as future? (Araújo 15).

Perhaps the answer is yes. The city of Belo Horizonte was, without any doubt, moved from the status of a politically motivated and scientifically designed utopia, framed by the nation's republican and positivist thoughts of civilization and progress, to that of a culturally and economically powerful center, with an innovative urban design, Niemeyer's architecture, Inhotim's vanguard conceptualization of art, and various other cutting-edge champions in the arts, such as Clube da Esquina, Grupo Corpo, Galpão, and Uakti. Along with the deeper roots of the state's ethos, cuisine as well as leisure styles and social habits, these art champions evidently support the city's strong profile against those of neighboring powerhouses, the much older cities of Rio de Janeiro and São Paulo.

The future idealized in 1897 actually came true as utopia, the good but non-existent paradise that the Greek word implies. From the dusty rural world of Curral del-Rei in central Minas Gerais to its present day capital's hustle and bustle, there has always been room for thoughts and expectations, those which the land's coined name, "beautiful horizon," symbolically suggests. In the meantime, the city has built its resistant and independent character, which suggests that the republic regime defenders may have indeed achieved, in due time, their goal of impressing the rest of the nation.

On everyday conversations, though, one can still hear a recurrent point of criticism: this is a great city, but it has no beaches. Seth Kugel quotes the prosaic reaction of some Belo Horizontinos to that grievance: "Não tem mares, tem bares." Loosely, it translates as "There are no seas, thus there are bars." More in tune with the name of the city, though, is Mineiro writer Rubem Alves's poetic response: "Minas' sea is not in the sea. Minas' sea is in the sky, for the world to look up and navigate without ever having a harbor to reach" (Alves).

Notes

1. Oscar Ribeiro de Almeida Niemeyer Soares Filho passed away on December 5, 2012, ten days before turning 105 years old. The Carioca architect's outstanding legacy in the city of Belo Horizonte is being expanded by the ongoing construction of his sophisticated project for Cristo Rei Cathedral, designed to seat 5,000 people.
2. Macedo maintains that Niemeyer's works in the 15 years that preceded the construction of the famous Pampulha legacy were both instrumental and foundational to all the projects he created before Brasilia (22-23).
3. There was such a fear of popular unrest, particularly among Ouro Preto inhabitants who felt strongly about keeping their city as capital, that the 1893 legislative sessions that led to the final of that deliberation had to take place in another city, Barbacena (Oliveira, *Belos* 24).
4. Echoing modernist Mário de Andrade's 1922 controversial poetry book about São Paulo's urban issues, *Paulicéia desvairada,* the mixed-genre CD, *Belôricéia,* was released by singer Helena Penna on Belo Horizonte's 100th anniversary.

Works Cited

Alves, Rubem. "Floripa." *Folha de São Paulo* 2 March 2010: C2.

Araújo, Laís Corrêa de, ed. "O nome é a marca." *Sedução do horizonte*. Belo Horizonte: Fundação João Pinheiro, 1996.

Assis, Joaquim M. Machado de. "Belo Horizonte!" Araújo 23.

Baker-Smith, Dominic. *More's* Utopia. Toronto: Renaissance Society of America/University of Toronto Press, 2000.

Bilac, Olavo. Araújo 26-29.

Dekker, Zilah Quezado. *Brazil Built: the architecture of the modern movement in Brazil*. New York: Spon, 2001.

Holston, James. *The Modernist City: An Anthropological Critique of Brasília*. Chicago: University of Chicago Press, 1989.

Kugel, Seth. "A Town Where All the World Is a Bar." *New York Times* 8 Oct 2007. <http://travel.nytimes.com/2007/10/28/travel/28next.html>. Web. 25 Nov 2010.

Lobato, Monteiro. "Belo Horizonte, a bela." Araújo 35-41.

Macedo, Danilo Matoso. "As obras de Oscar Niemeyer em Belo Horizonte." *Mínimo Denominador Comum: Revista de Arquitetura* 2: 22-35. *<http://revistamdc.files.wordpress.com/2008/12/mdc02-txt05.pdf>*. Web. 22 Nov 2010.

Milliard, Connie. "Intreview: Jochen Volz." Artinfo. 25 Nov 2010. <http://www.artinfo.com/news/story/34582/interview-jochen-volz/?page=1>. Web. 12 Nov 2010.

More, Thomas. *Utopia*. Eds. George M. Logan and Robert M. Adams. New York: Cambridge UP, 2002.

Needell, Jeffrey D. *A Tropical* Belle Époque. New York: Cambridge UP, 1987.

Niemeyer, Oscar. *As curvas do tempo: memórias*. Rio de Janeiro: Revan, 1998.

Oliveira, Jader de. *No tempo mais que perfeito: vida e sonhos de Belo Horizonte nos anos 50*. Belo Horizonte: [n], 2009.

Oliveira, Roberta de Souza Domingues. *Belos 111 horizontes*. Belo Horizonte, MG: Armazém de Idéias, 2009.

Penna, Helena. *Belôricéia*. N/l 1997. CD.

Scott, James C. *Seeing Like a State: How Certain Schemes to Improve the Human Condition Have Failed*. New Haven, CT: Yale UP, 1998.

Representing Durban in South African Indian Writings

Chetty Rajendra

> *To put it polemically, there is no such thing as a city…*
> *The city then, is above all a representation.*
>
> James Donald, 'Metropolis as text' (1992)

This article analyses the representations of Durban in Imraan Coovadia's *The Wedding* (2001) and Aziz Hassim's *The Lotus People* (2003). The purpose is to explore connections between the texts and the city as place/space. Writers use their unique lens through which they view their city, hence both the texts absorb and refract a different light on the common source. While the casbah (term used for the place where the Indians lived in the city) is a life-long passion for Hassim with its political activists and gangsters, it barely gets a mention by Coovadia whose text focuses on a personal story. The two writers of Indian descent, in defining their relation to Durban, also define themselves concomitant with the portrayal of the dispossessed and deprived, the victims of colonialism and apartheid in the city. The Durban portrayed in the texts is a 'little India' in an African city that the British colonists and the Afrikaner regime both claimed at different times – indeed the most contested city in South Africa. They fought each other for and in this city: The Zulu and the Boers (Battle of Blood River, 1838), the British and the Boers (Battle of Congella, 1842), the Zulu and the English (Battle of Isandlwana, 1879) and the Zulu and the Indian (Durban Riots, 1949).

Durban is represented as a complex space wherein nations are being crossed and lived within (it is considered as the 'last British outpost', the kingdom of the Zulus and host city to the Indian immigrants who came as sugar slaves in 1860). Questions of home and displacement, origin and homeland, cultural identity and migration collide in a powerful mix in Durban. The historical quagmire of apartheid and colonialism and more recently globalization, together with diasporic identity constructions, are theorized and positioned skillfully in Coovadia's and Hassim's texts. Certeau's (1984) theory on the various representations of space is an ideal lens to reveal the extent to which the narratives' repertoire of displacement is represented in terms of material history and conditions in Durban. Similar to literary elements of a text, the cartographic representations or maps are now being studied as a cultural text that is constructed by signs and power codes which are part of larger hegemonic discourses. Hassim transforms the landscape of Durban into a scheme for political commentary and the use of space for economic exploitation. Coovadia, on the other hand, through humour and satire foregrounds the concepts of home, diasporic identity, nostalgia and collective remembering without entering the political debates of the time. While *The lotus people* may be considered a historic epic and covers three generations of a family, *The Wedding*, a 'novelized memoir', focuses on an individual story of the impulsive arranged marriage of Ismet and Khateja and the bride's defiance of being sold like a 'box of vegetables' (43). They migrated to Durban so that Ismet can 'save' his marriage and 'Khateja the ice queen would melt' (120).

Both the novels depict not only a single family's journey from India to Durban, but also provide a valuable source of information about the experiences, struggles, feelings and thoughts of the South African Indian community – a history from the inside. The representations of Durban in the texts have elevated the texts from mere narrative to an aesthetic object that prompts a critical consciousness of spatiality.

Historical Background

Durban is - after Johannesburg - the second-largest city in South Africa. The third major city is Cape Town. Durban is on the east coast of the country in the province of Kwa-Zulu Natal. The timeline of human habitation in Durban goes back to long before the advent of recorded history in the region. While some of the earliest remnants of humanity are found in the nearby Drakensberg mountains, it is now established that prior to the arrival of the Nguni people and subsequent European colonialists, the area was populated by the original people of Southern Africa - now collectively called the Khoi/San. Then, several thousand years later, on Christmas day in 1497, Portuguese explorer Vasco da Gama arrived at the Durban bay, and called it "Terra do Natal", Christmas Country. The bay was surrounded by mangrove swamps and dense coastal forests. Only sporadically some pirates and ivory or slave dealers laid anchor, and it was much later, in 1824, that a proper white colonial settlement started, initially named "Port Natal". It was founded by merchants from the Cape Colony who had reached a contractual agreement with the mighty Zulu King, Shaka, who authorised them to establish a trading station. In 1835 the town was named Durban after the Cape Governor of the time, Sir Benjamin D'Urban. Time and again there were assaults and skirmishes by the Zulus, who - obviously - saw Natal as their tribal homeland and only tolerated the white settlers, because the town was of use to them as a trading station.

In 1844, Natal - with Durban - was incorporated into the British Cape Colony. In 1860, finding the Zulus to be uncooperative labourers, the British imported the first of several thousand indentured labourers from British India to take up work in the sugar cane fields. Along with them came "passenger" Indians who were not indentured, and who were free to engage in business.

The Indian Immigrants

The majority of South African Indians are descendents of indentured workers brought to the port of Durban in the British colony of Natal between 1860 and 1911 to work in the sugar belt. The indigenous Zulu people, relatively secure in their tribal economy, refused to market their labour. It was also the time in Natal when the Zulu warriors would victoriously wash their spears in the blood of over 1500 British soldiers at Isandlawana. It was India, a British subject, that offered the solution to the vacuum created by the emancipation of slaves on the world's tropical plantations. The immigrants and the African people were deprived of citizenship rights and subjected to gross exploitation by the British colonial authority and later by the apartheid regime.

For the immigrants, questions of origin, affiliation, cultural identity and migration collide in a powerful mix that has been called the politics of location by postcolonial theory (Frenkel 2). It would be interesting to get an answer to the question: At what point did the immigrants become indigenous to Durban, a place from which neither them nor their forbearers originate? Both Coovadia and Hassim theorise place and identities in Durban in relation to location, gender, politics and love. The positions held by the immigrants with regards to their identity construction is contradictory and shifts between an African (given the location of Durban) and an Indian (ties to the motherland) positionality, between the new homeland and a sense of displacement and loss, between the past life in India and the new present life in an unknown city and between the notions of race (dominant socio-cultural factor in colonial and apartheid Durban) and nationhood (African and/or Indian). Vikram, Ismet's friend in *The Wedding*, posits the ideal of a common ancestry – 'If we stick together as Indians, then the sky is the limit' (188). Ironically, they do not enjoy such solidarity in India with the class and caste system, and language and religious differences – 'So please Ismet , one word of advice that I can give for you. In this country you must not come with stories if you are this Bombay-Indian or that one Tamil, on what-what Gujarati-Indian' (150). It is the distance from the motherland together with the nostalgia that fuels the myth of homogeneity in India.

Space and Power

Michel Foucault's (1980) theory on the intimate connection between space and power, especially his theory of the Panopticon and its influence on the construction of modern cities finds resonance in Said's notion of "geographical violence" (Said 225). Foucault asserts rightly that 'a whole history remains to be written of spaces – which would at the same time be the history of powers – both these terms in the plural – from the greatest strategies of geopolitics to the little tactics of the habitat' (1980:149). The contested space of Durban, like all other cities, is not a neutral medium but has a history, with literature existing within a geographical and historical framework and further, space can be used as a tool of analysis in literary criticism (McNulty 5-6). Michel de Certeau's "Walking in the city" (1993), a theory that privileges the perspective of the walkers in the city, the people that cannot be governed by bureaucratic urban planning, will be used to explore alternative ways of engaging with city space. In other words, the 'big brother' gaze of the state and authorities from on high is undermined by the people that live in the city down below, they that own their habitus, the real makers and shapers of the city.

Fiction is an ideal medium for diasporic groups as the textual space is used to record and thus historicize the collective memory and to challenge the hegemonic memory and recorded history of the dominant power, in the case of South Africa, the colonial forces and later the apartheid regime. Shaw and Chase (1989) contend that it is through a nostalgic lens that the collective memories of diasporic groups are remembered. It is also through the process of re-membering that postcolonial writers are able to redefine colonial spatial history.

Foucault posits the notion of "heterotopias of exclusion", a fundamental exclusionary principle used in Durban to separate races geographically, economically, socially and politically. Black people (Indians, Coloureds and Africans), by virtue of their skin colour were marginalized by the white city fathers during the colonial period and oppressed during the apartheid era by the white supremacist regime – the materiality of power operated on the very bodies of the individuals (Foucault 1980:55).

Cartographic Representation

To discuss mapping and cartographic representation is not to abandon literary discourse altogether. Helgerson (1992) demonstrates how cartography and the epic came of age very early in Elizabethan England. In *The Faerie Queen* (1590-1596) Helgerson notes that 'every quest is said to originate and lead back to a single central court', and every river flows back to the 'courtly centre of power' (140). By substituting Durban as the court, Hassim creates the gangsterism, the commercial network and political resistance as the new power circulating in the city and lends to it some of the epic's heroism and majesty.

The cartographical representations of Durban are strongly evident in *The Lotus People* (2003). Certeau's (1984) theory on the various representations of space is an ideal lens to reveal the extent to which the narrative's repertoire of displacements is represented in terms of material history and conditions in Durban. Hocquard observes that the degree to which one knows a city is inversely proportional to the extent one actually sees it (Fester 84). According to Hocquard's strategy, one gets to know well a section of a city (a neighbourhood or a route frequently used), the memory of which knowledge lingers long after the perceiving presence departs the city, which subsequently becomes the city in the mind of the observer (Fester 84). Although visual perception forms the most immediate device by which the casbah is charted, history plays a key role as well as locating for the writers the city's cartographic points. Familiar landmarks trigger a flood of memories for Hassim like the Madressa and Ajmerie arcades, Sastri College, the West End and Himalaya Hotels, the movie houses, the Indian market, and apartments with their dark passages and courtyards.

The casbah on a Saturday morning was like no city anywhere on earth…

> Each street served a specific function. The eastern end of Victoria Street was theatre-land, the western half reserved mainly for the markets and grocery stores. Grey Street, from the racecourse to the West End Hotel in Pine Street, was the clothes-horses' paradise, offering an array of the most recent fashion trends from virtually every major centre of the world… Queen Street was a street of barbers on the one side and hardware and timber merchants on the other. Pine Street housed the best family owned tailor shops in the world; Prince Edward Street, the neatest sari houses and craftsmen jewelers. In between and at every corner was the inevitable tea-room, serving the best in chilli-bites and confectionery. (116)

There is a sustained emphasis on specificities of routes through the city in the novel and cartographical images proliferate in the construction of geographical space. The different streets performed different functions and formed territorial enclaves: economic hub, political rallies, entertainment, fashion, gangsters, markets, religious sites, etc.

> At the corner of Grey and Queen streets, occupying almost half
> a block, was the magnificent and architecturally famous Jumma
> Mosque, with its minarets and many domes (…) Adjoining the
> mosque, fronting onto Cathedral Road and directly opposite the
> historic Emmanuel Cathedral, were a row of cottages that had
> been consolidated into a large unit that served as a *madressah*
> for Muslim children. (115)

A major concern in Hassim's text is with issues of place and displacement
(Ashcroft et al 8) – "what these thugs in government are doing is beyond belief,
they're tearing decent people to ribbons with those killer dogs of theirs, they're
using their sjamboks to scar children for life (Hassim 539). The Group Areas
Act promulgated by the state in 1953 was the main heterotopia of exclusion
and it used race as the key category for spatial relationships in the city,
categories of inclusion and exclusion were created so that those labeled as
Indian were spatially segregated from white society and relegated to the 'Grey
Street' area of central Durban and suburbs specially for Indian people.

> Thousands of gracious and beautifully maintained homes,
> constructed and owned by Indian residents in the quiet suburbs
> of First Avenue, Mitchell Road, Florida Road, Cowey Road
> and their adjacent environs were expropriated and their
> occupiers given thirty days in which to vacate the premises.
> Compensation, determined solely by the government, would be
> decided on at some future date. It was a looters' paradise. The
> white financial establishment, in cahoots with the State, rubbed
> its collective hands in gleeful anticipation of enormous profits
> (100).

The apartheid government drew the lines of the Durban map to designate
different zones to the different race groups, for example Black African people
were moved to Umlazi and KwaMashu, Indian people to Chatsworth and
Phoenix, Coloured people to Wentworth and Sydenham. The white, male,
elitist gaze ensured that through cartographical means the city belonged to the
whites and legitimated a Eurocentric worldview of Durban.

A thematic map charts 'one class of feature, that feature being the
subject or 'theme of the map' on top of a base map so that it can reveal
'structures that would remain unknown if not mapped' (Robinson 57). By
plotting phenomena on an accurate base map, the terrain can be turned into a
narrative with a larger theme. The city is turned into a metaphor for the theme

represented and in Hassim's text, it is one of struggle and resistance of an oppressed community. This displacement and relocation of established communities is portrayed extensively in other South African fiction like Richard Rive's *Buckingham Palace: District Six* (1986) and Ezekiel Mphahlele's *Down Second Avenue* (1959). The forced removal of the Indian community from Cato Manor, a suburb in Durban, forms the essence of Ronnie Govender's *At the Edge and other Stories* (1994).

There is a representation of the particular discursive power of cartography within a larger economy of knowledge as well as topographical precision in the novel. The novel's composition is elevated beyond mere imagination, the writing can be equated with the rigorous method and precision of scientific practice. Hassim is not merely a writer fabricating stories from the stuff of imagination but a cartographer ordering Durban according to the rigour and detachment of scientific observation. The book is as much an archive of geographical fact as it is a narrative of imaginative fiction.

It is interesting to note that in both the texts under discussion, the key protagonists came to South Africa as passenger Indians, that is, they paid their own way and were not indentured labourers. *In the Lotus People*, the story focuses on Yahya Ali Suleiman who sets up home in the city, more specifically the Grey Street area that was reserved for Indians. The story revolves around Yahya, his son Dara and his grandsons, Sam and Jake. The story is based on real life families and real events and history is told from diverse perspectives and the voices of the different characters triangulate the historical events in the city for over an era. The fictional characters engage with the history of the city and country and engage with key political figures of the liberation movement like Mahatma Gandhi, Yusuf Dadoo and the doyen of Indian resistance in Durban, Kesavaloo Goonam.

Hassim uses Durban as a reference point, allowing a complete survey with all points related to the casbah and Grey Street. 'Grey Street and the roads leading off it became the focal point of the Resistance Movement (95). The genius of Hassim's mapping of Durban, is that every point on every route is related to the others because they are all, in the end, connected to the original source for this narrative, the casbah. The principal roads in the text radiate from Grey Street, the epicenter of the Indian community that settled in Durban (Chetty 112).

The text is not interested in simply painting a portrait of Durban as it appeared then. Rather, it represents an attempt to change the casbah from an actual historical space into a conceptual space in which the city becomes meaningful. The sight of the familiar places makes the narrator aware of the innumerable discrepancies between the past and the present and might be said to constitute for Hassim two maps superimposed upon each other. What is seen now often differs from what was known years before. On several occasions, the present holds nothing but recollections of places and people who had once marked the city, but who are now absent from it, chief of whom are the gangsters. The book can be read as lists of objects, persons and places. But by enumeration and the broad outlines that construct a cohesive whole, a cartographic conception of Durban emerges (Chetty 113).

Belonging to place

Bloom describes the nation as a coincidence, a cultural identity created through nothing more than a simultaneous residence in a geographically circumscribed location (Hegglund 179). Bloom's idea of national community is based on relation rather than essence, present circumstances rather than history. The map therefore does not present a preexisting community; it creates that community by abstracting a unified space out of a multiplicity of individually experienced places (Hegglund 179). Coovadia describes the place that his grandparents (Ismet and Khateja) journeyed to 'for personal reasons' and a new beginning and he weaves humour and history into the dialogue:

> So her husband brought her beyond her wildest dreams, to South Africa. To Durban on its northeastern coast, a beachy, subtropical Commonwealth city one million strong: one-third black, one-third white, and one-third Indian. Since Durban housed the largest number of Indians in a single place outside India, it was, excluding the subcontinent, the most rhetorical city in the world. (And thanks to its piebald, multistriped composition, the municipality of Durban inculcated in the mind of the expatriate Mohandas Gandhi, who was currently residing there, the outrageous conviction that each disparate subcontinental belonged to the same nationality – and so, in a sense, Durban created the nation-state of India.) (142-43)

Khateja was a free sprit in India, but the confinement in a small flat within the 'closed' Indian casbah in Durban cramped her lifestyle and made her feel claustrophobic. Ismet on the other hand, has become confident and tried to understand the new city so that he could 'control' and dictate Khateja's movement, forcing on her the role of student – 'Since the time they arrived on the shore actually he was busy with the nonstop lecturing to her' (156). He uses business to fill in his time and gains success in his venture as he surveys the city and creates a niche for himself first as a vendor, then as a vegetable and fruit seller and later as entrepreneur. In a vein of ironic inversion, Coovadia has situated Durban as the birthplace of modern India while simultaneously recreating South African history through inserting Indians centrally into the narrative (Frenkel 36).

Historically, the most common relationship that holds between a writer and a city is the one defined by any great object of desire: namely, that of the romance. The arranged marriage between Ismet and Khateja was troubled from the start since she refused to relent in any way, refused to comply and indicates to her mother-in-law, Rashida, that the investment in her was useless and worthless. Ismet's endeavour to break the stalemate with his new bride results in his migration to Durban:

> The place they found was in a block of flats on Queen Street, not far from the central business district, the Grey Street mosque, the market. There was a ground-floor tearoom, the stairways were cement blocks painted red, flaking red halls with a knee-high gray band, washing line strung up on chicken wire, black-eyed children with spades and buckets and dripping noses, the smell of cooking vegetables and evaporated butter, dimpled copper pots left out to dry by the screen doors, large circular women with red dots on their forehead. (144)

The personal reason for the migration is more a case of the taming of the shrew and it is Durban that eventually 'tames' Khateja. Ismet bargains with her that if he sends her back her family will force her into marriage with the madman, Ahmedu, and he is deluded into transforming her in Durban with his sexist assumptions:

> This was his idea: stand the fractious Khateja before an iron pot and paraffin stove, have her stirring with spoons one-two hours a day, washing meat, dicing vegetables..frying, ladling, marinating – at some point, indubitably, lo! a real traditional Indian-style home-country wife and gentle-figured lady would emerge from the membranes of dissension, would cast them off, chrysalis-like (or so Ismet imagined). (165)

The gendered meanings of home or recreating home in the context of migration and diaspora, emerge in the text through issues around cooking, objects and 'family' (Frenkel 35). The objects that they bring from India like the textiles, Koran and walking stick reinforces the nostalgia for home, it anchors immigrants in their new homes which they occupy as marginalized people.

de Certeau is concerned with the seemingly mundane everyday practice of walking through the city and Coovadia's easy humorous tale with its use of Indian English captures the ordinariness of the Durban casbah. For de Certeau, it is while exploring the city and getting lost in its dark crevices that the users are able to transform the abstract space of the city into a lived in and meaningful place. As Ismet walks through his new surroundings, the visibility of the city takes shape - they walk – an elementary form of this experience of the city; they are walkers, *Wandersmanner*, whose bodies follow the thicks and thins of an urban text they write without being able to read it (de Certeau 1993:153). It is Ismet that explores the city first on his way to and from mosque and the picture that emerges is no different from the streets of Indian cities, hence the new place has a feeling of home:

> He went straight past the jewelry stores with necklaces and Elgin and Madix watches on display in red velvet boxes, the *halaal* butchers selling cold meats and sausages, the Butterworth hotel on whose balcony men were drinking from dark green beer bottles. He was starting to feel perfectly at home. (176)

On Ismet's return back home, he gets lost in the new city and it seems as if the city is awaiting the imprint of an identity by the new sojourner; the city invites you to remake it, to consolidate it into a shape you can live in. One cannot experience the city without imagining it as well. Sicher (18) also notes that the ideologies of the city are embedded in architecture, institutions, hierarchies, and structures, and therefore urban experience cannot easily be separated from visual or symbolic representation of the city which encodes its various discourses in semiotic modeling of social space. One moulds the new city in one's own image, the soft city of illusion, myth, aspiration, and nightmare and transforms it, making it more real than the hard city one locates on a map (Raban 1).

> He went past Campbell's Automomotive Works, where men in blue overalls squatted on concrete amid pistons. He paid no heed to the Kubendra Universal Provisions & Refreshments Café with its shelves of brown bread wrapped in paper and the oven with a glass front full of curried chicken pies in foil

> flowers, hardly having noticed the warehouse on Stamford Road whose large rolling door was up, revealing dusty, white cloth sacks filled with sugar. A backstreet factory-surplus garment vendor accosted him and wouldn't let him go without a ten-minute lecture on bargain-basement pricing. Hurrying away, walking backward from the man who wouldn't stop with the chatting, he barely avoided treading on a nail that someone had left lying there in the street for anyone to impale himself on. (177)

It is Ismet's engagement with the marginal characters that are the most important in deciphering a city as in this case, the workers and vendors. The city is not really the habitat of the bourgeoisie, according to Walter Benjamin in *The Arcades Project*, it is also the home of the excluded character, those on the margins of society (cited in Gilloch 30). In Hassim's text as well it is the gamblers and the gangsters, the beggars and thieves, the poor and marginalized that are foregrounded. We also see it in Charles Dickens's *Great Expectations* where London is portrayed as a shameful place, being all asmear with filth and fat and blood and foam (165). It is easy for a new immigrant like Ismet to get lost in the city, more so the casbah, with its labyrinth of criss-crossing streets, homes above shops, and markets juxtaposed against factories and warehouses with the workers and the inhabitants flowing into the street. The city is an environment of anonymous crowds, where machines, arcades and the spectacle of consumerism would both disorientate and distract the urban dweller who has to be skilled to weave his/her way through the crowd. However, in spite of Ismet remaining anonymous like the crowds, closer to home we get a picture of a tightly knit Indian neighbourhood with support from Vikram and Pravina, and Khateja's grocer and butcher. Mishra alludes to this as the diaspora of exclusivism where Indians create self-contained mini-Indias in the colonies (422). It is a coping mechanism of the displaced immigrants and the need to put down roots among their own people in a foreign colonial space concomitant with its racism, exclusion and negative constructions of the 'other'.

Conclusion

Corner (213) maintains that mapping unfolds potential; it remakes territory over and over again, each time with new and diverse consequences. Michel de Certeau (1984) comments on the original intertwining of maps and stories in pre-Enlightenment cartography, invoking the itinerary as a formal mode that combines the temporal qualities of storytelling with the spatial imperatives of mapmaking as witnessed in *The Wedding* and *The Lotus People*. The map, de Certeau concludes, is a 'totalizing stage on which elements of diverse origin are brought together to form the tableau of a state of geographical knowledge' (121). De Certeau feels that they should be thought of as a stage upon which any number of 'performances' might take place.

Is Coovadia's and Hassim's reliance on mapping a modernist aesthetic strategy designed to give their novels the legitimating weight of fact and authenticity? Ultimately, it is the reader who is the only consciousness with access to the linking elements of the individual episodes and characters, suggesting that any community represented in the novel is an arbitrary rather than organic formation, resoled only by the surveying and judging gaze of the reader who can plot these diverse itineraries on a map of Durban.

Works Cited

Ashcroft, B., G Griffiths and H. Tiffin, eds. *The Empire Writes Back*. London: Routledge. 1989.

Chetty, R. "Mapping Durban in Aziz Hassim's *The Lotus People*." *Indian Writers: Transnationalisms and Diasporas*. Jaspal K. Singh and Rajendra Chetty, eds. New York: Peter Lang. 2010.

Coovadia, I. *The Wedding*. New York: Picador. 2001.

Corner, J. "The Agency of Mapping." *Mappings*. Cosgrove, D Ed. London: Reaktion, 1999. 213-52.

de Certeau, M. *The Practice of Everyday Life*. Trans. S Rendall. Berkeley: U of California P. 1984.

---. "Walking in the City." *The Cultural Studies Reader*. During, S. ed. London: Routledge. 1993.

Dickens, C. *Great Expectations*. London: Penguin Classics. 1996.

Fester, G.W. "Hocquard's Cartographies." *Symposium* 56 (2): 81-95. 2002.

Foucault, M. *Power/Knowledge: Selected Interviews, 1972-1977*. New York: Pantheon. 1980.

Frenkel, R. Writing South Africa in Diaspora: Imraan Coovadia's *The Wedding*. In Singh, J.K. and Chetty, R. *Indian Writers: Transnationalisms and Diasporas*. New York: Peter Lang. 2010.

Gilloch, G. *Myth and Metropolis: Walter Benjamin and the City*. Cambridge: Polity. 1996.

Govender, R. *At the Edge and Other Cato Manor Stories*. Pretoria: Hibbard. 1994.

Hassim, A. *The Lotus People*. Johannesburg: STE. 2003.

Hegglund, J. "Ulysses and the Rhetoric of Cartography." *Twentieth-Century Literature* 49.2(2003): 164-192.

Helgerson, R. *Forms of Nationhood: The Elizabethan Writings of England.* Chicago: University of Chicago Press. 1992.

James, Donald. "Metropolis as Text." *Social and Cultural Forms of Modernity.* Eds. Robert Bocock and Kenneth Thompson. Cambridge: Polity, 1992. 417-61.

McNulty, N. *Reading the City: Analyzing Literacy Space in Selected Apartheid Urban Narratives.* Unpublished MA thesis. U of KwaZulu Natal. 2005.

Mishra, V. "The Diasporic Imaginary: Theorizing the Indian Diaspora." *Textual Practice* 10.3 (1996): 421-447.

Mphahlele, E. *Down Second Avenue.* London: Heinemann. 1959.

Rive, R. *Buckingham Palace: District Six.* London: Heinemann. 1986.

Raban, J. *Soft City.* London: Hamish Hamilton. 1974.

Robinson, A. *Early Thematic Mapping in the History of Cartography.* Chicago: U of Chicago P. 1982.

Said, E.W. *Culture and Imperialism.* New York: Vintage Books. 1994.

Shaw, C. & Chase, M. *The Imagined Past: History and Nostalgia.* Manchester: Manchester UP. 1989.

Sicher, Efraim. *Rereading the City. Rereading Dickens. Representation, the Novel and Urban Realism.* New York: AMS. 2003.

Challenging the Global Megalopolis: San Francisco as Urban "Other"

Christopher Larkosh

What is the city today—that is, what is it really that each of us experiences as a city in the early 21st century? And where exactly do we place our own 'city limits': that is to say, where does the city that we call 'our own' both begin and end, if not begin again?

The ways that we b/order and delineate our understandings of urban space in language, narrative and thought, however differently, invariably tell us something important about ourselves: whether about how our terrestrial comings-and-goings play out both within the strictly defined administrative city limits of a single global metropolis and across the shifting boundaries of the metropolitan entities that we transit on a daily basis; the wide interconnected expanses of urban, suburban and rural spaces that make up the 21st century megacity; or even the personal archipelagoes of urban spaces that global nomads might piece together in both our own global travels and literary imaginations. At this point, the city as we imagine and live it becomes an undeniably modular construct, subjective and polymorphous in its shape and seemingly infinite in its combinatory potential.

With this in mind, it is increasingly impossible to ignore the 'Other' of any urban space, and that the putative 'outside' of any city, its ever-elusive elsewhere, is already 'inside': whether in the firm of ever-evolving multicultural neighborhoods, a global menu of media sources and consumer goods, if not the ongoing and irreversible global demographic shifts that continue to refocus attention on those persistent questions regarding the limits of citizenship, legitimacy and the ever-present possibility of alienation. Even if the idea of the "global city" has been circulating for some time in the form of by-now well known theoretical works (above all Sassen 1991), it is less possible (that is, if it ever really has been) to exclude other urban spaces from the questions that this research has posed, nor is it realistic to limit the criteria of presumed academic importance of these spaces to those determined by a short list of strategic economic, financial or political concerns, nor is it advisable to limit the intellectual point of departure from which research on this phenomenon is mapped out, being as it is still organized, collected and disseminated largely at a few prestigious academic institutions and publishing houses, most of them still, in spite of recent and remedial gestures, limited in geographical, linguistic, socioeconomic and cultural scope, and in many cases, generating discourses that emanate from highly securitized enclosures precisely to protect and separate these rarified spaces from the 'other' urban spaces that might otherwise come under greater consideration and thus gain the attention that they have all too often been denied. Then again, in spite of these very real structural divisions, this city, however academicized and segregated it may appear from certain textual perspectives, may in fact need no 'other', as both in its multiplicity and interconnectedness it remains as much the other as it might be imagined otherwise; i.e., as singular, knowable and still in thrall of the specialist voice of one who knows.

There is no doubt that this tendency remains in evidence in the US East Coast megalopolis: arguably the most populated continuous urban area in the Western Hemisphere (with approximately 55 million inhabitants), spread out across a dozen-odd US states and a federal capital district between southern Maine and northeastern Virginia. On a good day, a train can make the 450 mi/700 km trip along the transportation corridor from Boston to DC in about six hours, passing through the center of a number of urban spaces quite often thought of as cities in their own right, connecting onward to a series of bus and rail networks, interstate highways and international airports. Millions of us cross both the city limits and state lines within this megalopolis on a daily basis, adding to this mosaic of urban transit routes as the main evidence of its status as a single urban entity. While New York is recognized by most as the primary economic and cultural center of this megalopolis, one would be mistaken if one were to privilege, concentrate, or delimit its globality to there alone. The effects on continuing globalization disperse the markings of global culture far beyond these established focal points, and might even be more visible at times in smaller urban areas, where the effects of this ongoing process are often of more manageable dimensions.

Indeed, where does the urban network we live in truly begin or end? Certainly not in this contiguous megacity alone; whether through the global internet accessible on our mobile devices, or frequent air travel and the arrival of the "aerotropolis" (Kasarda & Lindsay 2011) as an airport-based model for the 21st-century city, the way that such interconnectivity shapes lived experience from one moment to the next constantly leads us to question to an even greater extent whether any kind of separation of one major urban center from another can withstand the pressures of global networks, especially those that the urban theorist Manuel Castells has identified as the "informational city" (Castells 1989).

As we are continually set into motion much as our information is, witnessing in both academic and personal terms this recurring phenomenon of global interconnectivity in other parts of the world—whether in China's Pearl River Delta, the Indo-Gangetic plain of South Asia, the Taiheiyo conurbation on the Japanese islands of Honshu and Kyushu or other East Asian countries such as South Korea or Taiwan, or in Latin American urban configurations such as the valley of Mexico, Bogotá or Caracas, US-Mexican border cities, southeastern Brazil or the River Plate—it becomes increasingly impossible for us to ignore that there is not necessarily anything particularly unique or primary about any particular metropolitan configuration, and that a interconnected global megalopolis has, in fact, already emerged as the form of urban space that most accurately characterizes the lived experience of a broad segment of human beings currently inhabiting our increasingly populated planet. With it will undoubtedly come new combinations of languages and cultures, as emerging economies and global regions shift the focus of economic activity away from the 20th century metropolitan centers of Europe and North America, and toward the dynamic megacities of Asia, Latin America and beyond.

One might suggest that we continue to live the form of connectivity that Deleuze and Guattari identified years ago in their seminal work *A Thousand Plateaus*: "if it is the modern State that gives capitalism its models of realization, what is thus realized is an independent, worldwide axiomatic that is like a single City, megalopolis, or 'megamachine' of which the States are parts, or neighborhoods" (Deleuze/Guattari 1987: 434-435). Indeed, one could argue that our peripatetic movement as urban subjects has already been irreversibly "deterritorialized," "nomadological" or "rhizomatic" for some time, and for this very reason, all the more transformational in scope by now. Moreover, as bands of global nomads establish contact with one another in an expanded set of urban centers and webs of communications at an accelerated pace, the sense of blur between them begins to intensify as well. Particularly when the transportation and telecommunications links to which many of us have become accustomed are momentarily interrupted (whether by the constants of political and economic inequality that make such global concentrations of wealth and power possible in the first place, to the recurrent spate of natural and environmental disasters, or violent conflicts and technological breakdowns that continually punctuate the hardly-seamless functioning of global exchange), it becomes all the more clear that the city is not even one geographically contiguous expanse on a single landmass, but a globalized archipelago of unevenly illuminated and pulsating populated spaces (however uneven in their interconnectivity) that stretches across all continents and already connects us with many, if never all of them. Even if one has never left one's own neighborhood, the urban landscape and its commonplaces still point toward this inescapable reality, through the transit and consumption of imported products, the buzz of satellite media and internet communications, and the juxtaposition of these once dispersed lived experiences of what we eat, watch, take home or share with others.

The only lesson we can draw from all this, then, is that there is not and never has been any single, clear, much less central, point of reference for the idea of the global city, no matter how much the promoters of the self-proclaimed indisputable intellectual, cultural and economic capitals of the 19th and 20th centuries (New York, London, Tokyo, Paris etc.) may continue to insist to the contrary. Quite often, such status is determined largely on the basis of cultural and academic models that privilege the exercise of power and leave less measureable forms of exchange at a relative disadvantage— whether artistic activity and literary inspiration, or the intensity of languages and cultures in contact with one another. New York remains one of the most ethnically segregated cities in the US, despite its repeated claims to having the world's most hybrid and cosmopolitan urban culture; Tokyo, while possessed of any number of examples of global consumer culture, is hardly an ethnically diverse society, with a smaller percentage of foreign immigrants than in virtually any other industrialized society. Even London and Paris, while undoubtedly cosmopolitan, have their own challenges of ethnic and socioeconomic segregation, as well as visions of globality and attendant models of cultural interaction still rooted, at least to some extent, in their late 19th and early 20th-century colonial empires.

So once the emphasis is shifted from discussions of prime economic, financial and political dominance to one of possible other spaces in which cultural and linguistic connectivity might be re-imagined, the possibilities for sustained critique of the "global city" approach might begin to find concrete materials for imagining urban centers differently. In this dispersed conceptualization of our urban context, to begin to develop a set of continually evolving countermodels to conventional understandings of the city might necessarily involve these immense extensions of other spaces, whether cultural, linguistic, ethnic or socioeconomic, carrying with/in them what 'the city' is or can be. How does the city that we may imagine we already know hold the *allopolis* within it, speaking other languages, shifting and blurring its internal boundaries, and presenting new cultural, linguistic and ethnic combinations that perhaps cannot be found anywhere else?

My Own "Other City": San Francisco

So what is perhaps most compelling about the other-city approach is how it places the author and the reader into a perspective in which both the point of departure, points of contrast, and the putatively alternative place to be viewed are necessarily made more explicit. After all, were it not for this perspective, we might not be even able to claim that San Francisco is necessarily an other city; after all, for so many who live here and other points on the West Coast and beyond, it is "The City" in the same way that so many others style themselves to be, both primary and indisputably central, at least to some extent in its own field of reference and the ways it tells and retells its own stories about itself. And while some of us may now be either back living in a corner of the East Coast megalopolis or shuttling back and forth between other cities in North America and beyond on a daily basis, San Francisco might still remain 'closer' to us on a practical and an emotional level than most of the other geographically nearby points on a global map: thanks above all to reasonably affordable air travel that often acts to diminish the importance of the most primary points of urban centrality on the basis of sheer proximity, whether New York, Boston, Philadelphia, Washington on the East Coast (not to mention Toronto, Montréal or Chicago), Vancouver, Seattle, Portland, Los Angeles, San Diego or San José on the West, or European and East Asian capitals. While we may still pass through them often, these nodes in our present continental map often manifest their importance as the transit points though which we depart to somewhere else. Admittedly, like so many others, our professional and personal commitments largely limit our experience of our continent's urban life to a largely dispersed perspective with a continually shifting set of transoceanic destinations beyond it, with all of the political and cultural implications that such a mapping would tend to imply.

Located just beyond the geological fault line that separates the Pacific Ocean from the North American continent, San Francisco is also part of a megalopolis, one that stretches down through the Bay Area to San José and the Silicon Valley, the Central Valley, to Los Angeles (the other point from which San Francisco is most commonly imagined as 'secondary' or 'other') and then down through Orange County to San Diego, if not all the way across the US/Mexico into Tijuana in Baja California, to form a conurbation that urban theorists have come to call "San-San." In this series of Spanish hagionyms re-employed as colonial place names, this California/West Coast urban corridor underscores its historical origins in the Camino Real and the Spanish colonial mission circuit it connected in the late 18th and early 19th centuries. A visit to one of those missions, and not only those now at the heart of California urban centers, but perhaps those obscure outposts now far from any nearby city (such as San Antonio de Padua, Soledad, San Juan Bautista, or San Miguel Arcángel) may well highlight more clearly the main components of these microcosms: not only its institutions of religious indoctrination, but also its invariably accompanying military presence, each of which acted in coordination with one another in the induction of a multiethnic Native population living in grass huts adjacent to the more permanent adobe structures (originally Ohlone, but subsequently joined by Miwok, Patwin and other indigenous groups) into a system of economic and ideological coercion and control in what was originally a Native village called Chutchui. However more sophisticated structures of social, economic and political organization might attempt to gloss over this fact in subsequent waves of conquest, consolidation of power and development, the remnants of these original structures remain part of this continuum, and however distant many of these missions remain from an identifiable urban center, they nonetheless made possible the city of San Francisco as we know it today: one of any number of indigenous and Spanish names, now left untranslated in English and other languages as they become an inseparable part of the US and global imaginary.

This linear sequence of missions as would eventually be supplemented by East-West transcontinental stagecoach and rail links after the region was annexed to the US in 1848 under the controversial Treaty of Guadalupe Hidalgo, that notorious document of broken promises to protect the rights of the postwar Mexican inhabitants, and then by those trans-Pacific maritime and air links that began with the first forays to open trade with Japan, an expanding missionary and economic presence in China, intervention in the internal politics of the independent Kingdom of Hawaii and its annexation as a US territory, at the same time that the US would occupy the Philippines, Guam and other Pacific Islands previously occupied by Spain as part of its victories in the Spanish-American War. Add to these the First and Second World Wars, as well as the Korean and Vietnam Wars, and San Francisco would be maintained as a center of deployment of military, economic and political power throughout the peak years of this 20th-century US Pacific hegemony. Each occasional geological or political earthquake, however major it might appear at the time, would only briefly interrupt, but never fully disrupt this apparent juggernaut of US imperial consolidation.

In light of these historical points of reference offered by way of introduction, it should nonetheless be made clear at this point that, like other cultural theorists who have re-envisioned the ways we write about urban space (esp. de Certeau, Augé), I have no interest in writing about any city, especially one we know as intimately as San Francisco, from the upper story of an academic building: i.e., simply by basing my critical observations on the quantitative analyses and academic investigations of others without any reference to my own specific personal connections to it, as I understand them. Disembodied and depersonalized academic models of urban space abound, usually legitimized precisely in the language of that institution and its methodological imperatives, and it is precisely this depopulated (if not explicitly ivory-tower) approach to urban life that I wish to avoid here. I remain most interested in San Francisco on the ground level, as an interconnected living and breathing urban space with uncertain regional and global boundaries: an ever-evolving cultural environment inseparable from a specific set of interpersonal memories and aesthetic preferences, which continue to posit our own human lives alongside those of others, both within and beyond this city's geographical borders.

Against the backdrop of this ambivalent, if brief, historical overview, the living among us can only count ourselves as late arrivals. As a city that already holds so many other cities within itself, San Francisco today often remains irreconcilably other to itself, its own story, its own ongoing conversation about itself. For this reason, it endures as my principal alternative urban hub, the place where I continue to return over the course of a lifetime, both to re-imagine the cultural and linguistic contours of our shared life stories, and perhaps even to reinvent our selves once again. San Francisco and the Bay Area always seemed to provide for me an inexhaustible supply of what was new or different, strange or future, a continual locus to move toward radically different ways of understanding both selfness and otherness, and it is for this reason that the city cannot but put be back in contact with my own personal contacts there for the purposes of this essay.

So in order to dislodge the predominant academic understandings of the global city from any subsequent interpretation, we may also need to displace the very city that we re-encounter here; out of the downtown areas or well-known touristic neighborhoods and into other spaces that provide many people with their main impressions of it: the Financial District with its elongated and controversial pyramidal landmark, the Transamerica building; the Civic Center as the focal point of a often chaotic exercise in representative democracy; supposedly recognizable 'ethnic' neighborhoods such as Chinatown or the Mission, however illusory this impression may actually be; or traditionally 'alternative' neighborhoods that North Beach was to the Beats, Haight-Ashbury to hippies, peaceniks and flower children, or the Castro to gay men, lesbians, bisexuals and transgender people. As such neighborhoods' traditional understandings of themselves continue to solidify and shift, not only for historical but also touristic and commercial motivations, it may be necessary to trace out the borders of such areas, to see how ever-developing understandings of intersubjectivity emerge in the interstices of such established urban spaces, and to continue to seek out and examine there what each of us calls otherness, not only on the other side of borders of space and identity, but also along the shifting lines of these borders themselves.

Many of these redefining urban border spaces might be identified within the city's landscape itself; for example, San Franciscans have often spoken in this way of the linear quasi-neighborhood called the Dolores Corridor sandwiched between the 'gay' Castro and the 'Latino' Mission, or watched as the dividing line between Chinatown and traditionally Italian-American and bohemian North Beach continues to blur. Even a short walk through and around the limits of the 1960s-era 'planned ethnic neighborhood'-turned-consumer and tourist complex called Japantown— with its block-long pedestrian street, its indoor mall featuring a wide variety of sushi restaurants and noodle shops, the Kabuki baths with its piped-in new-age music, the Kinokuniya Japanese-language bookstore, and high-end Japanese curio shops alongside dollar stores and supermarkets—would still come to reveal at second glance a much more complex cultural landscape than the name suggests: the Korean barbecue restaurants, video stores and day spa; Hawaiian consumer items such as baked goods and other food items, musical instruments, CDs, clothing and crafts; as well as the African-American jazz clubs, corner stores and art galleries that begin here to extend into the adjacent Fillmore district. After all, even Japan, especially that hypermodern urban space that some Western cultural theorists have repeatedly imagined as a prime example of "radical alterity" (esp. Baudrillard & Guillaume) has for some time ceased to be simply the incommensurable space that so many have imagined it to be: not only as Japanese continue to discover new cultural horizons in products as African-

American music and street fashion, Korean dramas and popular music, or trans-Pacific tourism, but also as wave after wave of imported Japanese urban culture continues both to hybridize and leave its lasting mark on the Western imaginary, leaving doubt as to where this 'Japan' being spoken of really begins or ends.

While the debate will continue as to what exactly are the predominant terms of this cultural interaction, it seems strange that the main vertical structure in this urban complex called Japantown, the elliptically-named Peace Pagoda, can remain so eerily silent on historical detail: perhaps a statement in itself of how war not only silences lives, but makes articulation of the resulting trauma all the more impossible. That said, if its terse inscriptions were in fact capable of speaking to the enormity of what this monument was erected to represent, it would have to bear witness not only to the horrors of the Second World War—whether the successive Japanese invasions and occupations of China, Korea and Southeast Asia, or the dropping of the atomic bomb on Hiroshima and Nagasaki—but also the deportation of the pre-war Japanese-American inhabitants of this very neighborhood to internment camps. While it is estimated that a third of the residents returned after the war, interpreting this amnesic late Modernist representation of 'peace' against the backdrop of this history sends an unintentional, and perhaps for this reason all the more disconcerting message: that it is the cultural specifics of memory itself that must be suppressed in order for peace to take center stage, be it here or anywhere else.

Another of the less examined spaces where this extreme cultural overlap and interaction can be experienced is in the adjacent suburban area of Daly City, home to one of the largest concentrations of Filipino people outside of the archipelago, so much so that it is often called "the Pinoy capital" (Vergara). To offer one example: any habitual visit to a local business by the name of Manila Oriental Market, always uncovers for us not only a wide range of Filipino food products, some with names already familiar to us, others, less so, often with unintentionally comic pronunciations or interlingual confusion: Ginisang bagoong (shrimp paste)? Mamon tostado (a toasted sponge cake)? Puto seko (a crispy rice cake)? As these examples may indicate, such consumer products in a supermarket display, in aisles marked with the trilingual English, Spanish and Chinese signage that has come to characterize the Bay Area, often serve to illustrate the Philippines' history of transoceanic interaction as well: whether with Spain, Mexico and the rest of the Spanish colonial empire; or with China and the rest of Southeast Asia; or with its most recent colonial master, the US, from which it won its independence in 1946 after an a long and often bloody struggle that reached with the 1899-1902 US-Filipino War. Through fifty years of US occupation and subsequent Filipino immigration, US imperial reach across the Pacific over the 19th, 20th and 21st centuries further complicates the final picture, eventually returning this cultural encounter to its own shores as a visibly multilingual and polysemic (if never fully postcolonial) cultural experience.

Walking up and down the aisles of this market, surrounded by and interacting with people from all over the Pacific Rim region, remapping culture can no by no means be imagined simply as a kind of speculative theoretical exercise, but more importantly at the very core of one's own continual and concrete lived experience. What to make of the unfamiliar packaged foodstuffs, each a symbolic challenge to how any of us may eat or otherwise consume today, within a set of culturally determined habits, preferences and tastes? How does reading a label or learning of a food's multiple origins give us a more conscious sense of the historical and cross-cultural currents in which we find ourselves? How do the communications we engage in, listen in on, and remember with each other here—whether in English, Filipino, Spanish, Ilocano, Chavacano, not to mention Chinese, Japanese, Korean, Vietnamese, Khmer, Hmong and all the other languages here, whether on packaging, in passing conversation or just in our associations—point toward this radical alterity, a being in place and time that is not only 'here-and-now', but seemingly and simultaneously, every other place, every other time?

Literary Excursions into Radical Alterity: Ferlinghetti, Anzaldúa, Cha

One might also ask how literary texts have collaborated in simultaneously constructing and disarticulating this radical alterity: San Francisco has produced a number of important texts in which the self is both explored and developed and is simultaneously imagined as other. In this "other-city" space, monolithic models of culture are continually called into question, while radically hybrid modes of imagining the self are juxtaposed against those hegemonic models created and disseminated by mass media and other institutional means of cultural diffusion.

To witness this by juxtaposing the works of authors who have written in and on San Francisco—such as Lawrence Ferlinghetti's collections of poetry, Gloria Anzaldúa's *Borderlands/La frontera* or Theresa Hak-Kyung

Cha's *Dictee*—yields an often overlapping collage of modes both of 'being oneself' and of imagining self as other: whether as a representative of a self-proclaimed counterculture, or as an embodied example of imagining the limits of language and culture differently. The question remains whether the other city—a city of others—can still be a project for one authorial voice or literary movement alone, or whether it must be comparative and collaborative by its very nature: one best envisioned across language and culture, space and time, and in conversation from the outset, in order to give a more complete sense of its ultimate possibilities.

After all, we are already far from the initial models of cultural mixity that first brought Ferlinghetti back from Europe and across the continent to center his literary and cultural project here: while it may still be to some extent "the most European city, the most Italian city, the most polyglot city, the most bohemian city" (23), the terms of this cross-cultural encounter have shifted irreversibly South and East over the course of a sixty-year literary and artistic career. The "Old Italians" on their park benches in North Beach are joined by the Chinese dragon from an ever-expanding Chinatown (one that is by now irreversibly our town, both on a local and global scale), as well as by the Black and Latino baseball players at Candlestick Park who, in hitting their home runs and running the bases, distract the poet from his reading of Ezra Pound: "this last of the Anglo-Saxon epics in the Territorio Libre of Baseball" (43). Even these poetic visions of an emergent, free and multicultural future, however powerful they may appear, would ultimately find an even more formidable opponent: in what Ferlinghetti calls on more than one occasion "corporate monoculture" (26, 79). In this context, one might ask what this poet is really proposing when he exhorts his reader to "work on a frontier, if you can find one" (29), as in the expanding reach of global capital, it is easy for him to imagine that there may no longer be any room in this city for poetry or other alternative forms of cultural expression. After all, for Ferlinghetti it is not San Francisco as a political or economic entity, but as a viable "other city" in alternative, if not overtly contestatory cultural and creative terms, that is now increasingly at stake here.

The border continues to arrive in other forms, however: whether as Anzaldúa's bilingual, lesbian and mestizo "borderlands/frontera", or Cha's transcontinental creative project that also gathers materials at the borders: whether of numerous East Asian cultures or the internal border called the DMZ (heavily militarized despite its name) that passes through Korea to this day. While Anzaldúa states "I carry 'home' on my back" (21), her bilingual English-Spanish texts plot out a broad range of cultural connections, not only with her own US/Mexico border region in South Texas, but also to cultural elements as disparate as Aztec goddesses or intellectual figures of 20th-century Mexico, all recontextualized by her life and literary activity in San Francisco. As she continually redraws the border to pass through herself, it extends to pass through this city as well: not only on a symbolic, but all too often on a visible, concrete level. In this geographical transfer of cultural identity, some questions still remain, however: how many of us can this border and its languages be said to pass through at this point, and perhaps more importantly, how have the terms of this cultural border crossing expanded exponentially beyond a single border or set of cultural terms to encompass a much more extensive vision of global, cultural and linguistic hybridity?

As a visual and multimedia performance artist, Cha had also articulated this question of cultural border-crossing years differently from her earliest work, not only in the terms of her own ethnic identity as the daughter of Korean immigrants, but also went far beyond them, re-inscribing both 20th-century history marked by war and the inseparable lived experiences of separation, pain and loss that accompany it through a fragmented verbal and illustrated visual narrative, one that also continues to point to the challenges of writing from a frontier, whether that in between languages and cultures or that between the written word and visual image. Whether through the inclusion of Chinese calligraphy or the map of bodily points used in acupuncture; an introspective look of her own study of yet another language, French, through the repetitive acts of written dictation; or the attempt to reconstruct her mother's life story as a teacher in Japanese-occupied Manchuria to her eventual immigration to the US represented in a passport photo; all interspersed with other historical narratives such as those of Greek poets or Catholic saints—all of these disparate textual remnants still remain at risk of being effaced: "words cast each by each to weather avowed indisputably, to time. If it should impress, make fossil trace of word, stand as a ruin stands, simply, as mark, having relinquished itself to time and distance" (Cha 177). However impermanent and fragile such words may appear at any moment, such work, especially when placed alongside others to be reread and reinterpreted, holds out the possibility nonetheless that these words will not be merely cast to the wind and forgotten, but gathered once again, reorganized and re-inscribed, especially when understood alongside those personal images and experiences that provide them with a additional layer of significance.

One Last Glance at the Global City
(and the Potential of Others)

Ultimately, the very concept of the global city, however convincing it may have been imagined from inside its own self-referential cultural network and through its corporate and/or academic interpreters, can by now be recognized as an increasingly deceptive intellectual construct, in spite of any lingering claims to their indisputable primacy. In contrast, other cities still provide concrete, complementary and alternative forms of globalized urbanity, perhaps more selective in their geographic or narrative scope at times, but perhaps for that very reason, no less compelling and worthy of scholarly inquiry. These other ways of experiencing the city may not necessarily pass through statistics of trade, capital flows, concentrations of power and other economic and political indicators of global interconnectivity, but what about the connectivity of communities, people, or ongoing lived experience? Why are these sensory, emotional, aesthetic and lived forms of global connectedness still not given a corresponding level of recognition in so many academic discussions?

Admittedly, much of what is experienced and lived as global in the city remains intensely interpersonal and transitory: whether it is a multicultural street filled with a visible mixture of people from all over the world, a market with products and services that originate in a wide range of global regions and cultures, communicating on one's laptop or smart phone in a busy international airport concourse in transit between cities on separate continents or reading in a quiet room alone, or perhaps most importantly, experiencing with others and discussing in concrete space and real time these complex forms of being in/between cultures, languages, and ways of looking at the world. These are all ways that the city will no doubt continue to be experienced in the coming century; not in a single language or from a sole perspective, but one irreversibly multiple and part of a fragmentary and shifting global narrative that varies in its focus and scope from one person to another. For some, the representative central node may well be San Francisco as it is in the essay; for others, it will be some other point on the network of global coordinates, one that we nonetheless continue to transit and appreciate all the same as an indispensible context for a more nuanced understanding of any other point on the global urban grid.

In the end, it is not always so all-important to pay attention to the tables and ranking of the world's cities to arrive at a ranking of those levels of globality that categorize urban spaces as such. At times, it is just as necessary to look at the intricate details of individual perception and complexity of lived experience to find forms of being in the city and the world, ones that at times rival or surpass those predicated by corporate monoculture, if not its academically mediated global interpretations. After all, capitalist globalization is not only present and predominant in the recognized urban hubs of the global economy, but also in the landscape and lived experience of smaller cities, the consumer offerings in its suburban box stores, the empty spaces of deserted factories, and even in the interstitial breaks and silences of these transformational flows of globalized cultures. And it is here in these very same spaces that we might begin to find not only the traces of what we might call the "other city," but also the incipient markings of an irrepressible, always re-emergent, and expressly radical alternative sequence of urban spaces, languages and cultures.

San Francisco-Providence, 2010- 2013.

Works Cited

Augé, Marc. *Un ethnologue dans le métro.* Paris: Hachette, 1986.

Anzaldúa, Gloria. *Borderlands/La frontera.* San Francisco: Aunt Lute Books, 1987.

Baudrillard, Jean and Marc Guillaume. [1984] *Radical Alterity.* Trans. Ames Hodges. Los Angeles: Semiotext(e), 2008.

Castells, Manuel.*The Informational City, Information Technology, Economic Restructuring and Urban-Regional Process.* Oxford: Blackwell, 1989.

Certeau, Michel de. *L'invention du quotidien. Vol. 1, Arts de faire.* Paris: Gallimard, 1980.

Cha, Theresa Hak-Kyung. *Dictee.* [1982]. Berkeley: University of California Press, 2001.

Deleuze, Gilles and Félix Guattari. *A Thousand Plateaus: Capitalism and Schizophrenia.* Trans. Brian Massumi. Minneapolis: U of Minnesota Press, 1987.

Ferlinghetti, Lawrence. *San Francisco Poems.* San Francisco: City Lights Books, 2001.

Sasken, Saskia. *Global City: New York, London, Tokyo.* Princeton UP, 1991.

Short, J. R. *Global Metropolitan: Globalising Cities in a Capitalist World.* London: Routledge, 2004.

Vergara, Benito, Jr. *Pinoy Capital: The Filipino Nation in Daly City.* Philadelphia: Temple UP, 2009.

Carnivalesque Osaka

Takayuki Yokota-Marakami

Although it sounds paradoxical, Osaka is often considered as the most cosmopolitan city in Japan, more so than the capital, Tokyo. It is paradoxical since more often than not a capital with its diplomatic institutions, political power and cultural hegemony is the most international city in a nation (London, Paris, Vienna, Bangkok, to name just a few). The cosmopolitan nature of Osaka city from time immemorial is described by many writers. For instance, an Osakite science-fiction author, Komatsu Sakyo[1] published an articled entitled, "Cosmopolitan City Osaka: Antiquity, Modernity, and Beyond," in which he points to the cosmopolitanism of Osaka, resulting from its convenient locus. In another essay, "Naniwa [the archaic name for Osaka] in Antiquity," he explains its geographical advantage thus: "Since [the reign of Ojin Emperor in the fourth century] Osaka, opening its gate towards the west and protected from the direct attack from abroad (because of its geographical position), was an 'international area' in the Asian Pacific zone" (32). His opinion is confirmed by an outsider as well. Alex Kerr, an American who loved the Kansai area (Osaka-Kyoto-Kobe-Nara and their vicinities) and lived there for more than half his life, writes:

> During the early Nara period [710-794A.D.], Osaka was Japan's window to the world, serving as the main port of call for embassies from China and Korea. . . . [N]umerous families from China and Korea emigrated to the Naniwa region, and Heian-period [794-1192] census show that its population was heavily of continental origin. . . . For several decades [in the sixteenth and seventeenth centuries] Osaka was again Japan's window to the world. (225)

The status of Osaka as the most "international" city in Japan, which has thus lasted for more than a thousand years, is now taken over by the capital. According to the statics by the Ministry of Justice (http://www.moj.go.jp/nyuukokukanri/kouhou /press_090710-1_090710-1.html) as of 2009, the prefecture that has the largest number of registered foreign residents is Tokyo, followed by Aichi (with Nagoya) and then Osaka. Also according to the statistics, the largest group of foreign residents in Japan is Chinese, followed by Koreans, Brazilians, and Phillipines. The statistics states that the Chinese residents have radically increased since the mid-1970s and became the biggest group in 2007, prior to which Koreans had been the largest group.

The statistical data clearly desmontrate the connection between the city of Osaka (or the greater Osaka area) and the Korean population. Osaka had the biggest alien population while the Koreans had been the largest group within Japan. This situation, probably, had lasted since the Yamato polity of 6-8 c. A.D., which extensively utilized the technologial/ bureaucratic/legistrative resources of the Korean immigrants. Ever since then, the Japanese- Korean relationship has remained tightly knit (for better or for worse), reaching its peak in the annexation of Korea in 1910. After this a large number of Koreans came (or, to put it better, were molibized) to Japan as cheap labor. According to the statistics by the Minstry of Law in 1974, 638, 806 Koreans were living in Japan towards the end the World War II. Most of them were from the poorer southern regions, notably, from the island of Jeju. The majority of them settled in Osaka. A historian, Kang Jae Eun explains this thus:

> The industrial city, Osaka, nicknamed Manchester of the East, which had been exporting the factory-made goods to Asian countries, was intent on recruiting Korean laborers immediately after the annexation. However, the sole immigration route for Koreans then was the ferryboat plying between Pusan and Shimonoseki, whence they spread to various parts of Japan. According to the survey of October 1920, Fukuoka prefecture, being close to the city of Shimonoseki and the industrial and coal-mining areas in the northern Kyushu island, had the largest number of Koreans. But after February, 1923, when the Amagasaki Steamship Company launched a regular service between Osaka and Jeju island, Osaka became the home to the biggest Korean settlement, especially with Koreans from Jeju. The situation has not changed to the day. (33)

The sheer economic motivation for immigration was replaced in 1930s by the military requirement. Eiji Oguma writes:

> After the break of the Sino-Japanese War, the government of Japan deported a large number of Korean laborers to the Archipelago (*naichi* [inland]] to compensate for the lack of labor force because of the war-related mobilization. In 1925

there were 130,000 Koreans in mainland Japan. The number
leapt to 1,190,000 in 1940, exceeding two million in 1945.
(241)

Thus, "internationalism" and "cosmopolitanism" of Osaka at its peak in the
first half of the twentieth century was an instance of colonialism. Such a
context is a "horizon of interpretation" for understanding a modern myth which
inspired three novels I shall be discussing in this paper: the modern myth,
based, however, on a "real" history, as regards the organized theft of iron, left
abandoned in the site of the weapon factory in the northern central part of
Osaka.

The Osaka Factory of Artillery was founded in 1870 in the former gound
of Osaka castle. (The Tokugawa clan in establishing its Shogunate government
in Tokyo [Edo], destroyed Osaka with its castle in two battles in 1614 and 1615.
This marked a shift of the political center from the West to the East, launching
rivalry between the two capitals (which was subsequently often conceived in
terms   of   rivalry   between   the   govermental   power   and   the
popular/civilian/mercantile section) in the next four centuries. The choice of a
site of the imperial factory of weaponry in the Osaka castle in 1870 is
significant in this respect and its symbolic meaning -designating the
domination of the Western Japan by the Eastern Japan- also has to be kept in
mind in intrepreting the "modern myth" in question.   The weaponry was
significantly enlarged during the Sino-Japanese war, the Russo-Japanese war
and the World War II, becoming the largest factory of arms in Asia. On the eve
of the termination of the WWII, on Aug. 14, Osaka was severely bombed by
the American air force and the Amory was almost completely destroyed. The
destruction was so devastating that the ground of the Factory remained
wasteland for twenty years after the war. In the meantime it came to be known
that the site retained a huge amount of scrap iron and other metals. The
outbreak of the Korean War led to the appreciation of iron price, which in turn
incited burglary of the former factory site. The organized group of burglars
began its nightly attack, causing conflicts with the police, at times subtle, at
others open. The group consisted largely of Koreans, living in the nearby
Korean bloc, and they came to be known as "the Apaches." Based on this
incident, three authors wrote novels: Kaiko Takeshi's *Nihon sanmon opera*
(Japanese Threepenny Opera) of 1959, Komatsu Sakyo's *Nihon Apacchi zoku*
(The Japanese Apaches) of 1964, and Yang Sok-Il's *Yoru o kakete* (Risking the
Night) of 1994. They are all by the authors, originally from the Osaka region,
the last being a Japanese-Korean.

In a collection of papers on the author of the first of the three novels, Kaiko Takeshi, a novelist, Oka Akira, states that naturalism with its obsession with human "interiority" had been a predominant literary movement in Japan until the new generation, to which Kaiko belonged, turned their attention to the "outside" to braze a new trail in literature (21-26). By "the outside" Oka might mean realities, historical facts, conditions, situations, etc. that have to be investigated (*shuzai*). Among the historical conditions that, Kaiko thought, directly addressed the literati of the time were realities in Asia, the most evident of which, during his career, was the Vietnam War. The sense of a mission of a writer eventually prompted him to volunteer to act as a foreign correspondent, stationed in Saigon, which almost cost his life when he dared to observe warfare in the front line. The experience was later turned into his masterpiece, *Natsu no yami* (Summer darkness; 1972) and other works. *Japanese Threepenny Opera* is another of his socio-historically inpired works.

The "outside" that Kaiko addressed in this novel was the Osaka armory and its vicissitudes, revolving around pre-modern conflict of Osaka (Naniwa) with Tokyo (Edo), its defeat and the subsequent status as the second city, Japanese imperialism during the World War II (and its military industry), the colonization of Korea, resulting in the Korean community in Osaka, the breakout of the Korean war, etc.[2]

The binary framework of outside/inside has thus been materialized on a variety of levels: Osaka, the previous center of Japan versus the new capital, Japan versus Asian countries, Japan at war with the world surrounding it (China, Soviet Union, and the United States), and, finally, the literary problematic of human interiority/psychology versus external socio-historical realities which environ a human-being, and so on.

Not only is the Osaka amory the record of such history that narrates the outside/inside distinction, but it also consitutes an outside to the city of Osaka itself within the city limit at present (of the time in a novel). It was an incredible anomaly in an urban space that refused to blend in the surroundings. This unnerves the hero Fukusuke: "N'empêche, que pouvait bien être tout cela, ces ténèbres, ce terrain mouvementé, et sur une telle étendue" (29)?[3] It thus remained alien and unknown to the inhabitants:

> C'étaient les vestiges de l'Enfer qui s'étendaient sous les yeux de Fukusuké. . . .Jusqu'à la date du quartorze août mille neuf cent quarante-cinq, la population d'Ôsaka fut tenue dans l'ignorance la plus absolue de ce qui se passit sur ce million et quelques de mètres carrés. Longtemps, pendant des dizaines d'années, un écran invisible de règlements draconiens, le mur

de palissades noires – au demeurant planches sordides –, des canaux sans fond furent dressés devant elle. (37-38)

This ghastly "unheimlich-ness" was, obviously, related to the association the armory evokes with the colonial warfare that Japan had performed *outside* the Archepelago with atrocities.

But the Osaka Armory was at the same time "inside." What is extraordinary is the proximity of such hideous darkness and infinite space to the center of the city: "Les ruines s'étalaient en plein cœur d'Ôsaka, entourées notamment par la Préfecture, une station de radio, le Château, la Préfecture de Police et un terrain de *base-ball*" (40). The founder of the Japanese modern army, Omura Masujiro, decided that the military facilities, including training schools and the Armory should be located in Osaka for various reasons such as that Osaka had a covenient basis for marine transportation[4] and that the military headquarters should not be in the capital so that the destruction of the political center in case of emergency might be avoided. He had the former Osaka castle site in mind and under his initiative, the foundation for the Osaka Armory was laid in 1870 (Miyake Chap. 1).

> Le grondement des roues des trains parvenait en longs échos tremblés, se répercutant dans cette gigantesque caverne obscure d'entre ciel et terre qu'enveloppait de toutes parts un silence de sépulcre. Pareil espace, pareille prolifération végétale à moins de cinq minutes de train de la gare centrale, au cœur de la seconde agglomération du Japan! Fukusuké essaya de se représenter grossière l'ampleur de l'étendue en s'aidant de la résonance creuse des roues des trans, de la résistance des herbes, du goût presque sableux du vent, mais dans celui-ci nul effluve, nulle saveur, rien qui annonçât la ville. (29-30).

But if the Amory was located in the unexpectedly central part of the megalopolis (in 1925 Osaka became the biggest city, in terms of population, in Japan, the sixth in the world, and that status remained for a few decades, during which Osaka was dubbed Dai-Osaka/Big Osaka), it was as unexpected that the Korean communities were also located in the heart of Osaka, right next to the Armory. The anomaly, the ugliness, and the obsenity (i.e. all that is not official and authentic) of the Osaka Armory is, obviously, a metaphor for the Korean community, which Kaiko describes relentlessly:

[I]ls [Fukusuke and the woman] pénétrènt sans tarder dans l'îlot des taudis. C'est à peine si cinq ou six minutes de train séparent cet îlot de la gare contrale d'Ôsaka mais, tout proche soit-il des néons, des bistros et des cabarets, de cette agitation de *souk*, de ce grouillis amiboïde, il présente l'aspect d'un véritable village. . . . tous les quartiers en bordure de la ligne constituent le maris de la ville, où se concentrent les petites exploitations industrielles ainsi que le quartier coréen. Où qu'on aille alentour, ce ne sont que caniveaux débordant de vase et de vomissures de riz qui recouvrent les rues d'une pourriture verdâtre. Tel était l'endroit où, sans se douter de rien, Fukusuké venait de mettre les pieds en chavirant ; l'authentique bas-fond, dans toute sa misère, sa grisaille humide et sa topographie aveugle. (19-20)

Just as the Osaka Armory is both external/alien to the city and internal/innate to it, the Korean quarters constitute both an alien intruder and an organic component, comprising Osaka, and therefore, the Japanese Empire. If the Koreans living in these quarters were the labor force that emerged in Osaka because of the annexation of Korea, the deportation of human resources, following it, and the recruitment by the Japanese government during the war (thus making it a case of an exploitation of Korean man-power that was used in the "exploitations industrielles [factories]" in Japan), the Korean communities, it can be argued, was an internal colony, both outside and inside, both foreign and native. The concept of *naikoku shokuminchi* (an "internal colony") has been used by many contemporary researchers of colonialism.[5] Here the more remote area within the "nation" that has been "colonized" is implied. I am further expanding this notion to discuss the Korean quarters in Osaka as a territory in the central part of the nation which, paradoxically, belonged to the "colony." The Koreans living in these quarters were mostly laborers mobilized by Osaka heavy industry, part of which was the Osaka Armory, which, ironically, was manufacturing the arms required for the colonialization of Korea and other Asian countries by Japan. This view (that the Korean quarters were an internal colony) is surreptitiously endorsed by the author, Kaiko, himself when he compares the quarters to "Casbah": "Quant au camp lui-même, c'était encore quelque chose d'assez fantastique! . . . [L]'îlot n'avait pas une population stable car, s'il comptait un nombre assez élevé de sédentaires, d'autres habitants s'y ajoutaient en prooprtion égale, malfrats, vagabonds, chômeurs, immigrés clandestines. . . . A cet égard, l'endroit mériterait le nom de «Casbah d'Ôsaka»" (43).

Now, if colonialism is about exploiting and devouring the weak, it is no wonder that this ambiguous locus within Osaka is closedly associated with epicurism and gluttony which appear to be the main motors that propel the narrative. When Fukusuke is invited to a job (of digging scrap iron at the former armory site) by an agent, the only instruction he receives concerning the job is that it is "an Apache work." Upon inquiry, this phrase is mysteriously paraphrased as "to laugh," then, eventually, as "to eat." "Eating," thus, metaphorizes an obscene, illegal act of stealing, i.e. insatiating oneself with the stolen property of the state (or, what had previously been the property of the imperial army). This metaphor is perpetuated in the novel by voracious eating and drinking that repeatedly take place before and after the "job" almost as a ritual.

At the initiation to the membership of the village, Fukusuke (an obviously Japanese name)[6] is treated a meal, consisting of a piece of meat and some vegetables at Mr. Kim's. The meat is so chewy that Fukusuke complains that it tastes like a tire. He soon finds out that the meat he was trying to masticate is a cow stomach (not in the normal diet of Japanese). A little boy who was serving him scorns his complaint, retorting: "We eat it everyday." Under "we" the Koreans are evidently implied. (Incidentally, the Korean boy speaks the perfect, i.e. *native* Osaka dialect.) Implied here is also a common notion that Koreans eat meat (especially, internal organs), to which Japanese have a negative attitude. Obviously, this has been one of the major rationales for discriminating Koreans, deriving from not only the Buddhist injunctions, but also from the discrimination towards the (Japanese) outcastes who had been engaged in cattle slaughter.

Gluttony, symbolized by meat diet, refers the narrative structure of the Apache legend to a carnival (when, literally, one is allowed to eat meat). Aptly, to eat is to laugh, to be festive, enjoy and liberate oneself. Such Bacchanalianism is, however, often considered as the general, regional character of Osaka itself (My intention is not to present some regional characters of Osaka society or Osakites as "reality." That would be as essentialist a gesture as to conceive of certain "national" characteristics that endorse nation-states and races. I am purely referring to the discursive formulations of such "characteristics," i.e. what are prevalently believed (and, subsequently, written), concerning Osakites). Osaka is almost unanimously acknowledged as the groumet capital of Japan. Training cooks spend the period of apprenticeship in Osaka and Kyoto restaurants before returning to work in Tokyo. Obsession in eating is considered as one of the most conspicuous traits of Osakites. The expression, *kuidaore*,[7] a proud slogan of Osakites, is often quoted to explain their behavioral pattern.

The culinary factor is not the only Bacchic element in Osaka. Carnivalesque laughter characterizes Osaka culture. As Kerr writes, "Osaka is where the fun is: it has the best entertainment districts in Japan. . . . It also has a monopoly on humor, to the extent that in order to succeed as a popular comedian it is almost obligatory to study in Osaka and speak the Osaka dialect" (217). "Entertainment" also implies sex-industry: "Osaka does not merely preserve old styles of entertainment, it constantly dreams up new ones. For example, Osaka premiered the 'no panties coffee shops' with panty-less waitresses that later swept Japan" (Kerr 221-222). The inventiveness of Osaka sex-industry is well-recognized and the new fads almost always originate in Osaka, not in the capital of Tokyo. In sex Osaka subverts the cultural hierarchy that it has been compelled to accept vis-à-vis Tokyo.

It is this Bacchanalian, rather un-Japanese, character of the Osaka region that renders the Apaches-Koreans once again both internal and external, i.e. both fellow-Osakites and alien Korean residents. The extreme vitality (and gluttony and Bacchanalianism) of the Koreans depicted in *Japanese Three Penny Opera* is made plausible by their voracious lifestyle (which in fact reminds the readers of that of the Osakites in general) and by their fluent Osaka accent (a language known for its vitality and vulgarity that well suit its carnivalesque culture). "Japan's national problem is homogeneity [of which Osaka is exempt. . . . Osaka maintains a spirit of fierce independence" (Kerr 223-224). If, however, as Kerr correctly remarks, homogeneity is Japan's national disease, homogenization is one of the most foundational political goals of any nation-state and, hence, its malady. Such relationship between Korean (epicurean) culture and the Osaka culture, between Koreans and Japanese, is what, possibly, allowed another novelist from Osaka, Komatsu Sakyo, to create a different legend, concerning the Apaches, taking Japanese as protagonists. Komatsu's *The Japanese Apaches* is a scientific-fantastic rendition of the legend. The Apaches, being isolated in the site of the Osaka Amory, adapt themselves to a new environment (the lack of normal food) and develop a capability to feed on iron.

The critic, Tatsumi Takayuki, uses Komatsu's novel as a source of an image of a cyborg humanity, central for his book, *Full Metal Apache*. The diatary thematics is emphasized from the very beginning. The hero is arrested for the charge of "unemployment." (He is dismissed from work. In the fantastic society within the novel umemployment is a legal offence.) He is to be dispelled to the site of the Osaka Armory as a punishment. Before being discharged there, he makes a rather lenthy tour in a police car all around Osaka without any reason: Temma, Sonezaki, Fukushima, Imamiya, Tamatsukuri, Morinomiya, etc., that reminds the readers of a carnival procession, and, finally, at Hoenjizaka, the hero spots his favorite noodle shop and murmurs: "Boy, I'd love a bowl of *ketsune*."[8] At the gates of the Amory, asked about his last wish (the imprisonment in the amory is tantamount to a death penulty), the hero says:

> "I'd like to have some rice with curry sauce. There's a restaurant on the corner of Umeshin street that serves rice with curry for four hundred fifty yen. I have really wanted to try it once. . . . Have you ever had rice with curry that costs as much as four hundred fifty yen?"
> "Four hundred fifty yen!?"[9] – The policeman popped his eyes out. "We've never even tried rice with curry for one fifty." (17)

The hero offers to treat the policeman with the dish if he agrees to make a stop at the curry shop. The officer is tempted, but in the last instance refuses. This policeman is later to be captured by the Apaches after the hero has become one of their members. All the captives are fed with iron. The hero recognizes the officer among them and talks to him.

> "Do you remember me, ol' pal?" . . .
> "This [iron] tastes pretty good. Not bad at all. It tastes like *kenchin* soup."[10]
> "Did you get to try rice with curry for four hundred fifty yen?" – I sat down next to him and asked.
> "Bro', give me a break." – He shrugged his shoulders. – "No way for a good-for-nothing like us. Scrap iron is much to our taste." – His eyes shone. – "What d'ya say? Wouldn't it be a good business if I open a café that specializes in iron in Nishinari or somewhere else.[11] I was thinking of making curry, using scrap iron."
> "Forget it. Ridiculous," – I said.
> "Curry with scrap iron! It'll take on!" – The policeman said, as if spelled by his own words. --" 'Pure *Indian* curry! Only in our café'…" (83)

Thus, gluttony is constantly related to and referred back to localities (*ketsune* noodle in Hoenjizaka, Indian curry in Nishinari, etc.), evoking, at the same time, grotesque humor of exaggeration (rice with curry sauce for thirty US dollars [as of now], curry with iron, etc.). Thus, food appears to be the almost central thematic of the novel, being the most important concern of the characters.

In the third section of the second chapter, entitled "How Did They Eat Iron?" the author Komatsu describes in detail the recipes for cooking fine iron meals: how to boil, what acid to use, how to make iron-*sashimi*, what sauce to use, how beautifully to dish up, etc.

The obsession in eating, naturally, leads to the carnivalesque infatuation in the lower dimension: "The excrement of the Apaches is known to be quite pure iron. The physiological process within the bodies of the iron-eaters is investigated energetically, but without any definite conclusion" (56).

We have already mentioned that the obsession with food, especially in a grotesquely exaggerated form, is carnivalesque aspects of Osaka region, or of Osakites and Korean immigrants. Bakhtin's theoretical formulation of the carnivalesque is applicable here. For Bakhtin, some of the key features of the Bacchanalianism are: blasphemy, obscenity, vulgarity, materiality, beating, bodily deformity, obsession in body in general, gluttony, excretion, subversion of ordinary reality and order, and so on, all of which are found in Komatsu's novel (and Kaiko's). "Eating and drinking are one of the most significant manifestations of the grotesque body. The distinctive character of this body is its open unfinished nature, its interraction with the world. These traits are most fully and concretely revealed in the act of eating; the body trangresses here its own limits; it swallows, devours, rends the world apart, is enriched and grows at the world's expense" (Bakhtin 281).

The Apaches eat iron and discharge pure iron that is sold for a good price. Aquisition of the capability to consume iron itself is the grotesque deformation of one's physical function. In a science fiction setting, Komatsu further develop the carnivalesque motif of devouring. And the language, just as in Kaiko's novel, plays the important part in constructing the Bacchic, too. Joviality caused by obscene laughter, emphasized by the vulgar Osaka dialect, is to be found throughout the work. "Osaka dialect is certainly colorful. Standard Japanese . . . has an almost complete lack of dirty words . . . . Osaka people say such vividly imaginative things that you want to sit back and take notes. Most are unprintable, but here is one classic Osaka epithet: 'I'm going to slash your skull in half, stir up your brains, and drink them out with a straw!' " (Kerr 224) Note that the "classic example" Kerr records is based on the carnivalesque motifs of violence and devouring.

> Ol' Okin suddenly stripped her butt, shouting, "Here I go!"
> "Ol' Lady, do you need to shit?" – The women around her laughed. "I ain't shitting," said the old bag assertively, "I'm showing my ass to the soldiers. I am sure they are all young lads with tiny cocks, not big enough for *that*. The women's slit

has opened any door since the time of Amaterasu.[12] It has a magic power. Upon seeing it, the soldiers will just clinch their fist and won't be able to shoot. Any guy, if he sees it, will not to be up to warfare."
All laughed out. "Ol' Okin, but where can you find a guy who gets knocked out by the sight of your grey-haired pussy? They'd just puke." "Shut the fuck up!" – Okin was offended. "Don't underestimate me. There were times when I made five guys cry for pleasure in a single night. There was even a guy who worshiped me, praying, 'Let me lick your pussy!' "After this, several women started stripping themselves, and then they all marched towards the police squads. (49)

The erotic is the constituent element of Osaka (and Japanese-Korean) Bacchanalia. The carnivalesque in the Apaches legend is inherited by the last of the three well-known narratives on it: Yang Sok-Il's *Risking the Night.* As the work is written by a Japanese-Korean novelist, the (colonial) situation of the Koreans in Japan is, naturally, problematized throughout the novel.

Kanamura [one of the main characters][13] ooked on *Funuke* [his nickname, meaning a coward in Japanese and gave him up.
"Dogs have tougher backbones than you. Are you really a Korean?"
Funuke simply didn't have a strong personality which is peculiar to Koreans. Kanamura was irritated by his sissy attitude. That's why he asked his nationality.
"Yeah, I am really a Korean."
"I've never seen a Korean like you."
"My *aboji* (father) and *omoni* (mother)[14] were killed in the bombardment in Fuse [a town to the east of Osaka]. So my Korean parents are not here anymore. But I am a Korean all the same."
Seeing that he does occasionally use Korean words like *aboji* or *omoni*, he must be a Korean after all.
"A Korean should have more guts."
"Let me ask you then. How come Koreans with guts remain colonized by Japan for such a long time?" (134)

Some of the typical post-colonial thematics are expressed in the quotation: the crisis of identification (The Japanese Koreans themselves cannot distinguish a Korean from a Japanese); the forfeiture of the (native/national) language, under which condition the Japanese Koreans can merely utter scattered Korean words such as *omoni, aboji, aigo* ("woe is me!"), *yopuchomu* (a denigratory term for a Korean), etc. and the Japanese Koreans carry Japanese names imposed by the Imperial government; the consequential, ironical situation, in which Japanese-Koreans can instance self-identification solely on the basis of what little Korean they know; self-depreciation as a colonized nation, and so on. But except for these problems-consciousnesses as to the colonization, Yang Sok-Il's novel proves itself to be an authentic successor of the two preceding novels. The intertexual relationship is clearly observed. As a matter of fact, although *Risking the Night* appeared more than three decades after Kaiko's *Japanese Three Penny Opera*, Yang personally participated in the Apaches movement and narrated the story to a poet, Hasegawa Ryusei, who, in turn, told it to Kaiko, who was searching for interesting material for a novel. The Ur-narrative was, therefore, with Yang (Takahashi 372). Therefore, it was Kaiko who adopted the unusual term, "to laugh," from Yang, who either was using it as an Apache himself or invented it as a literary fantasy. It is not that we have to be trapped in the problematic of Bloomian anxiety of influence, though.Yang explains the special usage of the verb, "to laugh" (in the sense of "to eat") among the Apaches in the sense described by Kaiko:

> Ito, who has been making a thorough inspection of the motor, finally made a decision and said, "All right. We'll laugh this."
> Ito decided to "eat" a motor, rather than searching for iron forever, after digging the ground in vain for hours.
> "What d'you mean, 'We'll laugh this,' " Kim, the novice, asked.
> "It means, we'll eat the motor."
> "Are we going to eat the motor?"
> "Idiot! We''ll take it out and sell it. Can't you even figure that out? What the hell are you here for? (54)

The carnivalesque aspects of the the two forerunners-novels are inherited in *Risking the Night* as well. The obsession in eating and drinking is clearly emphasized (together with its Korean connection): Apaches work hard (i.e. steal a lot) in order to earn enough money to order *sue*, a pork sausage, and *doburoku*, home-brewed vodka, prepared by Takashi's *omoni* (mother). The eroticism is given full impetus throughout this work as well, combined with the satiric laughter:

> "Good! Good! As *Omoni* of Takashi is a *houruromon* [widow],
> perhaps, one of us should sneak into her bed tonight."
> Takashima, with a reddened face, laughing vulgarly,
> approached her, as if a walrus in rut.
> "You can't come all together. Come one by one."
> *Omoni* of Takashi, apparently, was not against the idea, and she
> threw a glance at young Ko Sei Shu.
> "I bet you are a virgin. Come this evening. I'll cuddle and
> fondle you."
> Everyone burst out laughing.
> "Sei Shu, let Takashi's *omoni* make a man out of you!"
> Ito encouraged Ko Sei Shu.
> "Bullshit! I have plenty of women to choose from."
> "Don't bluff. Your expression just betrays that you're a virgin."
> Everyone burst out laughing again. Ko Sei Shu drank wine by
> himself with his back towards everyone else, murmuring, "I
> hate *yopuchomu* [Koreans]. They just talk big, but they ain't up
> to nothing."
> Leaving the complaints of Ko alone, everyone kept singing,
> dancing, and talking obscenities. (38)

The "images of the material bodily lower stratum" (Bakhtin) are paid much attention as well with obsession in excretion and its materiality.

> Tokuyama's wife was rushing his husband who had gone to the
> public toilet and would not come out.
> "How long do you need to be there? You have to hurry, or
> they'll take away everything."
> "Can't I just relax and poop?"
> "How many times have you got to poop?"
> "I poop when I want to."
> "Is there anything else you can do other than eating and
> pooping?"
> "Every one poops when he eats. What's wrong with pooping?"
> (22)

I have pointed out that in *Risking the Night* the Apaches are described as the "losers" of their native/national language (Of course, they are deprived of it by the (post-)colonial condition. My choice of the word for "deprivation" refers to the (post-)colonial self-depreciation that I have mentioned above and this marks the diegesis of *Risking the Night* throughout) Instead, they all speak in the horribly vulgar (but "authentic") Osaka dialect in a highly carnivalesque spirit (of deformation, exaggeration, disorder, obscenity, debasement, etc.). By their verbal trait, then, they behave as authentic modern Osakites (The Japanese-Koreans themselves cannot distinguish them from the Japanese). Earlier I maintained that the Osaka Amory was both inside and outside the city. Also I proposed the reading of the Japanese-Koreans (in Osaka) as both insiders and outsiders. The same is reconfirmed by the Japanese-Korean writer. By insisting this, however, I am not asserting that Japanese-Koreans have been completely assimilated. Rather, they are both authentic Osakites and complete aliens. I should also refer to the theory of the common origin of the Japanese and the Koreans, prevalent in the pre-war Japanese anthropological - archaelogical discourse. In the critically acclaimed book, *The Myth of the Homogeneous Nation*, Oguma describes the discursive history of the theory of the common origin which had proved influential in the pre-war colonial policy. He argues that this theory, rather unusual for the justification of the imperialistic expansion (which sees the colonized as the same people as the colonizers), was made feasible partially because of the (ethnic) similarity between the Japanese and the Koreans (374-376). Of course, this similarity does not essentially change the colonial burden of "mimicry" that Bhabha describes: "Almost the same, but not quite." The Japanese-Koreans are, I repeat, both identical and different.

This ambiguity opens up the possibility of regarding Osaka as a colony of a kind within the mainland Japan. With by far the biggest number of aliens in residence (Koreans) and the consequent tie with the Jeju island, Osaka was closely connected to Japan's external colony. If Korea was annexed to Japan by its imperial expansion, Osaka was affixed to Jeju.

This may open up a possibility of viewing Osaka as an internal colony, as it were, of the Japanese Empire, or of the first city, Tokyo as the center of the Japanese imperilialism. As a matter of fact, the relationship between Tokyo and Osaka (or any region in Japan other than Tokyo) has been in many a respect "colonial." Since the 17th century Osaka had been deprived of its political power and was under the constant military surveillance of Tokyo Shogunate who feared the rebellion of the anti-institutional force. It is true that Osaka enjoyed economic prosperity during Shogunate as a free port and it eventually became the commercial/industrial center of Japan (comparison of Osaka to Manchester has been pointed out [it is almost a cliché]). The common pattern of the second city, politically inferior, regaining its status in industrialization is observed here. The comparison becomes more convincing if we are to compare the Korean immigrants in Osaka to the Irish in Manchester in their "racial" (and, possibly, linguistic) affinity to the colonizers. But it was financial prosperity, bought at the price of political power (under Shogunate merchants were the lowest in the ladder of four classes with samurai at the summit). There were various forms of exploitations: military, political, and, finally, economic, too, as of late.

Another trait of "colonial" homogenization, of course, concerns the language as Osakites (just like any other local people in Japan) were forced to use the standardized language (upper Tokyo dialect). The literary consequence of this was that the standard Tokyo (Japanese) language has been imposed on the writings of modern authors as a narrative tool (a language that is to be used in narration). The creation of the national standard language (*kokugo*) and the vernacular style (*genbunicchi*) disabled the literati to write in dialects. The three Osaka authors that I have analyzed consciously resist this linguistic homogenization.

Yang, the Japanese-Korean writer, adds another dimension to this resistence. He (and many Japanese-Korean authors) further insert the "indigenous" Korean words out of their already quite inauthetic and scant verbal ability of their language of origin, which may not be their native tongue anymore. They can barely speak Korean except for some typical expressions: mother, father, alas, sausage, vodka, and so forth. But these expressions are "authentic" and "native" to them. Ashcroft writes of a metonymic hodgepodge in a post-colonial discourse with two languages (of the colonizer and of the colonized) interspersed in one single text (52). Yang's novel (and to some extent Kaiko's as well) demonstrates such a metonymy, but in a more complex manner: (colonial) Korean words mingling with Osaka dialect, bracketed by the Tokyo (imperial) standard language. Thus, in a "post-colonial" gesture of hybridity and the carnivalesque, Osakites and Japanese-Koreans (or the Osaka city and its Korean community) in a gesture of solidarity resist the pressure of homogenization and the standardization.

Of course, this is not to exculpate Osaka in Japan's imperialistic schemes and instances. Yet, what is signified by "Osaka" after all? Osaka as a place? Its geographic environment? Its infrastructures? Osaka administration? Osakites? Do we include a temporary resident like Tanizaki Jun'ichiro, Tokyo novelist? Or, for that matter, do we include Japanese Koreans? I leave these tormenting questions unanswered for now. It is to complicate the interspersing of the colonial and the imperial, the center and the marginal, the official and the unofficial, and so on. And it is a way out from the dichotomous framework of colony-empire, oppressed-oppressor, center-margin, foreign-native, Korea-Japan, etc.

Neither am I suggesting that Japanese-Koreans were (and have been) exempt from discrimination in Osaka (and elsewhere). The latter half of *Risking the Night* is dedicated to the description of the infamous Omura Asylum in Nagasaki, where Korean deportees were "temporarily" confined in a highly inhuman setting, symbolizing the Japanese oppression of Korea (as a colony). (The main character of the novel, Kim, is crippled there.)

With this reservation in mind, let us return to the issue of the ambiguity of Osaka as an internal colony, facilitated by its carnivalesque hybridity. As I have been pointing out, the carnivalesque is often considered as the typical regional character of the Osaka area: its hyperbole interest in erotic pleasure, valorization of gluttony, urge to destroy the fixed and accepted order (Komatsu writes of the "anachic nature of Osaka" [*Watashi no Osaka* 252]), affirmation of the unofficial, denial of conformity ("Osaka people are impatient and love to disobey rules" [Kerr 217]), obsession in vulgar humor, challenge to hierarchy, and so forth. All this leads to the heteroglossia of the second city, whereas Tokyo symbolizes the Japanese national principle of "homogeneity."

Homogenization and assimilation is the most typical strategy of colonialism. The Armory and the military headquarters were constructed in Osaka, not in the metropolitan area, in order to avoid the possible attack of the enemy and the consequent destruction. Note that both Hiroshima and Kokura (the original target of the atomic bomb, substituted by Nagasaki solely for the reason of the bad weather on the day of the bombing] had the military headquarters and the weapon factories. The peripheries are literally the war-front, which can be expended. If we are allowed to view Osaka as an internal colony within Japan, we are also authorized to see the standardizing and homogenizing force of Tokyo, i.e. of the central government, which Osaka resisted, as an instance of imperialism. And Osaka has constantly shown strong zeal in resisting nationalistic, imperialistic pressure of standardization, in standing out and in differentiating itself.

In fact, Osaka is often marked by its outspoken alienness, exteriority to homogeneous Japan, surrounding it. Kerr speaks of such an ambience, regarding the traditional downtown area of Shinsekai: "The minute you get out of the train station [of Imamiya, closed to Shinsekai], you realize that you are in another country. . . . The theme of Shinsekai is Cheap and Easy; in other words, this is not Japan" (218-219). This un-Japanese-ness is not necessarily restricted to downtown Shinsekai, but, more or less, the feature of the city of Osaka as a whole. The popular local rock-n-roll band, Urufuruzu, from Osaka has a song on its native city, "Osaka Strut" (1996). One line goes: "We don't need nothing (*nani*). We just love Naniwa (the archaic name for Osaka) 'cause it's the best. Compared to other cities, it is almost a foreign land"(102).

Thus, in inserting alien substances into organic Japan, Osaka reincarnates the spirit of post-colonial carnivalesque syncreticity, comprising inter-nationalism, cosmopolitanism, and hybridity, Osaka challenges the principle of homogeneity that Tokyo dictates. However, rather anti-climactically, the allure of the official, the authentic, and the Nation (represented by the capital city), haunts the people of the Bacchanalia. Both Kaiko and Komatsu glorify Osaka by describing powerfully vulgar, epicurian, vigorous Apaches that well represent this second City. Yang joins in the chorus of the carnivalesque disorder and challenge presented by Kaiko and Komatsu, towards the end of the novel. Strangely succumbing to the nationalistic logic of homogeneity, the hero expresses his yearning for Tokyo and the authority it embodies.

> Cho Yu Shin [probably, a double of the author himself] has given up life in Osaka and was constantly thinking about moving to Tokyo. It was not that he had a specific purpose, but still Cho Yu Shin, after all the jobs with the Apaches, was interested in trying his luck in Tokyo. His friends living in Tokyo somehow appealed to him as successes. (407)

Is this a defeatist assimilation of the colonized to the system endorsed by the colonizers? Or is this the post-colonial subversion of the power, that is, the strategy of the colonized to surreptitiously avail him/herself of the power of the empire without yielding to it? Or does this witness Yang's distrust of Osaka's ostensible hybridity and his criticism of it? Not surprisingly, the answer remains obscure. That Osaka is hybrid and syncretic means it is ambiguous and enigmatic.

Whatever the case, I would like to close the article, quoting the prayer that Kerr voices at the end of the chapter on Osaka: let Osaka never lose the status of being "the last bastion against the sea of ordinariness sweeping over Japan" (229). "Ordinariness to be imposed nation-wide" may be paraphrased in an academic jargon into impresialistic, homogenizing pressure from the political center toward any margin, but, perhaps, especially toward *the Other city.*

Notes

1. Japanese names are given with family names first, followed by first names.
2. It may be an apt place to reconfirm the matter-of-course theoretical presumption of this paper that both outside/inside and the first city/the

second city distinctions are constantly changing and historically variable. The status of Osaka as the second city (and its character resulting from that status) spans from the 17th century onward and it should not be essentialized

3. *Japanese Threepenny Opera* has been translated into several European languages, but, unfortunately, not into English. I will be quoting from the French translation, rather than offering my own rendition.

4. Be reminded that this is the reason that the novelist Komatsu gives for the cosmopolitanism of Osaka.

5. For instance, see Tamura, where the author analyzes Hokkaido as an internal colony.

6. It refers to a lucky charm (male) doll, named, "Fukusuke(-ningyo)," popular since the Shogunate. Therefore, it is not to be taken as his real name, but a nickname. It may symbolize his current poverty and misery as the doll is supposed to fullfil one's wish.

7. Kenkyûsha's Japanese-English dictionary defines it as: "bringing (financial) ruin upon onself by extravagance in food," citing a popular proverb, *"Kyō no kidaore, Osaka no kuidaore"* (People in Kyoto are extravagant in dress and those of Osaka in food). Consumption of blowfish (*fugu*) may also be relevant. Considered as the ultimate delicatessen, blowfish are consumed mainly in Osaka (60% of the entire national catch). Their livers are known to be especially delicious, though they are occasionally fatally poisonous. Fatal toxicosis from blowfish takes place in Osaka frequently, which does not discourage Osakites from making a suicidal attempt. The proverb, *"fugu wa kuitashi inochi wa oshishi"* (To eat *fugu* or to remain alive, that is the question) is expressive of the grotesquely carnivalesque (and existentialist) nature of Osaka culinary culture.

8. The abbreviation for *ketsune udon*, i.e. *udon* noodle with deep-fried tofu. It is supposed to be an Osaka specialty, and here it is called *ketsune* in Osaka dialect, not *kitsune* as Tokyoits would call it.

9. Four hundred fifty yen in 1958 when the Apaches were active roughly corresponds to 2,550 yen (around thirty US dollars) today, according to the conversion table of the National Diet Library. (A regular bowl of rice with curry sauce would cost around ten US dollars at a restaurant these days.)

10. *Kenchin jiru*, soup with stir fried vegetables, is believed to have derived from the Buddhist vegetarian dish.

11. Nishinari is the site for Kamagasaki, a slum area of Osaka, and for the Tobita pleasure quarters, almost the only remaining quarters of such nature in Japan. "Tobita survivies almost completely intact [as the traditional pleasure quarters]. There are no walls, but there is a precise gridwork of streets lined with low tile-roofed houses. In front of each house is a banner, and inside the entrance a young woman and the madam sit side by side next to a brazier. This is as close to Kabuki in the modern age as you can get" (Kerr 220-221).

12. This is a reference to a legend in Japanese myth. The Sun Goddess, Amaterasu, is offended by the God, Susanoo, and encloses herself in the cave, closing the entrance with a huge rock (*iwato*, a rock door). The world loses its light and Gods are in distress. They all gather in front of the rock door and begin to discuss the matter when the Goddess of dance and music, Amanouzume, starts sriptease, showing off her genitalia. The Eight Million Gods burst into laughter. Being curious, Amaterasu peeps out when the Mighty God, Amenotajikarao, pulls her out of the cave.

13. He is Korean, but carries a Japanese name. In 1939 the Imperial Japanese government issued a law, compelling Koreans (now considered the subject of the Empire) to create new (Japanese) surnames, register them, and use them officially. Such a colonial history is recorded in the narrative of *Risking the Night*:

    The groups were organized into three. Kanamura, Hirayama, and Matsuda became their leaders. All of them carry Japanese names, but they are Koreans. It appears that Japanese people cannot understand why Koreans carry Japanese names. This is the result of the enforcement of the Japanese government. In November, 1939, in colonial Korea the Imperial government issued a law to enforce Koreans to create Japanese surnames and register them in the form of the revision of the Korean civil codes on the basis of the imperial policy that subjects of colonies be incorporated to the subjects of mainland Japan as the Emperor's people. At that time there were Koreans who committed suicide in protest to such enforcement. Those Koreans who remained in Japan after the War have continued to use the Japanese names as aliases. (56)

14. The Korean words are transcribed according to the Japanese phonetic rendition. To be more exact, they should be spelled *abeoji* and *eomeoni*. In the subsequent quotations I will simply be quoting the Japanese transcription found in the text.

Works Cited

Ashcroft, Bill, et al. *The Empire Writes Back: Theory and Practice in Post Colonial Literatures*. London: Routledge, 1989.

Bakhtin, Mikhail. *Rablais and His World*. Tr. by Hélène Iswolsky. Bloomington: Indiana UP, 1984.

Bhabha, Homi. *The Location of Culture*. London: Routledge, 2005.

Kaiko, Takeshi. *Nippon sanmon opera* (Japanese Three Penny Opera). Tokyo: Bungei shunju, 1959. *L'Opéra des gueux*. Tr. by Jackques Lalloz. Paris: U.G.E., 1992.

Kang Jae Eun and Kim Dong Hoon. *Zainishi kankoku/chōsen jin: Rekishi to tembō* (Koreans in Japan: Their History and Perspectives). Tokyo: Rodo keizai sha, 1989.

Kawamura, Minato. *Umaretara sokoga furusato: Zainichi Chōsenjin bungaku ron* (One's Birthplace Is One's Native Land: On Korean Literature in Japan). Tokyo: Heibonsha, 1999.

Kerr, Alex. *Lost Japan*. Melbourne: Lonely Planet Publications, 1996.

Komatsu, Sakyo. *Nihon Apacchi zoku* (The Japanese Apaches). In *Komatsu Sakyō zenshū kanzen ban*. Vol. 1. Tokyo: Josai International UP, 2006.

Komatsu, Sakyo. "*Kosumoporitan shiti Osaka: kodai, gendai, sosite mirai e* (Cosmopolitan City Osaka: Antiquity, Modernity, and Beyond)." In *Watashi no Osaka* (My City, Osaka). Tokyo: Chuo koron sha, 1993.

Komatsu, Sakyo. "*Kodai no Naniwa* (Naniwa in Antiquity)." Ibid.

Miyake, Koji. *Osaka hōheikōshō no kenkyū* (The Study of the Osaka Armoury). Kyoto: Shibunkaku, 1993.

Oguma, Eiji *Tanitsu minzoku shinwa no kigen: Nihonjin no jigazō no keifu* (The Myth of the Homogeneous Nation). Tokyo: Shin'yo sha, 1995.

Oka, Akira et al. *Kaiko Takeshi: Sono hito to bungaku* (Kaiko Takeshi: His personality and works). Tokyo: TBS Britannica, 1999.

Takahashi, Toshio. "*Kaisetsu* (Commentary)." *Zainichi bungaku zenshū*: Vol. 7. *Yang Sok-Il*. Eds. Isogai Jiro and Kuruko Kazuo. Tokyo: Bensei shupppan, 2006.

Tamura, Sadao. "*Naikoku shokuminchi toshiteno Hokkaido* (Hokkaido as an internal colony)." *Kindai Nihon to shokuminchi*. Vol. 1. Tokyo: Iwanami shoten, 1992.

Tatsumi, Takayuki. *Full Metal Apache: Transactions Between Cyborpunk Japan and Avant-Pop America*. Durham: Duke UP, 2006.

Ulfuls. *Ulfuls Best*. Tokyo: Doremi gakufu shuppansha, 2009.

Yang, Sok-Il. *Yoru o kakete*. Tokyo: Nihon hōsō shuppan kai, 1994.

The Forgotten Landscapes: Redeeming the Dimension of the True in Contemporary Taiwanese Literature

Yu-chuan Shao

At the very end of his novel *Family Name from the Moon* (2000), Lo I-chun casts the reader into a prosaic everyday world. Calling this final chapter "The Wandering Journal," Lo closes the novel with excerpts from a journal written by the narrator's father, a first-generation émigré from China, and given to the narrator in his father's old age. These excerpts sketch his life in Taiwan from November 1949 to April 1950. When he first got the journal, the somewhat frustrated narrator expected an epic-like account of his family history, but it turned out not to be the family saga for which he had hoped, one that would finally lay bare the truth about the grand narrative made up by his father throughout his life about how he survived the turmoil of the civil war that broke out in China in 1949. Instead, the journal consisted of nothing but the father's story about everyday events at his school in southern Taiwan and, in between he told about his tedious everyday life and some of his hackneyed sentimental prose poems that reveal his homesickness, love and erotic feelings for his wife left behind in his hometown, along with his distress about his unknown future.

Coincidently, just a year ahead of Lo's novel, Wu He published his monographic novel *Remnants of Life* (1999), which dazzles and exhausts the reader with its/the mixture of history-laden reflections upon the Wu-she Incident and its remnants with the detailed account of the prosaic everyday life in the tribal village.[1] Pondering over what he sees in the lives of the young aboriginal woman next door and other villagers during his stay at the tribal village, the narrator reflects:

> Her brooks and hills, the fishing nets she puts under the stream rock, the bush where she stores her barbecue grills, and her gourds and the nocturnes she loves to listen to—there's hardly anyone here talking about "the Incident" in their everyday lives. Very few people at the village feel like living in the remnants of the Incident, even if in effect it is because of the Incident that they were relocated to this place called Chuan-zhong-dao, that they have learned to farm to make a living, and that how their lives here have turned this place

from strange, to familiar and then to indigenous. (*Remnants*
211)[2]

Poeticizing history- and trauma-ridden everyday life, this novel, in terms of
form and content, is very much like a philosophical treatise on the experiences
of the wanderers, who, like the tribal people and the narrator himself, have
lived in the eponymous remnants of history. The intimidating details of the
novel, bespeaking the stories of the wanderers, quietly and patiently manifest
themselves as a testimony to the remnants of history and life.

In contemporary Taiwanese writers such as Wu He and Lo I-chun, we see
a return to the everyday and prosaic lives of ordinary people and their lives as
wanderers. It is in such a return that fiction attempts to approach the true and
the anonymous and to address the remnants of history and life, which, very
often, may slip into oblivion for reasons both external and internal. Following
this literary return with the theoretical framework grounded in Rancière's
writings on politics and aesthetics, this paper aims to demonstrate how Wu
He's *Remnants of Life* may serve as a critical resource for rethinking the
distinction between nativism as a hierarchical order of intelligibility and
nativism as a rationality in order to work toward equality and emancipation.
For the capacity to see the distinction, I would say, enables us to act beyond
nativism as the dominant pattern of intelligibility and move toward a new
sphere of the sensible. The syntax of this paragraph was simplified.

I.   The Mute Speech of Details

In an essay on the excess of details in realistic fiction,[3] Rancière attempts
to demonstrate the working of aesthetic practices as a mode of social
emancipation that in his view, first took place in the nineteenth-century novel.
In the nineteenth-century realistic novel, he points out what we see is the
coincidence between the triumph of the novel and the "invasion of the prosaic
and idle everyday" (41). How do we account for such superfluity, which causes
a rupture in the narrative logic of representation? Starting with Roland
Barthes's article "The Reality Effect," Rancière lays bare the aesthetic and
social significance of so-called superfluous reality by exposing Barthes's
blindness, that is, what Barthes fails to see in his analysis of nineteenth-century
French novelists.

First, Rancière emphasizes that the new fictional cosmology emerging in
the realistic novel is also a new social cosmology. This social cosmology attests
to the presence of democracy: "democracy in literature or literature as
democracy" (43). Rancière thus explains:

> The "insignificance" of the details is tantamount to their
> perfect equality. They are equally important or equally
> pointless. The reason [that] they are so is that they concern
> people whose life is insignificant. The people clutter up the
> space, leaving no room for the selection of interesting
> characters and the harmonious development of a plot. It is
> exactly the opposite of the traditional novel, the novel of the
> monarchical and aristocratic times, which benefited from the
> space created by a clearly stratified social hierarchy. (43).

Hence the rupture of the logic of verisimilitude, in Rancière's view, points to the social basis of representative poetics. When the partition based on a stratified social hierarchy vanishes, fiction gets overfilled with "the insignificant events and sensations of all those common people who either were not counted within the representative logic or were counted at their (lower) place and represented in the (lower) genres fitting their condition" (43). For Rancière, the emergence of the uncounted points to the possibility for the re-distribution of the capacities of sensory experience in the new social cosmology that is brought into being through fiction.

Fiction designates "the relation of a referential world to alternative worlds" and that explains why fiction can serve as the space of equality and emancipation and thus manifest itself as the space of the true (44). Rancière thus elaborates: "This is a question of a distribution of capacities of sensory experience, of what individuals can live, what they can experience and how far their feelings, gestures and behaviors are worth telling to other individuals" (44). The equality effect that emanates from the capacities of sensory experience given to anybody does not indicate that all sensations are thereby equivalent. But "the frightening signification of literary 'democracy'" is that "anybody can feel anything" (44). For it is "this new capacity of anyone to live alternative lives which forbids the right subordination of the parts to the whole" (45). Critics, such as Barthes, who tend to view the excess of details as something superfluous and meaningless,[4] fail to translate both the aesthetic and the political import of parasitic images of idle everyday life. For Rancière, what is at stake in this excess is the conflict between two distributions of the sensible: the conflict between the hierarchical logic of the representative regime and the democratic logic of the aesthetic regime. And it is this "upheaval in the distribution of social temporalities" and of sensory experiences, this conflict in excess, that makes literature possible (50). Or, as we follow Rancière's line of thought, this is what enacts the politics of literature.

What can we hear from the mute speech hidden in the excess of details? In his book, *The Aesthetic Unconscious*, Rancière argues that the figures in artistic texts and works serve to prove the presence of the aesthetic configuration of unconscious thought: "there is meaning in what seems not to have any meaning, something enigmatic in what seems self-evident, a spark of thought in what appears to be anodyne detail" (3). He explains that it is through the aesthetic configuration that we get to recognize in those things of art "the existence of a particular relation between thought and non-thought, a particular way that thought is present within sensible materiality, meaning within the insignificant, and an involuntary element within conscious thought" (3). That is to say, aesthetics, as a particular regime of thinking about art, designates a type of judgment to redefine the territory of art and to make manifest thought in art that can be rather hidden, enigmatic, and confusing. For Rancière, the aesthetic unconscious does not indicate the pertinence of Freudian analytic concepts and forms of interpretation. Rather, the concept of the aesthetic unconscious points to the singularity of art: art as a form of revealing its thought through the representation of the sensible, or, to use Rancière's words, "art as the territory of a thought that is present outside itself and identical with non-thought" (6). To use Hegel's conceptualization, as Rancière notes, art designates "the immanence of logos in pathos, of thought in non-thought" (28).

Relating to the concept of the aesthetic unconscious, Rancière extends his analysis on art as a form of thought (and also non-thought) and thus sees the details scattered all over the space of the nineteenth-century realistic novel as a form of mute speech. Under the concept of "everything speaks,"[5] Rancière further elaborates in this book on the way prosaic details serve as signs encrypting a history, what he calls the first form of mute speech:

> Mute writing, in the first sense, is the speech borne by mute things themselves. It is the capability of signification that is inscribed upon their very body, summarized by the 'everything speaks' of Novalis . . . Everything is trace, vestige, or fossil. . . . Literature takes up the task of deciphering and rewriting these signs of history written on things. (34)

The second form of speech, Rancière notes, is the speech we encounter as soliloquy, "speaking to no one and saying nothing but the impersonal and unconscious conditions of speech itself" (39). This mute speech heard through the voices of the characters does not express the thoughts, sentiments, and intentions of the characters. As Rancière says, this mute speech designates "the thought of the 'third person' who haunts the dialogue, the confrontation with the unknown, with the anonymous and meaningless forces of life" (39-40). Taken in this manner, Rancière's formulation of the excess, superfluity, and muteness of the detail points to Barthes's error in his interpretation of the reality effect. The details, appearing in various forms of mute speech, are there to reveal the unconscious text of social history and point to the dimension of the true once they are mute and inconsequential, or, to use Barthes's words, "useless and meaningless."[6]

II. The Politics of Literature

What does Rancière intend by asserting that aesthetic disruption separates aesthetic democracy and notably literary democracy from political democracy? In what ways can such a distinction be connected to his proposition that there is "an 'aesthetics' at the core of politics that has nothing to do with Benjamin's discussion of the 'aestheticization of politics' specific to the 'age of the masses'" (*Politics* 13)? This proposition can be related to the pivotal conceptualization of Rancière's book, *The Politics of Aesthetics: The Distribution of the Sensible*, in which he argues how aesthetics does politics by means of establishing the connection between aesthetic practices and political practices. Like the political regime, the aesthetic regime always aims to disrupt the old regime of the sensible, according to Rancière. Then the answer to the following question becomes imperative: how does literature do politics?

"Literature 'does' politics as literature," Rancière argues (*Dissensus* 152).[7] The politics of literature, he writes, does not deal with "[the writer's] personal commitment to the social and political issues and struggles of their times," nor does it deal with "the modes of representation of political events or the social structure and the social struggles in their books" (*Dissensus* 152). To put it succinctly, the politics of literature according to Rancière means that literature as literature is involved in "[the] partition of the visible and the sayable, in [the] intertwining of being, doing and saying that frames a polemical world" (*Dissensus* 152). Drawing on Plato's idea of artisans and Aristotle's idea of citizens,[8] Rancière defines politics in ways that focus on the aesthetic core of politics:

> Politics is first of all a way of framing, among sensory data, a
> specific sphere of experience. It is a partition of the sensible,
> of the visible and the sayable, which allows (or does not allow)
> some specific data to appear; which allows or does not allow
> some specific subjects to designate them and speak about them.
> It is a specific intertwining of ways of being, ways of doing

and ways of speaking. (*Dissensus* 152)

Based on this conceptualization of politics and the historicity of literature,[9] literature, as the modern regime of the art of writing, represents a politics of literature grounded in the egalitarian principle of indifference to the hierarchical law of the old regime: it is "a specific partition of the sensible, a specific regime of speaking whose effect is to upset any steady relationship between manners of speaking, manners of doing and manners of being" (*Dissensus* 156).

Given that, how does literature do politics? And why, for Rancière, is it imperative that we separate literary democracy from political democracy? Rancière's thought on the politics of literature certainly sheds new light on the dilemma we have encountered in our attempt to frame the perception of a conflict-ridden common world by means of the discourse of identity politics, under the logic of which literature is reduced to political art, an aesthetic practice that is meant to address the political conflict of wills and interests. Under the logic of identity politics, social situations and characters in the fictional cosmology are expected to signify in a way that truthfully reflects the conflict of wills and interests which mobilizes the system of representative politics. In Rancière's view, it is literature as a unique regime of framing the intelligibility of the world that enacts the excess within the fictional world, the distance between art and life, and the dimension of the true, which can only be redeemed through aesthetic practices. Rancière thus writes on how literature does politics:

> Literature does a kind of side-politics and meta-politics. The principle of that "politics" is to leave the common stage of the conflict of wills in order to investigate in the underground of society and read the symptoms of history. It takes social situations and characters away from their everyday, earthbound reality and displays what they truly are, a phantasmagoric fabric of poetic signs, which are historical symptoms as well. For their nature as poetic signs is the same as their nature as historical results and political symptoms. This "politics" of literature emerges as the dismissal of the politics of orators and militants, who conceive of politics as a struggle of wills and interests. (*Dissensus* 163)

This elaboration on the politics of literature points to the conceptual and political significance of the schism between the two forms of politics: politics as a way to explore and bear witness to the hidden truth of a society in contrast to politics as a struggle of wills and interests.

What Rancière finds in the tradition of the novel starting from Balzac is something that he calls "the aesthetic revolution" that materializes the life of the anonymous and redeems the dimension of the true, which, as Rancière notes, is the very dimension great thinkers such as Marx, Freud, Benjamin, and the tradition of critical thought wish to bring to light. The aesthetic revolution, namely the new aesthetic regime, has turned the novel into a form that reveals the "symptoms of an epoch, a society, or a civilization in the minute details of ordinary life," the unconscious social text lying underneath the presentation of the prosaic everyday life (*Politics* 33). For the ordinary to become "a trace of the true," it has to be "torn from its obviousness in order to become a hieroglyph, a mythological or phantasmagoric figure" (*Politics* 34). To reflect upon the phantasmagoric dimension of the true is for Rancière the invention of literature: literature enacts a symptomatic reading which "[explains] close-to-hand realities as phantasmagoras bearing witness to the hidden truth of society," a plot invented by literature (*Dissensus* 164).

Given that phantasmagoric objects may point to the symptoms and contradictions of a society, literature as an aesthetic regime does not provide any direct political intervention into the reconfiguration of social situations. As a form that may disrupt the logic of an old regime and serve as a new pattern of intelligibility, literature itself is where politics is enacted, where the aesthetic regime aims to reconfigure "the map of the sensible." As Rancière illustrates in his analysis of the relationship between literarity and historicity:

> Political statements and literary locutions . . . define models of speech or action but also regimes of sensible intensity. They draft maps of the visible, trajectories between the visible and the sayable, relationships between modes of being, modes of saying, and modes of doing and making. They define variations of sensible intensities, perceptions, and the abilities of bodies. They thereby take hold of unspecified groups of people, they widen gaps, open up space for deviations, modify the speeds, the trajectories, and the way in which groups of people adhere to a condition, react to situations, recognize their images. They reconfigure the map of the sensible by interfering with the functionality of gestures and rhythms adapted to the natural cycles of production, reproduction, and submission. (*Politics* 39)

Grounded in the proposition that literature is meant to disrupt the naturalized order of the sensible, Rancière's theory of aesthetics points to the formation of a common world, that is, a space where the circulation of literary locutions and the quasi-bodies constituted by literary locutions form "uncertain communities that contribute to the formation of enunciative collectives that call into question the distribution of roles, territories, and languages" (*Politics* 40). In attempting to make what Rancière calls the non-part as a part of the old regime of distribution, literature aims to open up new possibilities and reconfigure the territory of what can be seen and said. The politics of literature, Rancière argues, enables us to reinvent a community that works toward the dimension of the true and thereby the possibility of equality and emancipation in that the aesthetic regime of the arts disrupts the bounds of the sensible. The space for equality and emancipation is made possible through dismantling the old regime of distribution, that is, by questioning the hierarchical order of the political regime that tends to honor one specific ethos.

III. The Forgotten Landscapes through Wu He's *Remnants of Life*

What are the forgotten landscapes Wu He's work wishes to reclaim? What issues do we intend to address by means of such a conceptual trope? What does this reading of Wu He alongside Rancière suggest about the forgotten landscapes in contemporary Taiwanese literature? It is a critical commonplace that forgotten landscapes, manifest in the writings of historical trauma, nation-building, collective amnesia, or identity crisis, have already dominated the space of contemporary Taiwanese literature (Chen 669-71; Liu 39-40). As Chen Fang-min points out:

> It is since the 1980s that Taiwanese writers have started questioning whether language can serve as the means to deliver truths, ... From the realistic literature of the 1970s to the postmodern period of the 1980s—all this can be taken as part of the chain reactions due to disillusionment with the nation-building project imposed by the nationalist party. (Chen 670)

> In the post-martial-law era, literature has become a very effective means of addressing those issues which were once suppressed by political or moral forces. In his reflection on contemporary Taiwanese literature after the 1980s, Chen Fang-min thus notes,

Entering the 1990s, Taiwanese literature is open to issues of all kinds. Gender and sexuality are the two subject matters that have been treated with the utmost care, depth, and intensity. . . . The topics related to sensual feelings or sexual desires were still suppressed in nativist literature, a huge milestone of the 1970s. It is in the 80s, thanks to the dominance of capitalism, that a new aesthetics was able to emerge so as to deal with issues simultaneously entangled in those involving ethnicity, gender, and class. . . . Using the body to fight against the power of the state, or using sexuality to reflect upon social situations has become a new path of literary writing. (Chen 671)

Chen's critical review provides us with a historical trajectory of Taiwanese literature of the post-martial-law era; in this monograph he also points out a number of ideological constraints that often lead not only to an aesthetic but also to an ethical impasse in the studies of Taiwanese literature. For Chen, such an impasse can be most clearly seen in the contested stances taken by local scholars on the issues of ethnicity and sexuality. In terms of ethnicity, there are two major difficulties worth our concern and effort. First of all, as Chen notes, Taiwan's intellectual circle is shaped and still dominated by the Han Ren (the Han Chinese)[10] and thereby the issue of cultural chauvinism and the disputes among the Han Chinese are looming.[11] The other thorny issue concerns biased critical treatments of second-generation mainland writers. Chen writes: "their writings, sometimes the writers as well, are condemned in that both the works and the writers tend to be examined and judged through the lens of 'nativism'" and thereby will often be labeled "resisting their Taiwaneseness" (*History* 41).

Through the writing of the remnants at a tribal village, Wu He's *Remnants of Life* provides a philosophical reflection on the entanglement between power and the regime of the sensible—what can be said and known. In its attempt to rethink nativism, this novel demonstrates the confines of nativism as a hierarchical order of intelligibility through a reflective account of the Seediq Tribe, an ethnic group that is, in Wu He's view, more entitled to claim "nativism" than the Han Chinese. Written in the form of a mixture of anthropological documents, philosophical fiction, and confessional writing, *Remnants of Life* reconstitutes the fragments of the Wu-she Incident and the everyday life of the remaining offspring of the Seediq people who survived it. Wu He published it in 1999, a time when Taiwan was mobilized by the dominance of nativist discourse. This false nativism, to use Wu He's words, has been widely used (and even misused) by leading politicians ever since the 1990s.[12] This novel can be seen as his implicit gesture to make problematic the implication and proliferation of such "nativism." As critic Yang Zhao points out, "Wu He's work on aboriginal peoples in a sense can be taken as his idea and pursuit of 'true nativism' and his way to contend with what he calls 'false nativism'" (264).[13] Ironically, however, various critics have claimed that the novel represents the triumph of nativism, as it best illustrates what nativism is. Critic Liu Liang-ya claims that "Wu He's novel redefines native consciousness by writing about aboriginal cultures that have long been oppressed by the Han Ren" (208). According to Liu, the novel has successfully demonstrated what nativism is trying to work toward by giving it more depth and inclusiveness. Taken in the manner of honoring nativisim, the novel is highly acclaimed for its unique and profound way of envisioning nativism through the prism of history and the present predicament of Taiwan's aboriginal peoples.

Contrary to such nativist thinking, this novel demonstrates that Wu He never stops questioning the intellectual and ethical bounds set by the logic of nativism. Unlike many other native Taiwanese writers who chose to stand up for nativism, Wu He, a native Taiwanese writer whose family has lived in Taiwan for generations, chose to remain quiet and live a secluded life during the 90s, when the population of the island country would be hastily labeled "nativists" and "non-nativists" (or "anti-nativists"), a dichotomy that can be seen as synonymous with the distinction between patriots and traitors. It may also be true that *Remnants of Life*, which I think testifies to Wu He's aesthetic and moral convictions, in many ways is still bound up with the intellectual impasse in contemporary Taiwan caused by the dominance of nativism, which, knowingly or unknowingly, often serves to draw a rigid line between political correctness and incorrectness. The impasse caused by the logic of political correctness, as critic Hao Yu-shiung notes,[14] still "confines the hermeneutics of Taiwanese fiction" (211). As *Remnants of Life* illustrates, such an impasse, working as a confined and even biased mode of intelligibility and sensibility, tends to reduce our capacity to acknowledge and address the truth of Taiwan, whose historical, cultural, and moral landscapes may turn highly confined—if not distorted—when seen through the lens of political correctness.

IV. Letting the Mute Speech of the Contested Voices Be Heard

Remnants of Life is a highly unsettling novel. And we may hardly be sure if it somehow unintentionally manifests the writer's unsettled feelings about the confined moral and intellectual frontiers of Taiwan today. The unsettling tone of the novel relentlessly bombards the reader with both the indeterminacy of its reflective discourse and the "excess" and "superfluity" of the details with respect to the reconstitution of historical scenes, the legacy of historical trauma, and the prosaic, idle everyday life of an isolated community. Read according to the logic of political correctness, this novel, often taken as the writer's ethical gesture of bringing back the silent victims, is meant to give voice to the struggle of a least powerful and most disregarded group in Taiwan. The defeated survivors of the Seediq Tribe and their offspring have lost their way of life, left with nothing but the *remnants of life*, a state of being that they simply have to endure. In his postscript Wu He states:

> This novel writes of three things. First of all, the novel is a quest for the legitimacy and appropriateness of the Wu-she Incident initiated by Mo-na Lu-dao and also that of the second Wu-she Incident. The second strain of the novel is concerning the soul-searching journey undertaken by the girl living next door during my stay at the tribal village. And the third aspect the novel engages with is the remnants of life I have seen and learned during my one-year stay at the village. (*Remnants* 251)

The novel's intense engagement with the representation of the culture and struggles of the tribe undoubtedly can be taken both as a political and as an ethical gesture.

Such an ethical turn seems elusively bound up with an ethics based on the logic of nativism and indicative of Levinas's notion of our excessive responsibility for the Other and the contemporary imperative for addressing the legacy of historical trauma. Published after the Revitalization Movements of the Aboriginal Peoples, which started in the 1990s, the novel certainly demonstrates Wu He's way—a least flamboyant one, I would say—to participate in the movements by making the stories of the anonymous tribal people heard and visible. But if such an implicit attempt shows the writer's ethical and thus political intervention into the discursive sphere which is morally and intellectually confined by the logic of political correctness, what can we make of the complexity of truths as revealed through the remnants of life at the village, the mixture of serious and lighthearted tones, the contested reflections on the possibility of seeking truth and justice, and the truthful account of the sensual and sexual on both the collective and personal levels? In other words, how do we make sense of such disruption between the gesture of political correctness and and that of political incorrectness? Why such excess of inquisition and interviews about the legitimacy of the Wu-she incident? And why is there such superfluity of details about prosaic everyday life in the tribal village? The incongruity between the solemn and lighthearted tones somehow weakens the political and moral grounding of the novel and troubles critics who tend to view the novel as the triumph of nativism.[15]

Such excess and superfluity, I would argue, is there to redeem the dimension of the true in the way the realistic novel redeems its own times as Rancière pointed out.   As *Remnants of Life* shows, the dimension of the true can be brought into being as the writer stays true to the flow of thoughts and feelings, confronts the contested perceptions and remains unbound by the dominant mode of thinking, the dominant regime that determines the distribution of the sensible today in Taiwan. The redemption of this dimension helps to transpose our understanding of a historical incident from the perspective grounded in the logic of political correctness to a new stance that will throw us into the phantasmagoria of truth to hear the mute speech of the traces of the true. As the narrator notes in the very beginning of *Remnants of Life*, the Wu-she Incident and its aftermath, the historical trauma that determines the destiny of the Seediq Tribe remains a hieroglyph, a mythological object that must be deciphered from an unbound perspective, unbound by current socially dogmatic positions. Drawn to the surviving tribal community, the narrator in a confessional tone thus starts the account of his one-year stay at the village. It is both a personal and a communal journey for deep reflection about the possibility of approaching historical and moral truths:

> It was perhaps in my teen years when I started reading about the Wu-she Incident. . . . And then many years later I learned, from a book regarding the history of the nationalist movements in Taiwan, that the Incident happened about a decade after Taiwanese people living in the plains had given up fighting against Japanese colonial rule. I guess there must have been good reasons to give up fighting by force and wondered why the message had never traveled to people in the high mountains? (*Remnants* 43)

And then in the brief sketch of his times the narrator humbly states the quest he feels obligated to fulfill by moving into the village:

> I was 28 when I was drafted into the army, and that was when I clearly sensed that on this land of ours there exists something we call "the State," an institution of power and violence that can, in ways palpable and impalpable, dominate both the heart and resources of this island country. . . . I left the army in 1981,

feeling the pain of being castrated by the army. Back then I didn't join the vibrant and time-turning political movements initiated by those activists who were fighting against the ruling party but chose to live a life of self-isolation at the northern small town Dan-shui. During my years there, I studied history and philosophy laboriously, for I was eager to understand the origin and meaning of the institutions such as the army or the state. . . . And I wanted to exorcize that heated young heart from me and stay calm and sensible enough for deep thinking over the legitimacy and ethics of the Wu-she incident. (*Remnants* 43)

The narrator embarked on this journey to learn about and meditate upon this historical event. Thus the novel constitutes a socio-historical cosmology that infills its aesthetic space with a multitude of thought fragments. These are evoked by written texts, oral history, tribal lore, interviews, small talks, and the writer's observations of all sorts of mute signs in the village—the ways people live their lives and ordinary objects scattered all over the village.

The excess of the fragments about the surviving wanderers manifests more than the writer's idiosyncratic style. It actually points to what Rancière sees in the realistic novel: the dimension of the true embodied through the speech of mute signs. The writer of a realistic novel, as Rancière points out, may work like a geologist, a naturalist, "[gathering] the vestiges and [transcribing] the hieroglyphs in the configuration of obscure or random things" (*Aesthetic Unconscious* 34). The mute speech we get to hear through Wu He's configuration of obscure or random things he sees at the village reflect the symptoms afflicting the struggling individuals of the trauma-ridden community. This novelistic discourse overwhelms as it keeps opening up the possibility of what can be seen and said and disrupts the bounds of the sensible.

The new frontier of visibility emerging from the mute speech in *Remnants of Life* redeems not just the history and life of the anonymous. Most of all, it redeems the space of dissensus. This space of dissensus, as Rancière notes, enables the redemption of the true as it ensures where the hierarchical order of the dominant regime can be challenged and disrupted by the aesthetic regime that works toward the principle of equality and emancipation of the individual and community. And this shows how literature does politics and how politics can still be viable. Rancière writes: "Telling the unconscious social text lying underneath—that also was a plot invented by literature itself. . . . The symptomatic reading that underpins the practices of historical and sociological interpretation was first of all a poetical revolution" (*Dissensus* 164). Through an intricate reconfiguration of the historical trauma the Seediq people have endured, Wu He provides us with a site of a poetical revolution. By disrupting an over-simplified mapping of the Wu-she Incident and its aftermath, Wu He challenges and at once expands the conceptual frontier of nativism so as to manifest the truths underneath the symptomatic social text. As the novel suggests, the history and culture of the native tribe remain anonymous and somewhat misconstrued in that the mode of addressing historical truth in the present time is largely shaped by a nativist logic that values the unification of divided political wills more than the revelation of historical truths. In its highly deconstructive account of the Wu-she Incident, *Remnants of Life* demonstrates its own limitations, as well as those of all other historiographies, in addressing the historical truths. And yet, at the same time, the deconstructive and self-reflexive tone of the novel enables the juxtaposition of diverse historical interpretations and thereby embodies the voices of the most defeated and silent in history—the Seediq children and their mothers who were forced to join the communal act of self-annihilation in the doomed battle with the Japanese predators.

By opening up space for deviations, as seen in the diverse mappings of the Incident provided by the villagers, *Remnants of Life* points to a more profound vision. It is a vision more than just giving voice to the anonymous. By framing "a new fabric of common experience, a new scenery of the visible and a new dramaturgy of the intelligible," as Rancière argues, fiction does not give a collective voice to the anonymous; instead, "it re-frames the world of common experience as the world of a shared impersonal experience" (*Dissensus* 141). As seen in the novel, the new fabric of common experience created by Wu He aims to disrupt the inadequate pattern of intelligibility and at once restore the community's capacity to see, to say, and to think through the rediscovery of the anonymous and the true. The defeated tribal people, as the novel notes, dislocated to Chuan-zhong-dao after the Incident and forced to take farming as their way of living, appear to be too disempowered to take part in the state-dominated project of historiography. Mo-na Lu-dao, the state-honored leader, has become the only cultural and spiritual totem left for the remaining offspring. They show very little interest in exploring the truths of the Incident in that almost all of those who witnessed the Incident are long gone as are other traces of this event. The monument in honor of national and tribal heroism does little for the defeated. By resorting to the mesmerizing power of alcohol, the remnant lives of the tribal village seem to defy time and existence. As the narrator reflects on their apathy about history and life:

Till the very end of the 20th century, almost 70 years away

from the Incident, the monument and the statue of Mo-na Lu-dao is now hovering over the playground of the elementary school where the massacres happened. Every year, on October 27, a group of people from Chuan-zhong-dao will travel to the site of the monument, their ancestral place, and participate in the state-hosted ceremony in memory of the Incident. They will bring food and their favorite kind of stimulant drinks mixed with rice wine for their hero Mo-na Lu-dao. From the talks given by the government officials, they now know that their ancestor Mo-na Lu-dao has become the spiritual leader of the entire Wu-she. Although no one seems to care, the legitimacy of the dubious Incident initiated by Mo-na Lu-dao is now confirmed by the government. (*Remnants* 45)

This account of the annual act of commemorating the Incident best epitomizes Wu He's deep feeling and thinking about the remnants of life, as the title of the novel so distinctively resonates with the readers. As he wishes to show the misery of the Seediq people—how downtrodden they are in the face of their history and their living condition, Wu He's will to address the dimension of the true and the political and moral dilemmas that evolve from the Incident is never compromised by his sympathetic eye. As he shows his understanding of the villagers who embrace heroism and tribal pride as the truth of the Incident, Wu He never fails to cast an unflinching gaze into the traumatic stories told by the mothers and those few who opposed such a suicidal battle as the Incident—their stories of how they were forced to take the lives of their children and then their own lives in the time of battle.

What is the mute speech that should and could be heard? This is a quest that is undertaken by the narrator so as to address all the truths which remain buried in the historiographies of the Incident confined in the logic of political correctness. During the narrator's investigation of the Incident, only two villagers disagreed with the official version. Both were from the Seediq Tribe—although each belongs to a different sub-tribe—and returned to their village after completing their college education in the capital city. For them, the Incident was caused by nothing but the tribal custom called *out-of-grass* (decapitation) and had nothing to do with the patriotic act of fighting against the Japanese colonial rule, which is highly glorified by the government so as to consolidate the unity of the aboriginal peoples with the Han Chinese. But such disagreement does little to reconstruct the Incident, as the novel indicates, since for them there is no such thing as "the Wu-she Incident," not to mention the follow-up Incident, or the so-called second Wu-she Incident, where the Seediq people massacred each other due to resentment provoked by the Japanese power. Such discrepancy and suppression that unsettles the restoration of historical truths lead to a fundamental question posed by Wu He: in what ways can we properly uncover and approach historical truths and for what purpose do we undertake the task?

Remnants of Life offers no simplified answer to that inquiry. All we can do and should do about history, as the novel suggests, is to map a larger meaning that does not patronize the victims but redeems the dimension of the true and the community's capacity to address it. For such dimension, I would argue, tends to be replaced by or mistaken for a hasty ethical act for the sake of truth and justice that the dominant political power already tends to see, reveal, and support. As the novel shows, there seems to be the unthought, the gaps in history and rationality, whose speech, though still mute, wishes to be heard and emancipated from the hierarchical order of the dominant power or the ethical order grounded in either tribal solidarity or the nationalist sentiment. This voice spoken to us through the narrator reveals the following:

> When I first became intrigued by the Wu-she Incident, I believed that the injustice of the massacre was antithetical to the dignity of resistance and the ritual of decapitation and that such opposition might be powerful enough to call dignity and ritual into question. But then I realized that the heart of the matter does not consist in the antithesis itself but in how we respond to the justification for violence in the name of dignity and honor, individual and communal. (*Remnants* 85)

The voice shows its own limited perception—seeing from the perspective of the now, as it claims—but this voice demonstrates its capacity to question a rationality that is limited to the logic of political correctness and ethical correctness.

Such inquiry, I would argue, is a necessary process for addressing the inadequacy of an ethics grounded in cultural pride and collective guilt. Questioning the ethical import of dignity brings no closure to the way we conceive of the Incident. Nevertheless, this inquisitive act disrupts the fixed order of the sensible and points to the possibility of thinking beyond the logic of nationalist or nativist discourse, which tends to value the wholeness of the nation, the tribe, or the culture itself more than any other aspect. The voice thus argues:

> Thinking from where I am, from the now, I tend to see

being—the preservation of life—far more valuable than the
legitimacy of fighting for dignity. During the course of my
reflective journey into the heart of this historical tragedy, I
have argued for the origin of *out-of-grass* and its historical
necessity, but now I am trying to argue against the distorted
thought suppressed by the defense of dignity. The now, where
I stand, will defend for the subjectivity of the individual and
question the justification for decapitation, regardless of the
worth of individual lives. . . . That is to say, if, in the case of
decapitation, we tend to think the autonomy of individuals
matters less, we are actually saying that being is meaningless
and thereby can be taken away anytime and that all else
coming from being itself matters little and thus can be
annihilated. . . . Hence the now is trying to fight against the
defense that decapitation is part of the tribal culture as
proposed by Ba-gan. For when we use the act of crushing
being for the purpose of preserving it, as seen in the practice
of decapitation, we help perpetuate the horror of being:
individuals are deprived of their autonomy and right to live
and will be doomed to live in fear of killing or being killed.
(*Remnants* 213)

In the attempt to lay bare the nature of violence—be it in a primitive or
civilized form—and the antinomy between being and dignity, Wu He shows us
the possibility and importance of thinking beyond the necessity of violence and
the preservation of dignity rather than life so that we may get to hear the mute
speech asking, "Why self-imposed violence? Why favors dignity more than
life?". For when a nation is mobilized to restore its pride, people may easily
lose the motivation and capacity to address such historically, ethically, and
emotionally complex issues as seen in the remnants of the Wu-she Incident as
pride and guilt very often compromise the will to address the true.

The paradox of redeeming the dimension of the true, I think, lies in our
capacity to address the complexity and irreconcilability of truths. But, as
Remnants of Life suggests, reflection about such irreconcilability is ethically
imperative. Making problematic the kind of justice anticipated by the victims
and granted by the government does not cancel out the historical and social
responsibility of the Japanese colonial power and the current Taiwanese
government, as indicated in Wu He's account of the predicament of the remnant
lives at the village that have to endure the misery caused by the aftermath of
violence and defeat. But, as seen in Wu He's critique of violence and hi

reflections on the meaning of those precious lives wiped away by both the dominant power and the minority themselves, a truly ethical act of redeeming the true should not be compromised by the logic of a guilt-ridden ethics that tends to present the dispossessed minority as innocent victims: an empty, homogeneous entity. As we see in *Remnants of Life,* this kind of perception—the victimization of the defeated—grows strong in the hierarchical logic of nativism as it tends to work toward the abstraction of the victims and the perpetrators. Wu He poses the question concerning how we may move beyond such dignity-and-guilt-bound regime of intelligibility that distributes and at once limits what is visible and possible to say about the true. And his aim is to dig into the nature of violence and the vision devoid of external and self-imposed violence by addressing the irreconcilability between violence imposed upon and despised by the victims and violence honored by the victims.

For Wu He, it is only through the voices of all mute objects—as irreconcilable as they can be—that the true dimension of history may emerge. And, in Rancière's view,   it is through hearing the complexity and profundity of the mute speech hidden in remnant lives that the effect of equality and emancipation can be made possible. He addresses the true in the same way as what Rancière sees in the phantasmagoria of the true as exposed in realistic fiction. Rancière thus notes: "[literature] finds symptoms of an epoch, a society, or a civilization in the minute details of ordinary life; it explains the surface by subterranean layers; and it reconstructs worlds from their vestiges" (*Politics* 33). As demonstrated in Wu He's tribal village, it is through an emancipated social cosmology brought into being by fiction that the community can be set free from the bounds of pride and guilt and thereby regain its capacity to ddress the complexity of the true.

es

The Wu-she Incident took place in October 27,1930. It was an insurgency nitiated by Mo-na Lu-dao, the leader of the Seediq Tribe, inhabiting in an-tou County in central Taiwan, as the Seediq people were trying to ht against the Japanese rule. In early December of the same year, most he Seediq people were either killed by the Japanese army or hanged 1selves, and the remaining hundreds of tribal people were relocated Wu-she to Chuan-zhong-dao, also in Nan-tou County.
ranslations of all the Chinese-written texts cited in this paper are

3.   This refers to the talk entitled "The Politics of Fiction," given by Rancière in 2009 during his visit to Taiwan. In a similar manner, in "The Politics of Literature," Chapter 13 of *Dissensus*, Rancière takes up the issue on the critique of a fascination for detail in Flaubert's prose and fleshes out the political meaning of such an aesthetic practice.

4.   As Rancière points out, Barthes argues in his article, "The Reality Effect," that the superfluity of useless details can be seen as an attestation of the real, "the real which proves its reality out of the very fact that it is useless and meaningless" (qtd. in 41).

5.   For Rancière, the meaning of "everything speaks" is twofold. It implies the abolition of the hierarchies of the representative order. It also indicates the great Freudian rule that "there are no insignificant 'details'" (35).

6.   In his reconfiguration of Barthes's view on the realistic fiction, Rancière spells out the paradox of the superfluity of the prosaic details that in Barthes's view are useless and meaningless. For Rancière, the paradox lies in the idea that those details will start to signify once they become useless and meaningless; that is, they speak through their mute speech.

7.   Rancière once again takes up one of his long-term projects that in his own words aims to re-establish "a debate's conditions of intelligibility," a debate concerning the nature of aesthetics and how and why aesthetic practices still matter in the contemporary scene (*Politics* 10).

8.   According to Aristotle, a citizen is a person who has a part in the act of governing and being governed. But for Plato, artisans refer to those who do not have time to devote themselves to anything other than their work. By relating to these two philosophers, Rancière thus elaborates on the connection between the distribution of the sensible and the aesthetics at the core of politics: "[aesthetics] is a delimitation of spaces and times, of the visible and invisible, of speech and noise, that simultaneously determines the place and the stakes of politics as a form of experience. Politics revolves around what is seen and what can be said about it, around who has the ability to see and the talent to speak, around the properties of spaces and the possibilities of time" (*Politics* 12-13).

9.   In Rancière's view, when literature is examined from its own historicity, it actually represents a new way of doing things with words, a new partition of the sensible, of the visible and the sayable. Literature is a new regime of the art of writing, a different kind of politics in contrast to the kind of politics embedded in the regime of representative art (*Dissensus* 153-54).

10. The Han Chinese are an ethnic group native to East Asia. It constitutes 98% of the population of Taiwan, but the majority of the population in the present-day Taiwan would designate themselves as Taiwanese vis-à-vis

Chinese, which is used as a political marker for the Han Chinese and all minority groups in Mainland China.

11. See p.41, *A History of Modern Taiwanese Literature.*
12. See the first chapter on ethnic Taiwan from the monograph entitled *Envisioning Taiwan* by Chen Gou-wei.
13. Here Yang Zhao is referring to the novel *Reflecting upon A-bon Ka-lou-si* (1997) by Wu He. Yang points out that this novel shows Wu He's critique of the dominant discourse of nativism and at once how Wu He is bound by nativism. The novel demonstrates his attempt to distinguish true nativism from false nativism but "his mode of thinking is still rather nativist, shaped by the principles of nativist literature, and the only difference is that his nativist setting is in the aboriginal community," as Yang notes (264).
14. Hao is one of the prominent Taiwanese writers and also works as a college professor in the Institute of Taiwanese Literature at National Chung Cheng University.
15. As Liu Liang-ya notes, Wu He sets a good example of how the Han Chinese may empathize with the minority groups, but such power of empathy is greatly diminished by the deconstructive tone accompanying the assertive one (197).

Works Cited

Chen, Fangmin. Taiwan xinwenxueshi [*A History of Modern Taiwanese Literature*]. Taipei: Lianjing, 2011

Chen, Quowei. *Xiangxiang Taiwan: Dangdai xiaoshuozhong de zuqun shuxie* [*Envisioning Taiwan: Writing Ethnicity in Contemporary Fiction*]. Taipei: Wunan, 2007.

Hao, Yushiung. "Woshishei?!: Lun balingniandai Taiwan xiaoshuozhong de zhengzhi miwang ["Who am I?!: On Identity Crisis in Taiwanese Fiction of the 1980s"]. Zhongwaiwenxue [*Chung Wai Literary Quarterly*] 26 (1998): 150-170.

Liu, Liangya. *Huoxiandai yu huozhimin: Jieyan yilai Taiwanxiaoshuo zhuanlun* [*Postmodernism and Postcolonialism: Taiwanese Fiction since 1987*]. Taipei: Maitian, 2006.

Rancière, Jacques. *The Politics of Aesthetic: The Distribution of the Sensible.* Trans. Gabriel Rockhill. London: Continuum, 2004.

---. *The Aesthetic Unconscious.* Trans. Debra Keates and James Swenson. Malden, MA: Polity, 2009.

---. "The Politics of Fiction." Yi meixue yu zhengzhi zhi ming: Rancière 2009 fangtaijiangzuo [*In the Name of Aesthetics and Politics: Seminars by Rancière, Taipei 2009*]. Taipei: College of Humanities and Social Sciences, National Chiao Tung University, 2009.

---. *Dissensus: On Politics and Aesthetics*. Trans. Steven Corcoran. New York: Continuum, 2010.

Yang, Zhao. "Bentu xiandaizhuyi de zhanxian: Jiedu Wu He xiaoshuo" ["The Emergence of Nativist Modernism: On Wu He's Fiction"]. *Remnants of Life*. Taipei: Maitian, 1999.   257-266.

Wu, He. *Remnants of Life*. Taipei: Maitian, 1999.

Dystopian Scenarios in Heterotopic Spaces: Paul Auster's *Man in the Dark*

Eduardo Barros-Grela
María Bobadilla-Pérez

In *One Thousand Plateaus*, Deleuze and Guattari articulated the concept of rhizome as a collective mechanism of enunciation within cultural theory. According to their seminal argument on the rhizome as metaphor for contemporary knowledge and society, human observation—and understanding—of culture implies a transgression of traditional modes of organization, and also questions the validity of vertical and hierarchical relations. Rather, according to their proposal, those relations are established according to patterns of planar horizontality, and require a vision of multiplicity, instead of the legitimized organization based on linear relations and binary oppositions. With their contribution, they fostered the construction of a solid–yet malleable–ground for subaltern cultural voices as legitimized discourses, and developed a mechanism of reciprocity among subjectivities. Also, their principles of connection and heterogeneity—resulting from the rhizomatic distribution of knowledge and space—problematized traditional cultural relations that supported a hegemony-resistance pattern, whose identity was determined by the existence of hierarchical relations. As Paul Auster's novel *Man in the Dark* seems to claim, though, the interrogation of contingent identifications of the self reveals a concealed spatiality that is subject to forms of intercultural production and fictional suspension, and provides a performative action upon the various dystopian reimaginations of the city that are enabled by the changing spatial paradigm facilitated by rhizomatic thought.

This article studies the cultural *anomalies* of Paul Auster's characters in *Man in the Dark*. This novel was published by Picador in 2009, and tells the story of an adult man, August Brill, who suffered a car accident and is staying at his daughter's house in Vermont while he recovers from his injuries. Suffering from insomnia, Brill uses the invading darkness of his room to build stories about alternative realities, which will interact throughout the novel with his own. In one of those stories, he *creates* Owen Brick, a young magician who answers to the stage name of "The Great Zavello", and who wakes up locked inside a huge cylinder functioning as a prison for Brick. He is oblivious to the reasons why he is confined inside a circular wall, but he does know he is part of a war and is confident someone from his army will come and help him. Sergeant Serge Tobak, in effect, arrives to rescue Brick and inform him about a mission he must fulfill: he must assassin someone named Blake, Bloch, or Black, in a space where 9/11 has never happened and no one has ever heard about a war in Iraq, but the whole country is immersed in a dark civil war. That person of uncertain name Brick has to kill is a demiurgic figure who during his nights of insomnia makes up the civil war the country is fighting, and must be eliminated for the war to end. Brick soon learns that the real name of that man is actually August Brill, and he is a literary critic who suffered and accident and is recovering from his injuries at his daughter's house, in Vermont.

Through the use of heterotopic spaces to recreate dystopian visions of the United States, Paul Auster succeeds in providing an imagined spatiality that questions traditional body discourses and identity manifestations by establishing rhizomatic spatial structures, that is, non-hierarchical mental spaces that undermine traditional conceptualizations of place as made up from fixed categories. Tim Woods, for example, analyzes Auster's use of space in *In the Country of Last Things* to approach closer to Soja's concept of spatiality[1], and claims that Auster's novels tend to focus on how space—in particular, locked spaces—and individual consciousness are related:

> Much of Auster's fiction pivots on spatial loci, on the actions of individuals within locked rooms, isolated garrets, enclosed spaces, circumscribed areas, and the effects of closure and openness on human consciousness: how a change in society's modes of production changes social conceptions of space and how, in turn, space constructs, and is constructed by, individual consciousness. (108)

Woods contribution to the discussion of Auster's novels' use of space alludes to their capability to create spaces of contingency generated from a constant interaction between the actual spaces and the social, mental, and political interpretations of those spaces made by characters. Those are spaces of transition, that is, spaces that situate themselves beyond the classical categorization of spaces as either perceived or conceived. Woods follows Soja's discussion of "thirdspaces":

> Thirdspaces are created by the effects of a changing culture, and are spaces of transition; transition between localities and over time. They elude the reflection of a single permanent power structure and are places of simultaneity and transience. They relate to both poles of binary conceptions of cross-cultural space and yet at the same time

entirely transcend them. More than a mental place, thirdspaces hold the possibility for socio-political transformation. (Soja 9)

Ana Isabel Gómez Vallecino agrees with Wood's view, and declares that Auster's characters are normally fragmented and dissociated from society, and live an existence of banality and lack of control. According to her, they are constantly looking for ways to escape from their constant crises, and reject looking inwards to their own consciousness. In this sense, these characters do project a transitional space that is foreign to traditional treatments of space. Auster's characters choose to create alternative spaces rather than confronting their own realities. However, those spaces are closely linked to the realities the characters inhabit, what instantly turns them into subjects belonging to spaces of transition. Christopher Donovan, in turn, provides a comparative approach to Auster's and Thoreau's works with regards to the influence of open and closed spaces upon human subjectivity. In his view, Auster's characters would use space as an instrument to define their own subjectivities, but they would have a minimal influence upon the configuration of that space. All in all, these studies succeed in pointing out and defining the spatial emphasis in most of Auster's characters, and provide a critical apparatus for the study of the mutual relations between space and subjectivity.

A logical continuation of the line of research initiated by these three critics would be focused on the investigation on how characters function in their relation with space, and also on how they create heterotopic spaces that, in turn, produce multiple identities for their subjectivity through a process of rhizomatic displacement, which will end up translated into an epistemological reterritorialization. Such a procedure can be studied through the different discourses of cultural identification in Auster's characters, who intend to embody the celebration of paranoia and melancholia as literary devices as they adopt *deferred* cultural spaces in a threatening apocalyptic scenario. These characters are, as aforementioned, displaced to an undefined, heterotopic, and apocalyptic space in order to establish a *deference* from their supposed spatial signifiers, and to establish a correspondence with the social mechanisms of displacement. Such a spatial transition can be read as a continuous reterritorialization of imagined spaces as places of identity production.

Rooting from Deleuze's principle of multiplicity, therefore, these characters' discourses question the relation of identification between territoriality and subjects/subjectivities, and then reconcile the performative function of their voices (as fictional characters) with the dystopian spaces they produce (as machineries of discursive production). This is evidenced by the narratological game established in the novel, which facilitates the fragmentation of the speaking voice and allows its discursivity to function as a transitional vehicle between the different narrative spaces: the decrepit and dark room in Vermont and the dystopic war scenario in Wellington. The characters in the novel aim to resignify canonical identity politics through the adoption of a political pose of transgression and parody, one that can only be represented through the de-signified denotative power of dystopian spatialities. A conversation between a disoriented Brick and a female character, Molly, shows the conflictive yet ludic and parodical tone of the narrative:

> Molly, Brick says, breaking the silence ten minutes into their walk, do you mind if I ask you something?
> It depends on what it is, she answers.
> Have you ever heard of the Second World War?
> The waitress lets out a short, ill-tempered grunt. What do you think I am? she says. A retard? Of course I've heard of it.
> And what about Vietnam?
> My grandfather was one of the first soldiers they shipped out.
> If I said *the New York Yankees*, what would you say?
> Come on, everybody knows that.
> What would you say? Brick repeats-
> With an exasperated sigh, Molly turns to him and announces in a sardonic voice: The New York Yankees? They are those girls who dance at Radio City Music Hall.
> Very good. And the Rocketees are a baseball team, right?
> Exactly.
> Ok. One last question and then I'll stop [...] Who's the president?
> President? What are you talking about? We don't have a president.
> No? Then, who's in charge of the government?
> The prime minister, birdbrain. Jesus Christ, what planet do you come from?
> I see. The independent states have a prime minister. But what about the Federals. Do they still have a president?
> Of course.
> What's his name?
> Bush.
> George W.?

That's right. George W. Bush.

Brick learns from Molly about the absurd political situation that has been adopted by the country, as well as about the cultural maladjustments of their confronted spatialities. The transgressive power of the dialogue lies on the playful references to political names that are well-known by the reader, who identifies the scene as totally parodical. The imagined spatiality fluctuates between the apparently logical state of the country according to Molly's standards, Brick's astonished look of that reality as compared with his own, and the reader's *omniscient* observation of events, which thus incorporates his/her own reality into the narrative.
Another instance of this invitation to transgress legitimate spaces appears at the beginning of the novel:

> I am alone in the dark, turning the world around in my head
> as I struggle through another bout of insomnia, another
> white night in the Great American wilderness . . . Bright
> light, then darkness. Sun pouring down from all corners of
> the sky, followed by the black of night, the silent stars, the
> wind stirring in the branches. (7)

These are the opening words in *Man in the Dark*, and they anticipate the double spatiality that will give format to this novel written by Auster: the spaces of light and the spaces of darkness converging in a contradictory common ground that destabilizes the reader's spatial expectations. Following the legitimate scenarios of dystopian science-fiction literature (Moylan and Baccolini 8), the narrator in *Man in the Dark* situates his readers/narratees in a dialectic position. Such a re-location allows him to speak freely about both the claustrophobic space that he physically inhabits—his room—and the psychotic spatiality that he deliberately constructs for his decrepit—and dismounted—identity. He is alone. Alone in the dark. A dark routine of light and obscurity that parallels that of his characters and that of his readers. In that sense, Auster's novel clearly uses the different manifestations, interpretations, and performances of space as mechanisms of identity dislocation and reality multiplicity, and it impersonates an amplification of the boundaries of reality.

Although many critics have rightly encountered in this Auster novel a celebration of realism[2] (Panzani; Greaney), the referentiality towards a discourse of heterotopia[3] becomes necessary when analyzing the different meanings of space within the text (space as geographical discourse, space as a mental narrative, or space as a *spectral* medium for identity interrogation). A critical approach to the first of these spaces must necessarily confront a set of stories in Auster's uses of urbanity and place-ness[4]—or dwelling—within the city environment[5]. As I anticipated earlier in this essay, in this novel, Auster uses a 72-year-old literary critic as the protagonist/narrator, one that has been *voluntarily* confined to the dark and oppressive limits of his room[6]. His place of confinement will generate a space of dystopian freedom of choice whose main function will be to liberate the author from his alienating space by killing him. The situation of a creative mind being exposed to a constrictive atmosphere is not new in Auster's narrative[7]. For example, his previous novel, *Travels in the Scriptorium*, presents a similar scenario, where an elderly person wakes up in a locked room with no knowledge or memory about the reasons for his imprisonment[8]. This man is asked to write his own story, only with the provision of a series of objects that are placed on a table at the center of the room within his reach to help him regain some memories from his concealed past (and, therefore, from his concealed identity). Similarly, in *Man in the Dark*, the protagonist is invited to *create* a story while he is secluded in his own apartment due to his personal circumstances and even his physical impediments (as evident by his state of corporeal decrepitude). In both cases, the spatial uncertainty and discomfort that define both protagonists' mental states are established from the beginning in order to implement in Auster's readers an empathetic claustrophobia:

> I would love to be able to walk up the stairs, go into her room, and talk to her for a while. Tell some of my bad jokes, maybe, or else just run my hand over her head until her eyes closed and she fell asleep. But I can't climb the stairs in a wheelchair, can I? And if I used my crutch, I would probably fall in the dark. Damn this idiot leg. The only solution is to sprout a pair of wings, giant wings of the softest white down. (13)

> The old man sits on the edge of the narrow bed, palms spread out on his knees, head down, staring at the floor. He has no idea that a camera is planted in the ceiling directly above him. The shutter clicks silently once every second, producing eighty-six thousand four hundred still photos with each revolution of the earth. Even if he knew he was being watched, it wouldn't make any difference. His mind is elsewhere, stranded among the figments in his head as he searches for an answer to the question that haunts him.

> Who is he? What is he doing here? When did he arrive and
> how long will he remain? (*Travels* 1)

In the first quote, taken from *Man in the Dark*, the protagonist and narrator shares his spatial torment with the reader/narratee who, due to his corporeal limitations, witnesses Brill's disability to physically move around a limited space of wood and concrete. The reader is thus invited to choose to create a hybrid space by using those giant wings provided by Brill's imagination, and to create a fusion of realities based on a structure of multiplicities.

The second quote also refers to a situation—in this case, taken from *Travels in the Scriptorium*—in which several spaces are visited to construct a transitional spatiality: first, the room where the old man is imprisoned; second, the heterotopic space of the camera that records his movements; third, the space where his mind is trying to answer to his identity interrogations; and last, the space of the reader who participates in the narrative game posed by the author. As in the previous quote, the reader shares the old man's restlessness caused by the uncertainty of his confinement, but at the same time acknowledges the existence of other spaces beyond the room described.

The descriptive tendency to design spaces of seclusion responds to Auster's intentions to transfer those physical barriers into mental states of limited freedom, a process that perfectly describes the transformation of space into spatiality as well. As Stephen Fredman states in his study of an earlier work written by Auster (*Ghosts*),

> Regardless of the imagery with which it is portrayed, enclosure within the room of writing invokes not just a sense of aloneness but a sense of claustrophobia in Auster's characters . . . Ultimately, what we have been considering as a poetic anxiety about the room of writing is revealed as a fear of death, a fear so acute that A. tries to evacuate his life out of the present in order to observe it safely, albeit in a disembodied fashion, from the future. (19)

It is obvious that, here, the freedom-seclusion dichotomy is key to understand Auster's narratives[9], but from an interpretation of the spaces created as mixed places where the different subjectivities merge. The reference to the character's alienation from his own corporeality implies again a sign of identity displacement as a tool of ontological interrogation. Either as a dislocation toward a different time or to an alternative reality, Auster's characters need to deal with the limitations of their spatialities in places of confinement, and look for a solution by creating heterotopic spaces of habitation. These spaces will be intimately connected to their material counterparts, and the characters in Auster's narrative will function in them as transitional liaisons. This can be clearly noticed in *Man in the Dark*, where Brill's presence in the intradiegetic story he has created is persistent:

> Because… because it was the only world I ever knew.
> But now you know another world. What does that suggest to you, Brick?
> I don't follow.
> There is no single reality, Corporal. There are many realities. There's no single world. There are many worlds, and they all run parallel to one another, worlds and anti-worlds, worlds and shadow-worlds, and each world is dreamed or imagined or written by someone in another world. Each world is a creation of a mind. (69)

Frisk's speech in this quote gives Brill a position of "relative omnipotence" within their reality, and subtly anticipates Brill's protagonism in blurring the boundaries between those different worlds. Both Frisk and Brick know now about the influence—and concealed presence—of that demiurgic figure in their world, and therefore become as well unintended transitional figures between both worlds. All of them—Brill, Brick, and Frisk—are part of a heterotopic space that exists only in subjective terms, but has an unequivocal influence on the worlds they inhabit. Brill's function in the story is to undermine the hierarchical relation that has been established between two of those worlds, and to put forward a new and horizontal relation in which characters' actions from within the story have a determinant effect on formerly external entities. The use of heterotopic spaces as a device to transgress traditional relations of power works in this novel in the sense that the "author"—or creator—of this new world is brought into the very spaces he is creating, what positions him in a space of restricted power: "He didn't invent this world. He only invented the war. And he invented you, Brick. Don't you understand that? This is your story, not ours. The old man invented you in order to kill him." (70)

The dialectics of power-resistance also work, thus, as a parody in *Man in the Dark*, as they aspire to create a heterotopic space of confinement, as Fredman clearly claims in the aforementioned quote. The "disembodied fashion," resulting from a spatial alienation of himself, makes of Auster's representative character an acting subject that performs his identity from an altered space. He is not just "observing his life" from somewhere else, but rather he is enacting a performance of his identity from a "line of flight" within his rhizomatic restructuring of space. The destabilization of the established relations of power between the different spaces allows Auster's characters to recreate the legitimate spatial structures as an accumulation of decentered compartments that interact with each other. A rhizomatic, rather than an arborescent structure, is then produced, and the relations of power and resistance among its parts are transformed into a horizontal complex of multiplicities. It is in this dimension that we can precisely address the connections between the aforementioned types of spaces (space as geographical discourse, space as a mental narrative, and space as a *spectral* medium for identity interrogation) and Auster's dystopian narratives.

Writing, for Auster's characters, implies the creation of a set of resources in order to escape from the secluded spaces they inhabit[10]. Those "places of refuge" become, however, imagined spatialities that are re-territorialized as *lignes de fuite*[11]; they are distorted transformations that find in dystopian scenarios the perfect spaces to develop their freed/secluded subjectivities. As seen in *Man in the Dark,* the dystopian alienation created by Auster's characters imply an inexorable seclusion within other spaces of contingency, i.e. spaces of performative suspension. The intricate relation established between the two spaces (inside and outside thc act of writing) destabilizes the fixed and essentialist nature of both, but, at the same time, it perpetuates the impossibility of any type of transgressive action in just one particular space. The influence of Brill upon his characters—and vice versa—in any of the worlds is limited to Brill's (or any of his characters') logic, so his—or his characters'—actions disallow any trace of performativity. Although the heterotopic space created by the transitional spatiality of the characters implies a liberation for all of them, their particular realities remain unaltered beyond their inert development, and are foreign to the characters' evolution within the heterotopic space. Brill refers to this inadequacy when he is occupied by bringing film references that can help his granddaughter's education. In particular, his remarks about the watch at the end of Yasujirō Ozu's *Tokyo Story* (1953) denote a partially unconscious knowledge about the limitations of spatial production:

> Noriko is sitting alone, staring blankly into space, her mind elsewhere. Several more moments pass, and then she lifts her mother-in-law's watch off her lap. She opens the cover, and suddenly we can hear the second hand ticking around the dial. Noriko goes on examining the watch, the expression of her face at once sad and contemplative, and as we look at her with the watch in the palm of her hand, we feel that we are looking at time itself, time speeding ahead

> as the train speeds ahead, pushing us forward into life and
> then more life, but also time as the past, the dead mother-in-
> law's past, Noriko's past, the past that lives on in the
> present, the past we carry with us into the future. (78-79)

Brill observes how the different alterations of reality, that is, the subjective
constructions of spaces, cannot escape from the burden of a history that
appears in the narrative as heavily protected by an unalterable time continuity.

Other traces of this aporia can be easily pointed out in the case of *Man
in the Dark*. It is again August Brill, the character that creates a new space
through his writing, who alludes to an alternate reality in which the history of
the US has been radically changed. In it, as aforementioned, the crucial
attacks against the Twin Towers in 2001 never happened, and a secession war
has been declared between antagonist US states instead[12]. As usual in the
narratives of Paul Auster, the alternate—dystopian—reality presented through
Brill's writing/imagination responds to a sort of space that would perfectly fit
in any definition of "dystopia" (Brooke; Gordin, Tilley, and Prakash; Lyman;
Slaughter). His ability to escape from an oppressive reality (let us not forget
that he acts as an illusionist in his alternative life as Brick, the character who
will be in charge of putting an end to Brill's life) will not take him to a
favorable environment, but rather to a vicious space of poverty, lack of
freedom, injustices, oppression, and repressive control systems. All of these
are, of course, functionally legitimized by the ongoing civil war precipitated
by the altered events. Auster's novel seems to follow here Gary S. Morson's
ideas about the *construction* of dystopias, as he places Brill, the writer in his
novel, to create lines of flight for his characters *to* function within historical
events[13]:

> In the men's room, he finally took the trouble to
> examine the money and was encouraged to see the face of
> Ulysses S. Grant engraved on the front of each bill. That
> proved to him that this America, this other America, which
> hasn't lived through September 11 or the war in Iraq,
> nevertheless has strong historical links to the America he
> knows. The question is: at what point did the two stories
> begin to diverge? (*Man in the Dark* 50)

Those historical events, as Morson suggests[14], are spaces of "contingency,
conflict, and uncertainty", where Brick (Brill's intradiegetic[15] protagonist) is
inserted as an anachronism, as a displaced participant of the dystopian space:
"Where was I? Owen Brick ... Owen Brick walking down the road to the city.

The cold air, the confusion, a second civil war in America" (*Man in the Dark* 14).

That dystopian scenario—within a heterotopic spatiality—confers therefore a different kind of voluntary alienation compared to that of traditional post-apocalyptic narratives. War, as an instrument of subjective development within the imaginary space of the intradiegesis, provides proactive patterns for dystopian characterization. In his discussion of *Brave New World* and *Fahrenheit 451,* Ángel Galdón explains the relevance of war scenarios in the anticipatory writing of dystopian literatures:

> At the last stage of the Cold War and along the 20th century the screen took into account the warnings of dystopian literature . . . In the third place, the past is a feature to be erased, depicted by the ruling power as a dark time prone to war and lacking morals. In fact, this past was, at the time in which the works were published, the author's and the readers' own time, linking the characters to the current socio-political context and creating empathy. (166)

Such a war setting is not *explicitly* exposed in Auster's environment when he publishes *Man in the Dark*, but his constant references to the war in Iraq and to the 9/11 events[16], as fundamental triggers of the multiplicity of realities *around* his novel, makes *Man in the Dark* a dystopian narrative inserted into the historical collective subconscious of his readership.

Auster thus turns to heterotopic spaces to introduce his machinery of postmodern[17] narratives, and uses the technique of the mirror as a producer of different and inverted spaces of reality to position the internal narrative of this novel. According to Foucault in "Des espaces autres," as it is well known, a mirror would be an appropriate form of heterotopia:

> In the mirror, I see myself there where I am not, in an unreal, virtual space that opens up behind the surface; I am over there, there where I am not, a sort of shadow that gives my own visibility to myself, that enables me to see myself there where I am absent: such is the utopia of the mirror. But it is also a heterotopia in so far as the mirror does exist in reality, where it exerts a sort of counteraction on the position that I occupy. (1572)

Auster's novel follows a similar pattern in order to construct the relationship between Brill and Brick, who are both reciprocal reflections of themselves. As in a mirror, Brill, through his writing, addresses his gaze towards his own reflection, Brick, *producing* thus an identity Other, an alterity that returns his gaze to reciprocate the same discourse of identity production to Brill. The (non)existence of such a parallel space in the mirror—in Brill's writing—would result in a legitimization of the real space as a "utopian reality." But Auster's intentional introduction of a *dystopian* environment at both sides of the mirror disallows the possibility of a reality other than the confluence of both. The heterotopic space in *Man in the Dark* becomes a *place* for transgression, as epitomized by the prevalent fluctuation of both realities throughout the novel. The Unamunian paradox[18] acquires full signification here, as Brick's drive to put an end to the parallel reality where he exists, by killing Brill, would legitimize the dystopian component of both spaces as the only coherent possibility. Such a spatial reconfiguration is precipitated by the aforementioned rhizomatic reconceptualization of space, which allows Auster to transgress binary relations in his narrative models, and introduce a structure of multiplicities, rather as a limitless *mise-en-abîme*:

> Putting his arms on the table, Frisk leans forward and says: Are we in the real world or not?
> How should I know? Everything looks real. Everything sounds real. I'm sitting here in my own body, but at the same time I can't be here, can I? I belong somewhere else.
> You are here alright. And you belong somewhere else.
> It can't be both. It has to be one or the other. (68-69)

Brick's incredulity about the possibility of belonging to more than one space at the same time refers to a paradoxical challenge to traditional forms of conceptualizing space, and at the same time presents a reaction against transcending the epistemological comfort of the status quo even in a situation of extreme necessity to change things.

In *"Another History": Alternative Americas in Paul Auster's Fiction*, Jesús Ángel González alludes to Auster's intention to create Brill's parallel reality as a response to a social necessity to *know* how things would have turned out should Al Gore had been—legitimately—elected as president in 2000. Varvogli and Simonetti have also stressed, according to González, Auster's writing shift since 9/11, "from a metafictional writer locked in his room to a political writer engaged with the world of American politics" (52). These references to a "social necessity" in Auster's late novels are, however, necessarily limited to this American novelist's use of space, as it has been shown in this essay. Auster puts forward a heterotopic space in which alternative realities are introduced as component parts in that rhizomatic multiplicity of *reality*, denoting an unavoidable and intricate commitment to ideological discursivities. All the spaces presented in *Man in the Dark* are repressive in essence, and there seems to be no possible escape from them. Auster's bidirectional lines of flight (i.e. the connecting lines between spaces) convey, necessarily, the radiation of dystopia to all the scenarios involved. When Brick is finding out about his role in the alternative world where he unexpectedly awakes, he is irrevocably exposed to, or rather implicated in, Brill's perceptions of their realities:

> He didn't invent this world. He only invented the war. And he invented you, Brick. Don't you understand that? This is your story, not ours. The old man invented you in order to kill him.
> So now it's a suicide.
> In a roundabout way, yes. (70-71)

Man in the Dark responds to a pattern of "roundabout spaces", in which actions are determined by the relation established between inhabitants of those spaces and the physical territories of subjects and subjectivities. The resulting heterotopian spaces are subject to permanent *reterritorializatio*[19], and its inhabitants are therefore constantly interrogated. Their identities make no sense—only as diluted subjectivities—in those spaces of contingency, and work as unfixed elements within an unfixed spatiality.

In this sense, Auster's late novels—particularly *Man in the Dark*—provide dystopian environments in order to represent his reconstructed reality[20]. Such a challenge is only possible, as I have tried to demonstrate throughout this study, by appealing to non-traditional forms of space, and both the Deleuzean rhizomatic (de)structure of space and the Foucauldian discussion of heterotopias—as well as their application to human spatialities (Soja; Lefebvre)—seem to fit in Auster's plans. He refers to the state of mind that his characters are obliged to adopt as *inert*, sedated spaces of identity suspension: "The effect is similar to anesthesia. The black void of oblivion, a nothingness as deep and dark as death" (72). *The horror*, the dystopian scenario in Auster's novel, is represented by the lack of agency that its characters exhibit. They inhabit those heterotopic spaces as inert bodies, which can only function as paranoid, melancholic *subjects* living in that "black void of oblivion," in that "dark nothingness." Auster is able to present to his reader this exact picture through a secondary character that has little to no weight in his narrative, but holds the truth of Auster's message in *Man in the Dark*: "An indelible picture, undimmed after all these years: the sight of that pathetic figure paralyzed by the pressure of events, a man gone rigid with despair as the city exploded around him" (81). Through rhizomatic structures, the main characters from *Man in the Dark* find a way to verbalize their Other identities, i.e. their displaced subjectivities, in heterotopic spatialities that are exposed to a constant process of deterritorialization and reterritorialization (a permanent resignification of the spaces that they inhabit and of the spaces that they create). To the question of why Auster resorts to a dystopian scenario to reproduce the spaces of contingency that emanate from their characters' minds, I have tried to respond by claiming that a rhizomatic (de-)structure must be applied not only to semantic referentiality, but also to the epistemological core of Brick and Brill. Their reciprocal heterotopic spatialities include dystopian and utopian views of themselves, resulting in a contradictory, yet coherent conglomerate of shared and fragmented subjectivities.

Notes

1. Spatiality [i.e. socially produced space] is a substantiated and recognizable social product, part of a 'second nature' [i.e. the transformed and socially concretized spatiality (socially produced space) arising from the application of purposeful human labor] which incorporates as it [i.e. socially produced space] socializes and transforms both physical and psychological spaces (Soja, 80).
2. Not in the traditional sense of the word, naturally, but within the discussion of realism in its relation with postmodernism. See Sterling-Folker's discussion on the Realism-Postmodern divide.
3. Although we also use this concept as conceptualized by Soja and Lefebvre, it is particularly relevant for this study in the original signification that Foucault conferred to it: "There are also real places–places that do exist and that are formed in the very founding of society–which are something like counter-sites, a kind of effectively enacted utopia in which the real sites, all the other real sites that can be found within the culture, are simultaneously represented, contested, and inverted. Places of this kind are outside of all places, even though it may be possible to indicate their location in reality. Because these places are absolutely different from all the sites that they reflect and speak about, I shall call them, by way of contrast to utopias, heterotopias." (1571)
4. See Fontaine Liu's article "On Place-ness of Place: 'Dwelling.'" *The International Journal of Environmental, Cultural, Economic and Social Sustainability* 5.1 (2009): 189-200.
5. See MacLeod's and Ward's essay about the use of dystopian scenarios within urban spaces. In it, there is a profuse discussion of estrangement as a social machinery of escape from within the city.

6. For further discussion on Auster's use of space as a tool for confinement, see Eduardo Barros-Grela, "Performances of Uncertainty in Spaces of Contingency: Aesthetic Confinement and Mechanisms of Silencing in Paul Auster, Haruki Murakami, and Park Chan-wook."

7. ⁷ Auster's prolific production has been notably peppered with references to isolated and oppressive spaces. Particularly clear are the cases of *Ghosts* (1986), *The Locked Room* (1986), *The Book of Illusions* (2002), or to a certain extent, *Sunset Park* (2010). Also, his film productions have repeatedly shown a leaning towards locked spaces (Álvarez López 95).

8. Jesús Ángel González accurately establishes direct connections between these two Auster's novels: "Auster's revision of American myths and their present consequences continues in *Man in the Dark* (2008), which is in more than one way a re-writing of *Travels in the Scriptorium,* to the point that Auster himself has talked about these two novels as a 'diptych', two short works that should be read together. We can find common themes and structure as well as a similar protagonist: an old man (now called August Brill, although at a point in the story some characters speculate that his name could be Blank) creating imaginary worlds to try to find a cure for his physical and psychological decline." (29-30)

9. For further information on the physical manifestations of fear, and their role as an instrument to control security, see Hildebrandt (6-7).

10. Debra Shostak provides an ample discussion on Auster's use of space and trauma (68-73), where she explains that Auster uses his stories to refer to ontological and epistemological uncertainty as a factor that influences the space within which the subject becomes conscious of his lack of presence.

11. Although it is not the intention of this paper to discuss in depth this Deleuzean concept ("lines of flight"), it is clear that it underlies the fundamental aims of the proposals that I am introducing here. I use this term as it is defined in *A Thousand Plateaus* in its relation to "multiplicities," i.e. as a *possibility* to interconnect the different spaces that make up that multiplicity. To see the original discussion on "multiplicity" and "lines of flight," see Deleuze and Felix Guattari, *A Thousand Plateaus.*

12. By "antagonist US states" I refer to Auster's division of states into secessionist and unionist states in reference to alleged political views according to the 2000 election results. After the polls, some states question the union and begin to declare themselves as independent, which gives way to a gruesome civil war (*Man in the Dark*, 8-9).

13. "Whereas utopias describe an escape from history, these anti-utopias describe an escape, or attempted escape, to history, which is to say, to the world of contingency, conflict, and uncertainty" (128).

14. Also, Merrifield (486) refers to the relevant role of space in the formulation of dystopias. For example, he refers to Mike Davis's study of Californian geographical history (*City of Quartz*, 1990), and claims that the more he describes the horrors of twentieth-century Los Angeles, the more readers are tempted to go there to live, "fascinated and mesmerized by its dynamics, by its perversity and absurdity".

15. Further information on narratology can be found, fundamentally, in the seminal text by Gerard Genette. Intradiegesis refers to the narrator's position at the same level as the characters that he describes.

16. See Houen, for instance, when he refers to Žižek's reaction to the Twin Towers attack, and he explains that "The Real which returns has the status of (an)other semblance: precisely because it is real, that is, on account of its traumatic/ excessive character, we are unable to integrate it into our reality, and are therefore compelled to experience it as a nightmarish apparition." (19)

17. See Harlass in his discussion of postmodernist fiction, where he claims that it reflects the author's crisis to confront reality, and makes Auster need to "incorporating the chaos of the world 'beyond understanding' into his fiction." (270)

18. In Unamuno's 1914 novel, *Niebla*, the main character decides to visit Unamuno and philosophically confront him about their existence. Also, Julio Cortázar's "Continuidad de los parques" (1956) reveals the same collapse of the utopian space of the novel when one of the characters in the book enters the reader's house with the intention of assassinating him while the latter reads his own killing.

19. I use this concept here following Deleuze and Guattari's discussion of multiplicities and territories (348-54).

20. See Houen's work (240) on the impact of 9/11 events upon the literary (re)productions of reality.

Works Cited

Álvarez López, Esther. "El ilusionista de las palabras: Paul Auster y su universo creativo."*Arbor* 186.741 (2010): 89-97.
Auster, Paul. *Man in the Dark*. New York: Macmillan USA, 2009.

---. *In the Country of Last Things*. London: Faber and Faber, 1987.

---. *Ghosts*. New York: Penguin Books, 1987.

---. *The Locked Room*. New York: Penguin Books, 1988.

---. *The Book of Illusions: A Novel*. New York: Picador, 2003.

---. *Travels in the Scriptorium*. New York: Picador, 2007.

---. *Sunset Park*. New York: Faber & Faber, Limited, 2011.

Barros-Grela, Eduardo. "Performances of Uncertainty in Spaces of Contingency: Aesthetic Confinement and Mechanisms of Silencing in Paul Auster, Haruki Murakami, and Park Chan-wook." *Relational Designs in Literature and the Arts: Page and Stage, Canvas and Screen.*Rui Carvalho Homem, ed. Amsterdam and New York: Rodopi, 2012. 387-399.

Cortázar, Julio. *Final del juego*. Madrid: Alfaguara, 2003.

Crosthwaite, Paul. *Criticism, Crisis, and Contemporary Narrative: Textual Horizons in an Age of Global Risk*. Hoboken: Taylor & Francis, 2010.

Deleuze, Gilles. *Rhizome: Introduction*. Paris: Les Éditions de Minuit, 1976.

Deleuze, Gilles and Felix Guattari. *Thousand Plateaus: Capitalism and Schizophrenia*. Minneapolis: U Of Minnesota P, 1987.

Donovan, Christopher. *Postmodern Narratives*. New York: Routledge, 2005.

Fredman, Stephen. "'How to Get Out of the Room That Is the Book?' Paul Auster and the Consequences of Confinement." *Postmodern Culture* 6.3 (1996): 54 pars. Web. 21 April 2010.

Foucault, Michel. "Des espaces autres." *Dits et écrits II, 1976-1988*. Paris: Gallimard, 2001.

Galdón Rodríguez, A. "Starting to Hate the State: The Beginning of the Character's Dissidence in Dystopian Literature and Films." *Altre Modernità* 3 (2010): 166–173.

Genette, Gerard. *Narrative Discourse: An Essay in Method*: Ithaca: Cornell UP, 1980.

Gómez Vallecillo, Ana Isabel. *Al borde del caos. Paul Auster y el realismo posmoderno*. Ávila: Universidad Católica de Ávila, 2009.

González, Jesús Ángel. "'Another History': Alternative Americas in Paul Auster's Fiction." *Comparative American Studies* 9.1 (2011): 21–34.

Gordin, Michael D., Helen Tilley, and Gyan Prakash. *Utopia/Dystopia: Conditions of Historical Possibility*. Princeton: Princeton UP, 2010. Print.

Greaney, Michael. "Sleep in Modern Fiction." *Literature Compass* 7/6 (2010): 467–76.

Harlass, Gudrun. *The Postmodern Structure of the Novels of Paul Auster*. Diplomarbeit: Universität Wien, 2010.

Hildebrandt, Mireille. *Controlling Security in a Culture of Fear*. The Hague: BJU Legal Publishers, 2009.

Houen Alex. "Novel Spaces and Taking Place(s) in the Wake of September 11." *Studies in the Novel* 36.3 (2004): 419-37.

Lefebvre, Henri. *The Production of Space*. Oxford: Blackwell, 2009.

Lyman, Stanford M. *Roads to Dystopia: Sociological Essays on the Postmodern Condition*. Fayetteville: U of Arkansas P, 2001.

MacLeod, Gordon and Kevin Ward. "Spaces of Utopia and Dystopia: Landscaping the Contemporary City." *Geografiska Annaler* 84.3-4 (2002): 153-170.

Merrifield, Andy. "The Dialectics of Dystopia: Disorder and Zero Tolerance in the City." *International Journal of Urban and Regional Research* 24.2 (2000): 473-89.

Morson, Gary Saul. *Boundaries of Genre*. Evanston: Northwestern UP, 1988.

Moylan, Tom and Raffaella Baccolini. *Dark Horizons: Science Fiction and the Dystopian Imagination*. New York: Routledge, 2003.

Panzani, Ugo. "The Insistent Realism of Don DeLillo's 'Falling Man' and Paul Auster's *Man in the Dark*." *Autres modernités/ Other Modernities*. Milan: Università degli Studi di Milano, 2011. 76-90.

Shostak, Debra. "In the Country of Missing Persons: Paul Auster's Narratives of Trauma." *Studies in the Novel* 41.1 (2009): 66-87.

Slaughter, Richard. *Futures Beyond Dystopia: Creating Social Foresight*. New York: Routledge, 2004.

Soja, Edward W. *Thirdspace: Journeys to Los Angeles and Other Real-and-Imagined Places*. New York: Wiley-Blackwell, 1996.

Sterling-Folker, Jennifer. "Discourses of Power: Traversing the Realist-Postmodern Divide." *Millennium: Journal of International Studies 33.3* (2005): 637-664.

Unamuno, Miguel de. *Niebla*. Madrid: Austral, 1963.

Varvogli, A. "'The Worst Possibilities of the Imagination are the Country You Live in': Paul Auster in the Twenty-first Century." *The Invention of Illusions: International Perspectives on Paul Auster*. Ed. S. Ciocia and J.A. González. Newcastle: Cambridge Scholars, 2011. 39–54.

Woods, Tim. "'Looking for Signs in the Air': Urban Space and the Postmodern in *In the Country of Last Things*." *Beyond the Red Notebook: Essays on Paul Auster*. Ed. Dennis Barone. Philadelphia: U of Pennsylvania P, 1995. 107-28.

Space and the Redrawing of the Canadian Imaginary in Black Canadian Literature: George Elliott Clarke's *George & Rue*

Betül Atesci Kocak

Introduction

Born in 1960 in Nova Scotia, the African-Canadian poet, and playwright George Elliott Clarke is one of the most important writers to present the life of black people in the Canadian province. He has studied Black literature of various countries and he gives special importance to his own native land, Nova Scotia. The writer states in the opening of the novel that during his childhood in Nova Scotia, he was continuously made aware of the fact that he was 'Coloured' both by his family and by white boys who called him and his brothers 'niggers' (3). Furthermore, the author introduces a didactic preamble that alerts readers to the history of the Black experience in Canada:

> It is impossible to believe slavery only a U.S. phenomenon and 'problem.' Indeed, in colonial Canada too, when it was one-part New France and one-part British North America, Africans were enslaved in what are now provinces of Ontario, Quebec, New Brunswick, Nova Scotia, and Prince Edward Island... In 1783, 3,500 black souls were evacuated by the defeated British to Nova Scotia at the end of the American Revolutionary War. (Even General George Washington's own slave, Henry, ran off to Canada.) Then, during the War of 1812-1815, another 2,200 African- Americans were summarily liberated by British forces, in field operations in the Chesapeake Bay region, and shipped to Nova Scotia – whether they wanted to go there or not. (Author's Note to the U.S. Edition)

The rural town of Three Mile Plains was an African-Canadian space created by the European settlers. In that place, freed slaves from American lands suffered from poverty where they generally lived in shacks or cabins. Black people living there were given limited options to improve their lives. Consequently, this made them search for spaces where they could fulfil themselves as individuals, just like the characters in Clarke's first novel. Each character in the novel tries to construct a different way to be accepted and included within the utopia of a tolerant, democratic, and a welcoming nation. One of Clarke's intentions to write this novel is to reveal a suppressed Canadian reality that left Black Canadians with hardly any choice to develop their potential.[1] Small-town life accounts for his family's reluctance to talk about the past. Thus, in writing *George & Rue*, he explains, he wanted to uncover this reality of his family that led his cousins George and Rue to murder a white taxi driver in order to rob a few dollars from him, and to their execution, a humiliating event that Clarke's family kept as a secret for decades. Clarke's reason to talk about black history and especially revealing it via his own family can be linked to Foucault's ideas on emplacement as a difficulty that results from the heterogeneity of the population:

> In a still more concrete manner, the problem of place or the emplacement arises for mankind in terms of demography. This problem of the human emplacement is not simply the question of knowing whether there will be enough space for man in the world- a problem that is certainly quite important- but it is also the problem of knowing what relations of propinquity, what type of storage, circulation, spotting, and classification of human elements, should be adopted in this or that situation in order to achieve this or that end. We are in an epoch in which space is given to us in the forms of relations between emplacements. In any case I believe that the anxiety of today fundamentally concerns space, no doubt much more than time (15).

When undertaking the study of spatial processes in the Canadian context, the term 'space' becomes tinged by the multicultural aspect of the nation. This paper will focus on place and space and their interactions with race and ethnicity in Canada as perceived by George Elliott Clarke's novel *George & Rue*, whose black protagonists engage a quest for place and belonging as they move between the rural and urban spaces of Canada in the first half of the twentieth century.

Heterotopian Spaces vis-a-vis Canada's Utopia
According to Ivison and Justin D. Edwards,

> Space ... is not simply a natural environment against which we struggle or onto which we impose ourselves, but is rather something that we play an active role in producing and

shaping. Thus, many Canadian writers, suggests Huggan, demonstrate 'an acceptance not merely of the immensity, but also of the malleability of space, of its potential for abstract reorganization.' (5)

The characters' attempts to create their own spaces in this novel show how they shift from their world of dystopias to a world of utopias. The way they follow can be regarded as utopian since their ideal is to exist as black individuals in the white dominated society of the late 1940s. As they cannot achieve this, they are left with no other choice but accept their diminished individual freedoms as well as the continual violence and inequality of their society. Due to the existing discrimination, the real-life characters are exposed to a repressive and controlling Canadian State. Neither the laws nor the nation contributed positively to their integration in the country's polity. However, the real life characters in *George & Rue* question whether they will be ever accepted in the heterotopias of Canada or instead, construct their own heterotopias.

In the Canadian imaginary Canada emerges as a place-to-be, perhaps encompassing heterotopias that needs to be continuously worked out in a space of flows. In the cultural plurality of the Canadian society, heterotopias are varied. *George & Rue* is a fictionally depicted real-life story of two of his cousins, George and Rufus Hamilton, who were executed because of murdering a white taxi driver in Fredericton in 1949. Clarke first talks about their life struggles that starts in one of the rural towns in Nova Scotia and ends with the brothers' final move to Fredericton which will later become the place where they were executed. In this novel, Clarke narrates how his real-life characters long for acceptance as they move between heterotopian spaces. However, as they are continuously rejected by main-stream Canadian society, George and Rue, as well as their parents Asa and Cynthy before them, try to create their own heterotopias. Foucault explains that in all cultures there are places that serve as a mirror to society, which he called heterotopias:

> Real places, effective places, places that are written into the institution of the society itself, and that are a sort of counter-emplacements, a sort of effectively realized utopias in which the real emplacements, all the other real emplacements that can be found within culture, are simultaneously represented, contested and inverted. A kind of places that are outside of all places, even though they are actually localizable. Since these places are absolutely other than all emplacements that they

reflect, and of which they speak, I shall call them, by way of
contrast to utopias, heterotopias. (17)

In the course of their short lives the real-life characters inhabit several
of the heterotopian spaces mentioned by Foucault —" the school, military
service, the honeymoon, old people's homes, psychiatric institutions, prisons,
cemeteries, theatres and cinemas, libraries and museums, fairs and carnivals,
holiday camps and hamams, saunas, motels, brothels, the Jesuit colonies and
the ship" (Dehaene 4) — and try to create some 'other spaces' of their own.'
Yet, in their search for a place and for identity as blacks these heterotopian
spaces consistently turn into dystopias for them.

Analysis of the Novel: Utopia, Dystopia and Heterotopias

1. Asa Hamilton

George and Rue's father, Asa Hamilton, is the representative of the Hamilton
fifth-generation in Nova Scotia and he is the third generation to work in the
small town of Three-Mile Plains that he calls home. However, Asa's home
differs from the usual protecting and loving meanings attached to home
because black people there were exploited to the point of starvation and
frustration. Asa works in Three Mile Plains as a butcher and his work requires
strength and violence. He continues using the same violence at home against
his wife and sons. Moreover, Asa feels that he has to fit the social
expectations of men as household providers now that he is a husband and a
father. In the first year of Asa's and Cynthy's marriage, the couple is happy
and in love with each other but with George's birth, the conditions worsen day
by day. They have neither enough money to take care of the new-born child
nor for themselves. With the birth of the second child, Rufus (or Rue), Asa
grows more violent as he starts to whip his wife and later his children, too. He
starts to project his frustration on his family. His life has a great correlation
with his past because he has bonds with the slavery of his ancestors. No
matter how much he dreams of a better life the burdens of the past impinge
upon his present:

> What neither Asa nor Cynthy knew was how much their
> personal destinies were rooted in ancestral history-troubles.
> Their own dreams and choices were passed-down desolations
> of slavery. African Nova Scotia and especially, Three Mile
> Plains were the results of slave trade and slave escape. ...
> "And could they afford self-respect? Well, they paid for it

with their backs, their legs and feet, their hands and arms"
(George & Rue 14).

Emasculated by these circumstances, Asa abuses his family in order to gain some sort of authority and control over them, and thus feel like a man, or the idea of what a man should be according to society. His harsh behaviour conceals the things that he cannot achieve in his life and he resorts to violence because he does not know any better. As a consequence of his brutal behavior, Asa does not receive any respect or love from his sons or wife, who would gladly escape from his reach if they could. In order to escape Cynthy's dissatisfaction with him and his fear that she could run away from him, further emasculating him, Asa finds a brothel in Windsor town an alternative heterotopian space, a borderland where race relations are suspended as he can buy the favors of a white prostitute, something that momentarily allows him to feel empowered as a man: "There, no one cared if a raven and a dove commingled. There, liquor was being sold, hog was being sold. So when he waxed violently tired of Cynthy, her Montreal mania and her cash complaints, Asa rented hisself a creamy tart" (32). In this brothel, his relation with the woman called Purity explains that in her, Asa found love, peace and quiet. Purity is a woman from the French-speaking countryside who could not speak any French, a marginal person. In this sense, it is possible to say that the two resemble each other.

The brothel is defined by Foucault as one of the 'extreme types of heterotopias' (22). Thus, Asa's leaving home to visit the brothel shows him stepping from his current dystopian world into a heterotopian space, a reality which is both real and unreal as he may think he finds affection in Purity. The fact that Purity is white signals his acceptance into white society, trespassing racial barriers, as well as social class borders.

2. Cynthy

In the novel, Cynthy stands for the African-Canadian woman's point of view and experience. She dreams of the life that the Canadian social system allegedly grants to women in general: to become a loved wife, have a family, be admired and respected. However, these things are impossible to attain for a black woman living in rural Nova Scotia. Her happy days in the beginning of her marriage pass quickly and giving birth to two children under very poor conditions and her husband's whippings make her miserable. Violence, added to the poverty they experience results in Cynthy's creating her own dreamed space, away from the dystopian space of Three Miles Plain. Montreal becomes her heterotopias, as she envisions herself in a Lincoln wearing a red dress that makes her as attractive and beautiful as the women in the city. Montreal becomes the space where her dreams and desires can be fulfilled:

> What was Montreal? Her Harlem, her Heaven. From movie magazines and cousins, she knew it was rum that was fire in the mouth and satin in the belly. It was women who could cross ice- black ice- on stiletto heels and never fear losing their balance... Montreal was frontier Paris, a Habitant Manhattan. (20)

Longing for sophisticated city life makes Cynthy more aware of Asa's deficiencies. Her husband, whom she was in love with once, is now perceived as brutal, ugly, rude and poor. The more she desires a loving husband, the angrier and more desperate she becomes. Thus, Montreal emerges as the place of opportunities as well as the fortunate marriages with handsome and beautiful couples, an urban space where her husband could not fit: "Problem was, it looked like Asa ain't got no drive; times too, he didn't even look good... He was so ugly, in actuality, Cynthy thought, that she could wear out a whole dictionary to describe just how sorry her husband was... She wanted to be petted, fondled, praised, kissed, licked, lapped, tickled, teased, spoiled, and made love to like in glamour magazines" (19).

Cynthy is so influenced by trendy magazines that her idea of city life is totally determined by the consumerism, affluence, fashion and enjoyment advertised by the capitalist system. She makes possessing equivalent with happiness as she thinks the more she possesses, the happier she is. Her strife to buy the red dress signifies her absorption of capitalism and of the belief that she can create a new identity for herself. Once she owns that dress, the meaning of life would be different for her. She thinks that she gains an expensive and charming look with it. However, the dress does not help her to be admitted in the city but just serves as the object to make her feel that she fulfils her dreams. Clarke emphasizes in the third part of the book that the red dress is "an emblem of civilization" for her as she feels more trapped each day in the chaos at home and in the rural Nova Scotia and that dress would make her as attractive and beautiful as women in the city. Consequently, she buys the dress with the intention to have a place in society because she fits neither at home nor in the city.

Cynthy behaves as if she is not black since most of the time she despises both the black women and men in the neighbourhood. Nova Scotia and her marriage are Cynthy's particular prison. In the world she creates for herself, she feels both relieved and included in the Canadian society by rejecting the real space she is in. According to Foucault, prison and some other places such as rest homes and psychiatric hospitals "can be called heterotopias of deviation: those in which individuals are placed whose behaviour is deviant in relation to the mean or required norm" (18). Cynthy is a proper type for this explanation. She cannot be defined as a loving mother except for the times when she reminds herself that she is a mother and she tries to play that role as a feigned or fake identity: "Times, Cynthy remembered to play mother. When Georgie was twelve, she sewed him a quilt got from twenty-pound sacks of Five Roses flour. She was goodness itself-when she could convince herself to be maternal" (34).

Her desire to possess more money, and to live in Montreal, an urban heaven of sophistication and glamour, support the idea that Cynthy represents the capitalist figure in the novel. Her growing desire for the life in Montreal makes her leave home one day. In addition to her dreams, she wants to take revenge from her husband who burns her red dress which is her emblem for fulfilment and meaning of life, the key that opens the doors of Montreal. Though her dreams turn into dystopias, she keeps being a continuous struggler.

As the country improves, black people's desire to be accepted within the nation increases. They do not want to be excluded from having a Canadian identity in the expanding and promising land. Ivison and Edwards claim, "As Soja and others have argued, the ascendancy of the city and urbanism as a way of life has led and is leading to the incorporation of ever-vaster swathes of land, and ever-larger populations, into urban spatiality" (10). The growth of the city is so immense that it impinges upon the rural in a way that the urban seems to reject its rural source. Hence, when the blacks are consistently barred from the urban space, they try to create their own spaces. Consequently, as Cynthy is aware of this circumstance, she chooses to make love with lots of men and at the end she ends up leaving with 'Reverend' Dixon, who represents for her "a promise of a red dress and a train ticket to Montreal" (36). Thus, in order to access the utopias of the urban, she needs to give in her body to a white man. Dixon, she thinks, has money and power, a nice outfit and he is living in the city so he can help her to find her place in the urban space. However, after a short time, she comes back 'home' with just a new coat which shows that she again fails to achieve her dreams. The way she dies indicates how far apart she is from her aspirations, as she dies of a heart attack while cleaning the toilets.

3. George Hamilton

George Hamilton, born in 1925, is the first child of Cynthy and Asa Hamilton. With his birth, the family, especially Asa thinks "that's when sweetness turned ugly," (9). That suggests a different idea to the general belief that a new-born baby brings happiness. He is born at the time when the family is suffering from extreme poverty. Both brothers are born in December, into a cold and gloomy atmosphere which points out the challenge of survival. As a child, George suffers a lot from the violence at home as he and his brother are continuously being whipped by their father. He starts to work in the farms from a very early age and contrary to his brother Rue, he is happy doing the farm work. Though they are in charge of doing hard work as young children, George is always content with these kinds of jobs because in the fields he gradually learns how to make money from the farm work as he says: "Here was happiness (29)" referring to the farm.

From the very young age, the children are brought up with the worry of earning enough money to eat and are obviously affected by the frequent quarrels between Cynthy and Asa. They always hear about the problems related to poverty, experience the abuse of Asa and the boys are affected by their mother Cynthy who all the time yearns for a life in Montreal. The reason why the boys grow up with a responsibility to earn money is that they are made to bring all the money they earn to Cynthy until the time they start to smoke.

The two brothers are also mistreated at school. It is obvious from their clothes that they are poor since they have to go to school barefooted in spring and fall and wear double moccasins in winter. Under these conditions, it is impossible for them to have pens, pencils, papers or crayons no matter how much they envied the other students' school stuff. All they can do is to share the things with the other students. In these tragic times of poverty, their teacher is another threat for them because once she gets angry, she would "stick three-inch-long fingernail in their ears" (30). George thinks that school is like a "boxing ring." Rue once fights his teacher and also, they fight with the white boys who throw chalk to the brothers "to make them white" (30). As a result, the brothers are expelled from the school in the third grade. The discrimination they are exposed to gradually makes them use their physical strength whenever they are in trouble.

The presentation of the ship as heterotopia appears after George's quitting the army where he was made to peel potatoes all the time, different from what he expected. Leaving the army, he takes the ship to the West and visits lots of countries, which makes him change his mind about the rural life and that way, the ship enters his mind in the Foucauldian sense:
and if one considers, after all, that the boat is a floating piece of space, a place without a place, that exists by itself, that is self-enclosed and at the same time is given over the infinity of the sea and that, from port to port, from bank to bank, from brothel to brothel, goes as far as the colonies in search of the most precious treasures they conceal in their gardens, you will understand why, from the sixteenth century until the present, the boat has been for our

civilization, not only the greatest instrument of economic development (I have not been speaking of that today), but also the greatest reserve of imagination. The ship is the heterotopia par excellence (22).

Upon his return to Canada, George is arrested ashore. Unable to figure out why, he thinks that they may have arrested him because of his dark skin. His claiming that he has been to South America, England, North Africa and Siberia does not work out to change the army's decision to accuse him of deserting, besides being 'a negro that never mops the floors without being whining' (76). The army asserts many excuses to justify his arrest. They call him a 'bad' guy who is "unlikely to become an efficient soldier" (77). They even disclaim the official paper which showed that he is a healthy boy claiming that he has "Psychopathic Personality" with a "negative attitude toward the army" and also that he is of "doubtful stability" (77). The army's racism causes George to look for another way to make his living as he heads to Montreal, his mother's dream city. For George, Montreal also seemed to mean a lot: "So Georgie boarded the Ocean Limited and clickety-clacked northwest to that 'Paris of the Saint Lawrence: Montreal.' That ex-fur trade, beaver-pelt metropolis boasted Coloured bars, Coloured dancers, brown-sugar beauties, and brown-sugar dandies. Strolling Sainte-Cathcrine Street at night was like promenading an avenue of tinfoil and diamonds"(78).

George is attracted by the black 'beauty' that Montreal offered. The city offers the things that he lacks in rural Nova Scotia. For that reason, he thinks that he can make a life there with Blondola. Hence, the ship bound for Montreal encapsules his attempts to move in space and eventually find his own place where he can be accepted as a Canadian. However, George is again too naive, believing that he could overcome the racial discrimination that kept black people back: "When Georgie tried to find work, there was none for a black boy. Yes, he could shine shoes again; he could carry bags– again; he could wash dishes – again. But he craved better. He tried to get on Haligonian docks stevedoring, but nothing doin for a Negro" (83). Regardless of his attempts, it becomes clear that George gets closer to a world of dystopias contrary to what he expects.

Prior to his overseas experience, George was like most Canadians in that he thought of himself "in connection with the land." As W. H. New claims, Canadians "are fascinated by distance and scenery, park and farm, property and region, river system and mountain range, 'cottage country', religious codes involving nature, and the staples they can produce from the land and use in trade—all this in a largely urban society (17). However, after his sea voyages George realized that it was necessary to move to a larger city with his family if he wanted to prosper. Yet, the space the family experience in reality and the one they have in their minds are very different from each other because they will be pushed to ghetto urban spaces in Fredricton. The city turns at this point into a heterotopian delusion in Foucault's terms: "There are others, on the contrary, which look like pure and simple openings, but that, generally, conceal curious exclusions. Everybody can enter into those heteropian emplacements, but in fact it is only an illusion: one believes to have entered and, by the very fact of entering, one is excluded" (21).

Nevertheless, when George and Blondola moved to Fredericton after getting married, Fredericton seems to be a new start for the family. Though the couple has a small shack, they are happy to live together and their little house becomes George's heterotopia. After various attempts to find a job in the city, George returns to working in the fields on the outskirts of the city. The couple has a happy life until the day Rue arrives at their house.

4. Rufus Hamilton

The second child of Asa and Cynthy Hamilton, Rufus or Rue Hamilton, is different from his elder brother George. His inevitable destiny is the same as George's, that which Asa inherited from his father: "only scraggly land, not even haggard love to give" (10). For his mother, he is different and important because he reminds her of the white man she once met whose name was Rufus, and she believes that the name will keep the Montreal dream alive. For this reason, Rue becomes for Cynthy the embodiment of another space created to fulfil her dream. But the case turned out to be different from her expectations in the rural town of Three Mile Plains as Rufus and his brother grew up in an environment full of sorrow, lack of love and respect, hardship and poverty. So, these made his name fit more into Rue other than 'gorgeous' Rufus: "Now there were two living babies amid the graveyard that Three Mile Plains could be, if they didn't get out. Cynthy called the new baby Rufus, or Rue. But he was a bother – rufous in tint and rueful in mood. Too much like his papa" (20).

Clarke stresses that Three Mile Plains and the graveyard is almost equal because there, black people are only made to work without having any opportunities to prosperity and comfort. There, they can never talk or ask about their rights as human beings as all expected from them is hard work as if they are machines without feelings. As the writer explains, no employer cared for them, which resulted in frequent premature death:

> Plains Negroes had to go into Windsor to work. They went to the gypsum auqrries, to the textile mill, the apple orchards, and into the mansions, all for pennies. In the gypsum pits, they saw buddies "axidentally" dynamited- arms, legs, flying through the air, or dropping dead of lung cave-ins, their

breaths whitened by gypsum that blackened the guts. . . .
Privation was there in the boulders, in the starving hog, in the
men mistakenly blasting each other into amputees for a wage
of twenty-five cents a day, and calling themselves lucky.
Some died broken, but everybody died broke. The people had
to make their history with their sweat." (16)

The novel emphasizes that black people can be put up with as long as
they work hard and suffer that makes the cemetery becomes their heterotopia.
It becomes the place that all black fellows share with the nation. As Foucault
states: "The cemeteries then no longer constitute the sacred and immortal
belly of the city, but the 'other city,' where each family possesses its dark
dwelling" (19). Since the characters are aware that the conditions they
experience in Three Mile Plains are not promising, they start the new life
doomed to failure from the beginning that's why though they are alive, they
know that a life full of disillusions and dystopias await them. However, death
equalizes blacks and whites as time is suspended into eternity in the cemetery.
As Foucault explains,

> The heterotopia begins to function fully when people find
> themselves in a sort of absolute break with their traditional
> time; one can see that the cemetery is indeed a highly
> heterotopian place since the cemetery begins with this strange
> heterochronism, that, for the individual, is the loss of life,
> with this quasi-eternity in which he incessantly dissolves and
> fades away (20).

Different from his brother, Rue is always more defiant, aggressive and
violent than George. Once he slaps a white teacher when she calls him "a sly
little nigger boy!" (30). This behaviour caused him to be expelled from school
at the age of eleven. In the fights with the white boys, he is more brave and
violent than George because he has an attitude as if he doesn't care about
anything and anyone just because he understands that neither his family nor
society care about him. For this reason, he does not cry when Cynthy leaves
him and George on a cold winter day. He is aware that to the family and
society, he and his brother mean nothing. As a result, he chooses to be
aggressive and violent:

> Rue shed no tears at Cynthy's vanishing. He already
> understood that "I love you" equals two parents and a bastard:
> I, you, and Love. Jawgee and Rufus was just black boys

blackened further by Depression. They were two pieces of
shit that Cynthy just had to put somewhere. The falling snow
hammered a prison into shape around them. Snow belted
them like their father's hand (37).

Though their mother returns later, it does not mean anything to him.
Consequently, he is another figure to create his own heterotopian spaces. In
his gloomy life there is one place that he can find relief and happiness: The
abandoned house he uses as a shelter and which contains a dilapidated piano
on which he can nevertheless improvise and sort of compose his own life,
something that nobody has allowed him to do yet. Music becomes his
consolation and makes him turn to art where no one judges him because of his
colour, family and poverty and he does not need to struggle to do his music as
it already provides freedom and opportunity to express himself:

> The piano became his confessional, his brothel, his hospital,
> his church, his army, his canteen, his library, and his school.
> It was refuge from a lust-busted-open shack on Panuke Road.
> Rue loved to feel and hear his fingers striking handsomely
> against a half-playable keyboard, with no knowledge of
> mistake or failure or trespassing or vandalism (40).

Rue reflects back the notorious heritage of his family by kicking Asa in
one of his attempts to beat Cynthy. In that fight, it is difficult to say that the
two are from the same family because they fight almost to death and Rue
insults his father using racist term, as if he were not black like his father. He
starts to use the same words the white pupils and teachers call him. He calls
his father 'nigger' and 'dog' as an insult: "I'm a-gonna break ya, nigger...
Stay down there like the dog you are" (46).

After their parents' deaths, the two brothers start to think about what to
do with their lives. Though the war revitalizes the business and economy in
1942 there are not proper jobs for the brothers as the economic boost serves
for everyone except for the black people who suffer from racist discrimination:

> Since their whole family is now in a cemetery, Rue and
> George begin to study how to live better. They think on it in
> the morning, ponder it in the evening. They could look at
> each other and at Three Mile Plains and see only more
> struggle, more suffering, more sickness. But the Not- Again
> World War was on, opening up jobs everywhere; the war
> seeded warehouses of ready caskets and treasure chests. (52)

Rue's first experience in love is with a black girl called Easter. The relationship they have is rather naive because both feel very excited, happy and full of hopes. Rue fell in love with Easter the moment he saw her and he immediately thought of changing his life, quitting alcohol, etc. He thinks that he can get out of Three Mile Plains with Easter because he knows that he can trust her. Though both are black, Rue is aware that Easter is different from him: she comes from a wealthy and respected family, and has lots of clothes, white friends, stylish furniture, cars and horses. For him, Easter is like a cure because she is always optimistic and believes that Rue could become a musician if he wanted and studied. Hence, the piano and Easter are the only things Rue can find relief in, and freedom to create his own space. Despite having a prosperous life as a black in Nova Scotia, she wants to move to Halifax and become a nurse, buy a nice house, get married and have lots of children. Though her dreams sound luxurious to Rue, he embraces them as his own and decides he can work in the Canadian National Railway[2] as a porter. So, now he is dreaming of becoming both a porter and a pianist, two of the few professions blacks are allowed to take at the time.

Rue's dreams come to an end when he learns one day that Easter has died while crossing the river with her horse on the wooden bridge over the Avon River. After Easter's death, Rue cannot stay in Nova Scotia as everything reminds him of her and that's why he heads to Halifax, to the industrial and urban city. There, he meets a man called Googie who owns a brothel and believes that "the wage of vice is profit" (65). Soon after he meets him, Googie offers him a job as a pianist. Rue's flawed music—he learned to play only on a half piano in that old house in Nova Scotia –nevertheless manages to convey his blues. In those days he feels that he belongs to somewhere. The place is not a proper one, but the important thing is that he is doing something with his music without anyone interrupting. Playing the piano gives him the chance to express himself through music. He is still missing Easter a lot and does not want to get involved with anyone, although he would eventually become Purity's lover. One day Purity told him about the man who looked like him without knowing that he is Asa's son. Rue goes crazy the moment he hears this, realizing that he has made no progress at all over his despised father, and his intentions of revenge on his father cause him to whip Purity, the white whore, until she is the same skin colour as him. The event encapsulates Rue's difficulty to do away with his family's past and with the burden of historic racism.

George and Rue: Two different mind-sets, a shared fate

Having accepted the stereotype of the bad nigger once he has experienced the social constrains that prevent him from becoming an average Canadian, Rue rejects George's advice to work and one day when they can hardly find anything to eat, Rue offers George to rob someone after attacking him thinking that "There was no other way to make a dollar"(105). As the streets are very crowded that day, they decide to call a taxi and rob the driver. When the taxi comes, George is shocked because the taxi driver is the man who had driven George and Blondola home when their first baby was born. That white taxi driver had been very kind to the black couple as he "was also trying to improve his self" (99). Though his attitude may seem normal, the man is very conscious of racial differences and of the couple's otherness. However, he tries to overcome racism by being nice to them, although he cannot help being prejudiced.

In contrast to Rue, for whom the assault on Silver only means "I's getting cash and my clothes out the cleaners" (128), George is reluctant to hit the taxi driver, and he keeps telling Rue: "Ain't hittin Silver. He's been a pal" (122). However, he eventually hits him with a hammer and Silver dies. The few dollars the brothers get from him go, in George's share, to pay for the hospital expenses caused by the birth of his second child; but also, George keeps some of the money to go to the brothel. Thus, the brothel appears once again in the novel as a heterotopian "space of illusion that exposes all real space, all the emplacements in the interior of which human life is enclosed and partitioned, as even more illusory. (Perhaps it is the role played for a long time by those famous brothels of which we are now deprived)" (Foucault 21).

After the event, George confesses the crime to the police and the court finds them guilty and they are given death penalty. Before the day of their execution, the jail in the novel is depicted as follows:

> George, Rue, and Plumsy was all herded-separately-into the east entrance of the jail, a two-storey grey-stone structure with wood-planked, tin-clad ceilings painted either cream or indigo, and placed into one of the four separate second-floor cells, with 1840-era solid wood floors hammered down with homemade nails. Each cell had white-painted radiators, red-brick walls painted black, and black-painted, inch-thick iron-bar doors, and back windows, generously sized at three feet high and two feet wide, but bisected and segmented by a double row of iron bars painted cream. Here light could sluice in; no one could slide out. (170)

The jail the brothers are put in resembles Bentham's Panopticon in the sense that it restricts the communication with other inmates in other cells, but makes the inmates totally visible to the jailer: "The panoptic mechanism arranges spatial unities that make it possible to see constantly and to recognize immediately… Full lighting and the eye of a supervisor capture better than darkness, which ultimately protected. Visibility is a trap" (Foucault 200)

Rufus was pretty sure of his own self and stayed calm while responding to the questions. However, though in general Rue was away from revealing his senses, with the question about India, the girl he wanted to marry, he talked about his dreams and his love that could never come true: "We wanted to marry here at the Lord Beaverbrook Hotel, in a two-piano ceremony. She was going to wear a ritzy, white lace Victorian gown, while I put on jazz." (184) In these sentences, Rue showed that India, their marriage, and jazz (or music in general) were the only places that he felt home and free that's why he did not talk about India till they asked him. He wanted to preserve 'home' like his peaceful and unspoilt space.

In the jail, George continuously looks forward to being rescued and makes the Bible his guide. His turning to religion and making the Bible his own heterotopia shows how he struggles to be forgiven by the white court. He possesses and rereads the Bible to find relief and repent from his sins. Besides, he wants the court to realize that he shares the same religious belief as they- the white people- do. He states that he is a 'converted and convicted Christian' with the last hope of a survival.

From the novel, the characters emerge as dislocated and uprooted. Though they tried hard to escape their dystopian world into a world of heterotopias, racial discrimination played a crucial role in preventing their integration in society. Their quest resembles a vicious circle in which they come back to the point of departure, not different from the conditions they had inherited. Thus, the brothers remain trapped in their alterity, while exposing the relationship between space, race, and the construction of identity in a historiographic redrawing of the Canadian imaginary. Thus, the current multiculturalism myth is problematized while bringing to the foreground the importance of bearing in mind the intersection of time and space with race and ethnicity.

Notes

1. Furher information about Clarke's family, apartheid and his ideas on his novel *George & Rue* can be found here:
   http://www.youtube.com/watch?v=faJBHmD7oXc

2. In the novel, Clarke underlines the difference in naming the railway: "Coloureds called it the Canadian Negro Railway because it employed Canadian Negroes as porters. The Canadian Pacific Railway was called the Coloured Peoples Railway because it hired West Indians, Negro Americans, and "real" Indians" (56).

Works Cited

Clarke, George Elliott. *George & Rue*. New York: Carroll & Graff Publishers, 2006.

Dehaene, Michel and Lieven de Cauter. *Heterotopia and the City: Public Space in Postcivil Society*. Paris: Editions Galimard, 1997.

Edwards, Justin D. and Douglas Ivison, ed. *Downtown Canada: Writing Canadian Cities*. Toronto: University of Toronto Press Incorporated, 2005.

Foucault, Michel. "Of Other Spaces." *Heterotopia and the City: Public Space in a Postcivil Society*. eds. Michel Dehaene and Lieven de Cauter. Paris: EditionsGalimard, 1997. 15-29.

---. "Discipline and Punish: The Birth of the Prison." *Panopticism*. New York: Penguin, 1997.

New, W. H. *Land Sliding: Imagining Space, Presence, and Power in Canadian Writing*. Toronto: University of Toronto Press Incorporated, 1997.

Writing Spaces: Travel, Global Cities and Landscapes
Editors: I-Chun Wang, Mary Theis, and Christopher Larkosh

The Cape of Desire and the Sea of Mirror: Buddhism and Ecology in Seungwon Han's *Lotus Sea*

Won-Chung Kim

Since the publication of *Buddhism and Ecology* in 1997, Buddhist ideas have been increasingly regarded as a viable alternative for consumption-oriented Western culture. But Buddhism has been, in fact, one of the most important considerations for many writers and thinkers from the early stages of ecocriticism. Even the first law of ecology that everything is connected with everything else is directly resonant with Buddhism's most important doctrine of dependent origination (연기법 緣起法). Arne Naess' philosophy of deep ecology, for one, is heavily indebted to Buddhism. The extent of influence that Buddhism has had on deep ecology is so vast and far-reaching that Ian Harris's argues that "Deep ecology itself represents a Buddhification of Western metaphysics" (205). However, the opposite also holds true. In East Asia, Buddhist, Taoistic, and Confucian ideas are sometimes mixed together and are almost indistinguishably present in the minds of people, governing their view of the world and nature (Kim Won-Chung 133). Ecologically reinterpreted Buddhism and traditional religious idea from East Asia have provided an opportunity for people to view their own cultural heritage in a new light, because they have been deeply embedded in the societal culture of the region and peoples' (un)consciousness. Seungwon Han's *Lotus Sea,* a novel published in 1997, shows how Buddhism can play a crucial role in overcoming the ecologically devastating effects of anthropocentrism and reaching universal reconciliation.

As one of the most prolific writers of Korea, Han has published more than 60 books. Since his debut in 1968 with "Wooden Boat" from Daehan Daily, Han has published more than 40 novels, 12 collections of short stories, and 3 books of poems. Most of his novels portray commoner's lives, their struggles and agonies in living by the seaside under the irresistible and overwhelming surge of change, with particular attention to the rapid transformation of the traditional village due to modernization and industrialization. In his works, Han repeatedly portrays the lives of the people of a seaside village very realistically. However, he does not stop there; he works to investigates it further through a mythic and shamanistic vision. As Korean literary critic, Taedong Lee argues, Han's novels successfully embody the unconscious life energy of Korean people, whose thoughts and behaviors are deeply influenced by a traditional shamanistic world view and Buddhism

(196). Environmental issues are one of the key subjects Han emphasizes in his writing. In "A Ruined Village" Han shows how the Korean War and following modernization, especially the reclamation project have ruined the livelihood of a small village, and how eros can play a remedial role in rebuilding these broken relationships not only amongst human beings but also humanity and nature. "My Sister and a Wolf" (1980) graphically depicts the miserable consequence of the overuse of agricultural pesticides. As a pioneering work of toxic discourse in Korea, the novella warns that our random use of chemicals will bring not only extinction of other species but also the demise of our own life. In "American Bullfrogs" Han investigates the deadening effect of human greed and possessiveness on the ecosystem, comparing human beings to American bullfrogs who have become a headache to Korean ecosystem. Being imported to Korea for edible meat, they have no natural enemy and have grown ferocious destroyers of local habitat. The wide spectrum of environmental issues these novels investigate positions Han as one of the most important ecological novelists in Korea, alongside Se-Hui Cho and Wonil Kim.

The center of Buddhist ecology is the idea of dependent origination (연기緣起) and compassion (자비慈悲). If the former is the epistemological recognition of the fundamental law of the universe, the latter is a practical norm for our behavior to the ten thousands things of the world. Insisting that this *Paticca Samuppada* (dependent origination) is at the heart of Buddhist understanding, Allan Hunt Badiner explains, "it suggests that all things–objects and beings–exist only interdependently, not independently. This is the emptiness of *sunyata* – that nothing has a separate existence. In Buddhist perception, everything is alive and influences everything else. All of nature is vibrating with life, even the air" (xvi). In order to fully understand the application of Buddhist philosophy to ecocriticism, it is essential to first understand the Three Dharma Seals (삼법인 三法印) – which is at the core of Buddhism. The Seals indicate that first, whatever exists in the phenomenal world is impermanent, or all formations or conditioned things are impermanent; secondly, things are in existence only by conditions – in other words, there is nothing in the whole universe that has a permanent self-entity or self-nature; third, nirvana is quiescence free from birth and death, or *samsara*. Compassion, as one of the two pillars of Mahayana Buddhism, along with *Prajna* (반야 般若), means showing loving kindness toward all living beings who are in misfortune or suffering. Because most characters in Han's novel are devoid of these two virtues, they act like *mara* (which translates as devil, but, in fact, refers to our own discriminating, deluded mind), turning the world into a battle zone of their own selfish desires.

Regarded as one of the best works of ecological literature in Korea, *Lotus Sea* unfolds a story of conflict between family members battling over the property of their father – who has been in a coma for almost a year. As a former representative to the National Assembly, Joocheol Park's life fits the mold of any other corrupt politician; he has exercised his authority to obtain concessions and indulged himself in debauchery. Each of his three sons was born of a different woman, and the strong enmity between them complicates the distribution of his property. Joocheol's plum orchard, located at the cape overlooking the sea, takes center stage in the novel. In the novel, the contrast between land and sea is the most conspicuous, and this contrasting landscape provides the author with an opportunity to investigate the characters' mindsets. The cape is a liminal place; though it is located within the land, it is also bound by the sea. In a sense, the fact that the cape is a liminal place at the very end of the land, where there is no more ground to go, drives people to reveal their secret desires more explicitly. As Korean literary critic Eungbaek Ha notes, the sea, for Han, is the home of not only his physical being, but also his literature (136). To Han, the sea is a world of primordial energy and stands for nature itself. As the place where all life originates, it embraces even the confusion and chaos of the world. Therefore, the sea is an immense world of infinity and represents humankind's yearning for flight out of our small, finite world (Kwon 406). In this sense, the land and the sea in this novel can roughly stand for civilization and nature, respectively.

The opening scene of the novel, in which the youngest son Yoonseok mercilessly cuts plum trees with a chainsaw, characterizes the types of behaviors people are exhibiting toward the land:

> Out of the crying sound, whether of the chainsaw cutting off the base of the trees, or of the trees being killed, dark green juice, as if vomited by the juice machine, flows out. The trees which were alive just before cry and cough blood at the mad attack of the chainsaw [...] Their cry shakes the sky, the land, and the sea, covering the world with green blood. (5)

Though the author says the chainsaw is "mad," it is not the chainsaw but the man cutting the trees who is really mad. Yoonseok wholeheartedly devoted 15 years of his life to growing the plum trees. His cutting down the trees under the excuse of turning the plum orchard into a fish farm is, therefore, not an act of sheer madness, but a carefully calculated one to gain exclusive possession of the farm. Against Yoonseok's chainsaw, Yoonho, the second son, holds an air rifle to drive his younger brother out of the farm and claim it for himself. The dispute over the cape is about to develop into a serious crime at any moment. By placing this cruel scene of destruction at the very beginning of the novel, Han adds another dimension to the story. The family members' desire to own a piece of land is indicative of humanity's desire to possess and use nature at will. The two weapons the two brothers brandish – chainsaw and rifle – have historically been the most powerful weapons used to bring indigenous people and nature under siege. In this sense, green blood is a perfect symbol for the agony and pain nature suffers under humanity's indiscriminate development of the earth.

Through the novel, Han demonstrates that peoples' unrestrained desire results not only in the disruption of family relationships, but also leads to the devastation of nature. Most characters in the novel are possessed by some kind of darkness. The author's words that "Yoongil (the eldest son) was becoming a deranged devil" (17) can equally be applied to most characters in the novel, except Tomalee, who has "the eye of mind which can see through people, whether their thoughts are honest or not" (95). The darkness that has paralyzed Joocheol into a coma is nothing but the physical embodiment of this darkness. Han's own words on the back cover of the book sheds light on understanding the nature of this darkness:

> The cry "open your eyes" is the koan of this novel. Because of peoples' desires, the world is devastated. It is a warning to the anthropocentric humanism. In the novel, I've tried to say that the world is made not only for humankind but also all the animals and plants and even for microorganisms. *Lotus Sea* is intended for the cosmic reconciliation between humankind and nature.

This darkness of desire in peoples' minds makes them blind to see true nature of things and pursue their own interest indiscriminately.

Han employs the technique of alternating voices to highlight the dire state of humankind's groundless hubris in the ecosystem. Among the 16 chapters, the odd chapters are narrated by the young chickadee, while the even chapters are by a third person omniscient writer's point of view. By alternating different perspectives, Han is able to present a more balanced picture. The bird's comment and narration works like a chorus from Greek dramas, mostly making fun of humanity's extreme selfishness. By giving a voice to the bird, Han turns his novel into a dialogical text. Because the bird stands for nature in the novel, nature is no longer "an analyzed object or utilized object" (Barnhill 203) but earns the statue of Bakhtinian anotherness. According to Bakhtin, "Anotherness enables dialogical interchange. To be another instead of an other is to be a speaking subject" (Barnhill 203).

While defining the concept of anotherness, Patrick Murphy also argues that "I want instead to think about the concept of anotherness, based on the Another —not the Alien and not Stranger, but the brother, the cousin, the sister, and not just the human ones, but all the creatures with whom we share the plant" (35). Serenella Iovino also notes, "ecological literature can act as means of ethical and epistemological liberation" (54) by "giving a voice to whatever is without a voice" (Italo Calvino 98, cited in 55).

The voice of the young male chickadee carries the view of the world apart from humanity and it, thereby, breaks open the small enclaves of the human world. His words are bitter but wise and represent the voices of the other, the object of humanity's attack under the name of development. The following two passages aptly summarize how humanity is viewed by other beings in nature:

> The young male chickadee shuddered at the word of development that came to his mind. Human beings who try to develop this and that recklessly are the most horrible creatures in the world.   His father left a will to be careful of them. (14)

> Human beings are capricious. Whatever they had set their minds to do, they have done it by any means. When they wanted, they filled up the sea, and they also tore down the mountain when they wanted. Ridiculously, they think that all things in the world were made only for themselves. (15)

The adjectives the bird uses to describe humanity such as "the most horrible," "capricious," and "ridiculous" shed light on how wretched being we have become in our reckless pursuit of our selfish desires. But the bird's most poignant indictment is against the anthropocentric hubris, which thinks "all things in the world were made only for humanity." This unwarranted arrogance is ridiculous and self-suicidal in the ecosystem.

This hubris stems from humanity's ignorance about the interrelatedness and interconnectedness of all things in the world, one of the key concepts of Buddhism. Because nothing can exist by itself and nothing can have its own unique beingness (무자성 無自性), a thing can keep only a temporary beingness, and even that only in relationship to numerous other things. Therefore humanity's arrogance that it can live without the help of others and exploitation of others is an unforgivable sin in the ecosphere. The chickadee's criticism of human arrogance is relentless but accurate:

> Wherever they put their feet, nothing could survive [...] they would change original forms of things. Complaining that duck's legs are too short to see, they try to splint a stick to them, while trying to cut crane's legs short saying their long legs must be cumbersome. Humankind is a strange race indeed. They measure things only with their own yard, and think egotistically. They will not consider other's view or position even a little bit. They even think about god whom they adore from their own point of view. (30)

As the above passage suggests, this kind of egoistic thinking leads humanity to violence to others and itself, as well. Considering that the chickadee is looking for a place to build nest to lay eggs, his saying that "Alas, this place commands a good view, the sky is clear and dark blue, the sea ripples indigo, poplars grow dense and salty wind caresses my heart [...] Everything is perfect, but here is no peace. It is not a place to build a nest" (6) shows clearly how the world has changed into a kind of dystopia to other beings except humanity.

The driving force of environmental degradation and industrialization is symbolized as measurement in the novel. Measurement divides the land to set boundaries and is usually followed by development. But the author reverses our presupposition about measurement by associating it with the devil:

> Angels, being mixed this way or that way, live harmoniously without taking measurement, while devils have to measure everything. If you leave a thing as it is without taking measurement, it is a world of irrationality, but it becomes a world of rationality when it is measured. Rationality is devil's painted face and his trumpery magic. When people measure land and build fences, conflict arises. (68)

Our over-confidence on the reason and abuse of measurement has brought two consequences; it removed all other dimensions from the world except what is seen, and it also has made people become irrational by an ironic turn. As Blabberer, a mouthpiece of the author in the novel, says, "Because of rationalists who are unwilling to believe in the things they cannot touch with their own hands, the world has become this strange place" (42). By reducing all things to the level of what one can see and hold, the world is completely desacralized and exposed to merciless exploitation.

From the perspective of Buddhism, all conflicts in the novel are caused by three poisons or three evil roots of greed, anger, and ignorance (탐진치

貪嗔痴). Padmasiri De Silva's explication of three poisons in "Buddhist Environmental Ethics" is really illuminating:

> In general, the Buddhist sees greed (*lobha*), hatred (*doda*), and delusion (*moha*) as the root cause of all suffering. Excessive greed finds expression in life orientations bound to extreme sensuality and hedonism (*kama-tanha*) and in limitless expansion and possessiveness (*bhava-tanha*). Hatred is expressed by a destructive and violent attitude toward oneself, others, and the natural world (*vibhava-tanha*). Destructive patterns of consumption generate unending cycles of desires and satisfaction. (17)

In the novel, all the family members fight for the piece of land out of greed. And their greed develops into a madness, in which they are willing to go as far as kill each other. In fact, all the crimes in the novel including adultery, fraud, and kidnapping are instigated by nothing other than this greed. Blabberer's words that "Money, money, money, money, money, don't fret so much about it. Money is good, but it is not everything" (115) aptly summarize the hidden motive of the family members' actions.

This mind of three poisons is symbolized in the novel as the darkness enthralling most characters in the novel. This darkness narrows people's attention to themselves and makes them blind to see their own true nature and other people's concerns. The grandfather's state of paralysis serves as a metaphor for their mental state. It is the same darkness which Tomalee tries unflinchingly to expel, by shining a flashlight into his grandfather's eyes. As Han says, this darkness or gray light from the devil is not a light at all, and merely breeds an illusion. Most characters in the novel are following their false, illusory egos; their mind and words are so perverted that they say one thing and mean another. Yoonseok's speech below is a typical example. Though he intends to make a fortune by turning the plum orchard into a fish farm, he positions himself as a sincere ecologist and oriental philosopher:

> I, Yoonseok Park, have tried every means to make this farm something like the beginning and center of the world, the fountain of Oriental thought. Humankind must recognize and live within the relationship with all things that they have built from the very moment of their birth in this way or that way. If one tries to deny the relationship in which because of this that exists, or because of that this exists and live alone, the relationship is bound to break. If it breaks down, he or she is

> bound to die. The logic that I have to live and, therefore, you
> have to die, will bring catastrophe to everybody [...] In that
> case, natural enemy relationships and symbiotic relationships
> would collapse. The order of the universe is just the same.
> (166)

It is really ironic and pathetic that Yoonseok is the very person who tries to kill others and break the relationship in order that only he may prosper. Pointing out the limit of the Western philosophy, he insists that "I will take this place as a new site for Oriental thoughts, because humanity can be saved only by returning to them" (140). But his real motive is to make a fortune by turning the orchard into a fish farm and then eventually developing the farm into a resort. This quack ecologist, blinded by false gray light, does not know that he is shamelessly contradicting himself. As Jongsung Kim notes in *A Study of Ecological Consciousness in the Modern Novels of Korea*, Han is criticizing through Yoonseok's behavior the hypocrisy of humankind's immersion into anthropocentric view with a minimal knowledge of the ecosystem without any real ecological consciousness (108).

The cure for this darkness is the light of Tomalee's flashlight. Because of the darkness of people's unrestrainable greed, the world has become a hell. This world is not much different from the nether world of hungry ghosts and animals to which Joocheol mentions he has been. There, everyone gets surgery so that his or her throat becomes as tiny as the eye of a needle. Having no way to satisfy their hunger, these mad *pretas* roam the hell. According to Buddhist philosophy, these hungry ghosts or spirits are ascribed to this state because of their craving and jealousy in their former lives. But Han suggests that the members of Park family and by extension most people in the world, live this life of hell in this world, because they are under the grip of demonic greed. In this sense, Yoonseok's confession that "Perhaps more than 12 demons are taking their seats in me, and they make me not to feel any regret" (139) is worth listening to. Like the chainsaw he brandished to cut down the plum trees, his giant greed does not know any stopping and destroys not only the environment but also the lives of people around him. The white poplar standing beside the orchard defines this attitude as the devilishness of human beings. But the real irony is that the poplar is trying to learn and imitate this devilishness of humankind, while condemning it vehemently as the very cause of ecological crisis (Koo 86).

While the cape is the battlefield of selfish desires, the sea is a place where one can reflect on the true nature of oneself and relationship with others. Humankind's absurd arrogance stems from ignorance that all life forms in the universe are inextricably interdependent and interconnected.

Furthermore, Buddhism teaches that our present life is causally connected with our doings in our previous life. In this sense, Buddhism even dissolves traditional boundaries of the mundane and supramundane realms. The law of dependent origination governs not only this world, but the world after death, and this is the core of the lesson Joocheol learns while he was in the nether world. Therefore what is most important is to acknowledge this connectedness and enlarge one's scope of attention beyond oneself into other living things. After recovering his sense from the coma, Joocheol emphasizes the importance of becoming one:

> The fountainhead of the universe destroys everything with time. To know its power and become one with it is called yoga. In it, pleasure and pain are one, rose and ditch are one, and a bump of gold is one with dust and rock... He who knows this has arrived at the origin of the universe. In order to get there, one has to renounce all desires and free himself from all attachments. Then, he is able to control himself. (235)

Yoga is to reach at the state of Buddha's sea mirror, as Blabberer rightly notes (235). It amounts to renouncing the discriminating intelligence (분별지 分別智) and seeing things with eyes that are clear and undisturbed by one's selfish desires. Seungtaek Lim, a professor of Buddhist philosophy at Kyungpook National University, argues in "Yoga and Buddhism" that yoga "suppresses the sensory organs, mind, and intelligence in order to attain at a state of calmness" (n.p.). By renouncing one's subjective will or desires, one can see the things as they are.

The perception of the true nature of things as they really are, leads people to be awakened to the idea of selflessness and the *sunyata* of all things. Joocheol's words that "we have to return empty-handed as we had come empty-handed. I have nothing to give to you except this empty nothingness "(236) show his complete change from a man of extreme greed to a man of Buddhist wisdom through suffering in the hell. Ian Harris's claim that "The condition of extreme individualism, conceived as a final stage in the disease of the Western self can only be arrested by the kind of radical restructuring to which Buddhism alone holds the key" (202) rings true in Han's novel. The Buddhist remedy for the three poisons is three supreme disciplines (삼학 三學) – precept (계 戒), meditation (정 定) and wisdom (혜 慧). Buddhist scholar, Seokho Choi, gives an ecological reinterpretation of these disciplines that serves as an important insight about how we can free ourselves from the powerful grip of greed and live harmoniously with others:

> Precept is to set a norm for living with others and keep it.
> Meditation is to feel satisfaction not by controlling and
> possessing objects but by controlling one's own indiscriminate
> greed. Wisdom is to acknowledge the interdependent
> connectedness of all beings and practice these disciplines for
> the happiness of all beings as well as for oneself. (333)

These three disciplines are, metaphorically, the light of Tomalee's flashlight,
with which he casts away the darkness paralyzing his grandfather. Only these
key disciplines will be able to exorcise the twelve devils living inside of
Yoonseok and instigating him to do hideous things.

The sheer contrast between the geographical sites, the cape and the sea,
constitutes the basic frame of the novel. While the land – more specifically,
the cape – symbolizes the place of conflict and greed, the sea is a place for
reflection and self-renouncement. It is a paradox that the waves are high in the
land but calm in the sea:

> When the waves are high, the sea cannot reflect things of the
> universe correctly. So does the sea of our minds. The waves
> are our desires. If you calm down all desires, all things are
> reflected clearly. This spot is where one can imagine the mind
> of Buddha. Look over there! The sea reflects the sky like a
> mirror. Doesn't it reflect mountains, ships, and people's minds
> also? This is called Ocean Seal, a symbol for the mind of
> Buddha who has entered to the state of enlightenment. (201)

The waves Joocheol mentions must be the waves of humankind's greed,
which prevents people from seeing their true nature. Han suggests that the
first step for universal reconciliation is to clearly see what kind of beings we
have become in our indiscriminate pursuit for more material wealth.
Possessed by unrestrainable desires, we have become most horrible and cruel
creatures to our fellow beings in the ecosystem. Only in this ocean seal, one
can wash away his or her greed and glimpse into the mind of Buddha.
Tomalee's repetitive cry of "Open your eyes" throughout the novel is nothing
but an urge to get out of the hell of one's greed. It condemns the myopic
anthropocentricism of humankind and helps open our eyes and practice
compassion to other beings –not only human beings but also animals and
plants–who share the ecosphere with us (Kim Wookdong 205). When
Moonkwon Chung argues that this cry is a cry for a new world view,
especially for a Buddhist worldview (117), she alludes to the Buddhist idea of
dependent origination and the *sunyata* of all things.

Topographically, the shape of the farm resembles a lotus flower, surrounded by petal-like mountains and sea. The lotus flower represents a place, where one can be cured and learn the wisdom of mutual living, as Blabberer says, "when one is able to look at the lotus flower in a proper way, all his or her diseases will be cured" (199). Lotus flowers bloom out of mud, and they have been a traditional symbol for the mind of Buddha. Through Joocheol's last words, Han demonstrates that our narrow egocentric vision of self-gratification can be cured by the universal vision of interconnectedness. Joocheol's parting statements indicate that we are all part of an enlarged Sangha (승가 僧伽), not just a community of Buddhists, but a community of all beings of the earth. This recognition urges us to restrain our reckless desires and practice compassion toward other beings. In this enlightened vision the human world, the natural world, and the spiritual world are reinstituted as a holistic universe in which each is closely connected and interdependent (Kwon 409). Han suggests that universal reconciliation is possible only when all constituents are willing to renounce their illusory desires and practice the heart of compassion. But in this depraved world – in which even the white poplar, "poisoned by the drug of humankind's humanism" (242), preaches that all creatures should learn the devilishness of human beings to survive – this reconciliation is difficult to achieve. Perhaps that is the very reason why the author has chosen not *the lake* – the usual place where lotus grows – but *the sea* as the place where this precious lotus of Buddha's wisdom will bloom. Though the lotus is extremely hard to find, once we do find it, Han argues that its exquisite fragrance will detoxify us from the poison of anthropocentricism and take us into the pure land of harmonious living.

Works Cited

Badiner, Allan Hunt. "Introduction." *Dharma Gaia: A Harvest of Essays in Buddhism and Ecology*. Ed. Allan Hunt Badiner. Berkeley: Parallax Press, 1990. xiii-xviii.

Barnhill, Landis David. "Great Earth Sangha: Gary Snyder's View of Nature as Community." *Buddhism and Ecology: The Interconnection of Dharma and Deeds*. Ed. Mary Evelyn Tucker and Duncan Rhuken Williams. Cambridge: Harvard UP, 1997. 187-217.

Calvino, Italo. *The Uses of Literature*. Trans. P. Creagh. San Diego, CA: Harcourt Brace Jovanovich, 2001.

Choi, Seokho. "Environmental Problems from the Perspective of Buddhism." *Changjakkwa Beepyeong* 19:2 (Summer, 1992): 316-334.

Chung, Moonkwon. "The Embodiment of Ecological Imagination with a Special Emphasis on Seungwon Han's *Lotus Sea.*" *Inmunnonchong of Baejae University* 14 (1999): 103-118.

Ha, Eungbaek. "The Sea of Movement, the Sea of Calmness." *The Life and Literature of Seungwon Han*. Ed. Cheolwoo Lim, Donghwak Lim, and Eungbaek Ha. Seoul: Moonydang, 2000. 136-152.

Han, Seungwon. *Lotus Sea*. Seoul: Segyesa, 1997.

Harris, Ian. "Buddhist Environment Ethics and Detraditionalization: The Case of EcoBuddhism." *Religion* 25 (1995): 199-211.

Kim, Jongsung. *A Study of Ecological Consciousness in Modern Novels of Korea*. Ph.D. diss. Korea University, 2003.

Kim, Won-Chung. "Taoistic Ideas in A.R. Ammons and Seungho Choi's Ecopoetry." *Comparative American Studies* 7:2 (June 2009): 128-139.

Kim, Wookdong. *For the Literary Ecology: Green Literature and Green Theory*. Seoul: Minumsa, 1998.

Koo, Za-hee. "Realization of Ecologism through the Order of Jeophwagunsaeng." *The Journal of Korean Fiction Research* 25 (2005): 77-101.

Kwon, Myunga, "Three Stories about the Sea, the Desert, and the Moon." *Jagga Segye* 9:3 (August, 1998): 406-415.

Lee, Taedong. "The Movement of History and Life Force." *The Life and Literature of Seungwon Han*. Ed. Cheolwoo Lim, Donghwak Lim, and Eungbaek Ha. Seoul: Moonydang, 2000. 192-196.

Lim, Seungtaek. "Yoga and Buddhism." Beopbo Sinmoon (July13, 2011) <http://www.beopbo.com /news/view.html?skey=%C0%D3%BD%C2%C5%C3&x=28&y=12&page=6&section=93&category=171&no=66567>

Iovino, Serenella. "The Human Alien. Otherness, Humanism, and the Future of Ecocriticism." *Ecozon@* 1:1 (2010): 53-61.

Murphy, Patrick D. *Ecocritical Explorations in Literary and Cultural Studies: Fences, Boundaries, and Fields*. New York: Lexington Books, 2009.

Silva, Padmasiri De. "Buddhism and Environmental Ethics." *Dharma Gaia: A Harvest of Essays in Buddhism and Ecology*. Ed. Allan Hunt Badiner. Berkeley: Parallax Press, 1990. 14-19.

Writing Spaces: Travel, Global Cities and Landscapes
Editors: I-Chun Wang, Mary Theis, and Christopher Larkosh

Remapping the Roots:
Specular Routes and Spectral Homescape

Jiayan Mi

I. Reconfiguring Poetics of Homescape as National Space

The unique sphere known as "jia," or home/family/house, occupies a central space in Chinese culture; it is a combination of both the private and public spheres, signifying the architectonic unity of the domestic and national spaces (namely, "guojia," or the state-family). *Jia* is the essential locus of the ethico-moral value system in traditional Chinese society. However, the emerging modernity at the threshold of the twentieth century has led to the dissolution of traditional spatial boundary, thereby causing a radical displacement and a spatial deterritorialization in the minds of the Chinese people. It is exactly the loss, absence, and the collapse of the traditional notion of home that triggers the scenarios of home-seeking and home-making, giving rise to a new discursive formation of "the native home/land," known as "xiangtu wenxue," or the native-soil literature in modern Chinese literature.

Central to the modern preoccupation with the native home/land is the fact that the downfall of the old home takes place exactly at the same time as the demise of a dynastic imperial China and the birth of a new nation-state in modern Chinese history; thus the quest for a new home goes hand in hand with the making of a new nation. The obsessive spectacle of the native home/land, I argue, is to create a nationalist narrative of nation-building. What lies at the core of the pervasive home/land narrative in modern Chinese literature is the cultural imaginings of a new home as ideal space for a modern nation.

In this paper, I discuss two representations of the home/land narratives in Lu Xun's well-known short story "My Old Home" (1921), Shen Congwen's travelogue *Random Sketches on a Trip to Hunan* (1934), in an attempt to reveal how the native, local, regional home experiences are translated into "China narratives," i.e., how the native home/land is culturally and politically incorporated into the national agendas. I argue that the obsession with the home/land narratives articulates a collective wish for a post-home self-relocationality on the one hand, and on the other, reflects the contending ideologies of representing, remapping and re-narrating a heterospace for constituting a new nation-state. In this sense, the home/land narrative that proliferates through the whole twentieth-century Chinese literature provides a negotiable space for competing discourses, either as a reinforcement of, or as a challenge to, the Chinese national identity.

However, modernity offers double binds: namely, its power to free people from the restraints of their socio-geographical attachments to a specific locality, from a stable home grounded in a sedentary agricultural society; and its power to uproot, dislocate one's dwelling, thereby producing persistent feeling of separation, trauma, and lack in the psychological, emotional and cultural world of the migrants. Such drastic dislocation is generally experienced as homelessness or as homesickness. To be in the state of homelessness triggers a strong desire to search for a new home, a true dwelling place; and homesickness is a desire to return to one's native home, s nostalgia for a good time in one's past and a belief that it can be recuperated. In modern Chinese literature, the motif of searching for one's home is pervasive, as shown in one exemplary text of Shi Tuo's *The Orchard Town*:

> We indeed want to see our hometown. It is a natural feeling inherent within us which becomes the very cause of our unrest… We keep searching for this old dream—a shattered dream of both desolate and sweet. In our heart, each recollection is a blossom of flower, a secret flavor, and a short song mixed with clouds and sunlight. Although we already knew that the buildings in the past have collapsed to ruins and wastes; graves already cleared away; trees already cut down; and the little trees we planted have filled the hungry stomachs of the goats—a view that everywhere prevails the melancholy, mourning and all kinds of emptiness, we still could not help searching for the home from the ups and the downs… (1938 in 1956: 2)

This mixture of both "desolate and sweet" emotions and the afflicted condition of being "melancholic, mourning and empty" precisely characterize the *zeitgeist* of early modern China, a time when the home was lost, absent or shattered while a new home was not yet   made.

As a result, modern Chinese literature is obsessively haunted by the specter of the home, and most modern Chinese writers start their literary careers from their native towns. They are either pleased by the beautiful prospects of their homeland or depressed by the wretched scenes of their old home. For the former, they are willing to return to their homes; for the latter they turn away from them. Return-to-the home and turn-away- from-the-home are two emotional postures as well as two representational modes particular to the investments in the projects of home-seeking and home-making in modern China. The upsurge of nostalgia in modern Chinese literature precisely reflects the national reconstruction of Chinese cultural identity after historic trauma and a national reconstruction, which focuses on the torturous journey of self-definition and self-discovery made possible in acts of homecoming.

In facing the disappearance of the old home, questions such as "What kind of new home is it going to be?" "What is a new mode of home to be for a modern China?" and "How is such a new home to be built?" are raised by the new intellectuals. To find answers to these questions, they make "field trips" to their native places, which are often located in the peripheral countryside, making a homecoming journey that is usually described as "*youzi huangxiang*" (the return of the drifters) in modern Chinese literature (Chen 1989). Thus, we witness a particular figure who recurs in modern Chinese literature—a modern intellectual, whom Leo Lee designates as "the solitary traveler" whose itinerary of returning is not linear but twisted, filled with shocks, tensions, and fragmentations (Leo 1985). The "solitary traveler," as Yingjin Zhang aptly observes, is inevitably caught "between tradition and modernity, between ignorance of the country and knowledge of the city, between a passion for one's hometown and a repulsion at its indolence, cowardice, and cruelty, between a nostalgia for the forever lost world of childhood innocence and a disillusionment with present scenes of corruption and deterioration" (Zhang 1996: 52).

Such a dilemma casts a new light on the perspective of looking at the home, either subverting it or rediscovering it as a new home. Briefly put, with the inscription of the home narrative in modern Chinese literature, the geographically remote regions called *xiangtu* are brought into the nation's focus, which is further extended to the agenda of searching for a "post-home" identity and building a new modern nation. In this way, as home and nation converge, the local becomes national, translating "native experiences" into "national narratives;" and reconfiguring home scenes as national scenes in which national subjects are called forth and constituted.

In what follows, I investigate how the native, local and regional experiences are translated into "China narratives," i.e., the native home imagined as a national home, in Lu Xun's short story "Guxiang" (My Old Home) and Shen Congwen's travelogues. Instead of considering the home as a locus of ideality, I treat it as a cultural artifact, a construct of volatile signification that is made to articulate a contending collective wish and national imaginings. As for the country tour and home returning, I conceive the trajectory of the journey as a mode of cognition, a "cognitive mapping," to borrow F. Jameson's term, a spatial perception that helps one to position or reposition one's self by "inventing new geotopical cartographies" in a changing geopolitical landscape (Jameson 1991; 1995). It is evident, as I will show in the paper, that the returned natives always modify, reconfigure, and remap their positions vis-à-vis the country folks and the home scenes.

II. Lu Xun: Deterritorialization and the Imagined Home Space

Lu Xun, the founder of modern Chinese fiction, starts his literary imagination with his hometown and thereby inaugurates what is often called "xiangtu wenxue," or "literature of the native home," in modern Chinese literature. More than half of Lu Xun's stories (fourteen out of twenty-five) are set in the town of S—his hometown of Shaoxing—and in Luzhen, his mother's place of origin. The rural hometown not only becomes his most effective means for exploring the national malaise in his stories but also the source of creative inspiration. Central to Lu Xun's fiction is the narrative of the homecoming, telling of a return journey by a "self-exiled intellectual" to his hometown after many years' absence (Hsia 1961). These homecoming narratives, such as "My Old Home," "Village Opera," "New Year's Sacrifice," "The Loner," and "In the Tavern," are often initiated by the first-person narrator, an authorial persona who reflects a social way of seeing when he re-encounters his country folks and home scenes. The inscription of the I-narrator into the home narratives is paradigmatic in that it introduces in the event of homecoming a third point of view, a critical witness or a detached observer, who dramatizes as well as mediates the tensions between the self and the other, the authentic and inauthentic, and the proper and improper, and who is "situated morally between the crowd and its victims" (Anderson 1990: 88). Among these homecoming stories, "My Old Home" (1921) is an exemplary text that illustrates Lu Xun's perception of the home and his reconfiguration of the homecoming journey as a national agenda.

Guxiang" ("My Old Home") begins with an anti-heroic mode of homecoming. For what welcomes the returnee are not homely, cheerful, and jubilant, but desolate, ghostly, and bleak scenes, scenes evoking an elegiac atmosphere seem to show that the home had just been uprooted. Thus, the homecoming is to embrace not life but death; it is not to enjoy homely peace but to encounter danger and risks. Such a return signifies an adventure into the heart of darkness in order to witness its final moment of collapse and to mourn its loss and demise.[1] So the story goes with the I-narrator who, after twenty years of urban life, is returning to his native home by boat on a cold winter day for a final farewell. He discovers that the aura of the idyllic and cozy home cherished in his memory has disappeared, and what comes into his sight instead is a desolate and gloomy old home. However, the "marvelous scene" (*shenyi de tuhua*) of his old home does flash back to life for a second when the narrator's mother mentions his best childhood playmate, then a ten-year old country boy Runtu who, in the eyes of the narrator, knows everything about the natural world—how to hunt animals under the moonlight, catch birds in the snow or pick up shells by the sea, and who enlightened the young mind of the narrator to the wonders of a greater world. The narrator's momentary nostalgia for his "beautiful old home" is immediately shattered when he reencounters the adult Runtu who comes up to greet him respectfully as "master" (laoye), an old term of address that bears deep social hierarchy and class differences. This re-encounter with Runtu shocks the narrator and brings him deep disillusionment because the clever "young hero" to whom he looked up in his childhood has now changed into a "wooden puppet" (483): his face is heavily wrinkled; his hands "coarse, clumsy and chapped;" and his dress shabby.

Even more shockingly, beyond this physical deterioration the narrator discovers Runtu's spiritual stupefaction: now he is no longer high-spirited and eloquent but silent and speechless like "a stone statue" (483). As a superstitious father of six, Runtu, now worn out by hard life, is burdened and squeezed by "famines, taxes, soldiers, bandits, officials and landed gentry" (Ibid.). Deeply disillusioned by the drastic changes in his home and his childhood buddy Runtu, and clearly recognizing that a communication gap—"an invisible high wall" (485)—exists between himself and his country folks, the narrator feels a strong sense of alienation, and returns to the city without regrets, as he stated in the story, "This time I had come with the sole object of saying goodbye... to say goodbye for ever to the familiar old home" (476). On his way back to the city, the narrator expresses his hope for the future, making pleas for four modes of new life, "a life we have never experienced" (485): no barriers (*gemo*) such as that occurring between himself and Runtu in the younger generations; no "restless toiling" (*xingku zhanzhuan*) like the narrator's own life; no "toiling to the point of stupefaction" (*xingku mamu*) like Runtu's, and no "toiling for the sake of dissipation" *(xingku ziwei)* like others. But to the question of how to realize the new hope, the narrator has no direct answer; or maybe he is searching for the answer because the story ends with his remark that his new hope is "distant and elusive" (*mangyuan*), that is, lies in the unknown future.

As mentioned above, Lu Xun creates a strong anti-home narrative to register his narrator's traumatic return to his old home, where he had experienced alienation and displacement rather than security and warmth. The home, as the I-narrator reveals through his roundabout sojourns, has degenerated from "idyllic tranquility" to present desolation, so that the itinerary of the narrator is a journey from a mnemonic *extra*-ordinary home to an *ultra*-ordinary home in real time, a kind of defacement that disenchants the auras of the romanticized childhood home evoked by the narrator's nostalgia. In order to show the deterioration of his old home, as many scholars have already observed (Wang 1993; Fang 1986; Xu 1981; Mei 1998), Lu Xun forcibly constructs a dyadic structure of sharp contrast between the idyllic home of his childhood and the dreary home of the present. Seen in this light, the dyadic contrast between the past and the present merely reflects the general sentiment of nostalgia, which Fred Davis calls "the first-order nostalgia", namely, a belief that things then were better, more beautiful, healthier, happier, more civilized, and more exciting than now" (1979: 18). If that were the case, it would certainly devalue Lu Xun's mission in writing this story because as a social Darwinist and an iconoclast Lu Xun would never embrace the nostalgic celebration of the "good and fine" past. On the contrary, the radical Lu Xun always insists that a modern intellectual should break away from his/her old past with no regret, and should ultimately overcome his/her "homing instinct." Only in this way can s/he achieve intellectual maturity and a rational critique of a sick China. Therefore, I would argue that Lu Xun inscribes in the story a triadic structure not of contrastive juxtaposition but of retroactive disavowal, i.e., the negation of what temporally precedes. The triadic structure of negation is constituted by three types of the home: a past home as remembered; a present home as witnessed and a future home as imagined.

Since the story opens with a distant view of a catastrophic scene in the narrator's old home—cold late winter day, cold wind, a few desolate and lifeless villages scattered far and near under the somber yellow sky, and with a closer view of the narrator's bleak house—"broken stems of withered grass on the roof trembling in the wind"—thus a dreary, miserable and ruined home of the present is immediately framed by the narrator's subjective point of view, which dictates the flow of both   backward and forward yearning. Facing such a depressing present home, the narrator naturally feels nostalgic for his childhood home: "Ah, Surely this was not the old home I had been remembering for the past twenty years" (476). With this complaint and particularly when the name of Runtu is brought up by the narrator's mother, a remembered home of the past emerges—"this childhood memory sprang into life like a flash of lightning" (479), where a "marvelous scene" is witnessed:

> A round golden moon was hanging against a deep blue sky, and beneath it a spread of sandy seashore planted with emerald green watermelons stretching as far as the eye could see, and standing in the midst of all those melons an eleven or twelve-year old boy, a silver ring around his neck, pitchfork in his hand, was thrusting with all his might at a Zha

(badger), which with a quick turn, escaped through his legs. (477)

Such a colorful, sweet, cozy and healthy picture of the past home evoked in the narrator's mnemonic flashbacks sets up a strong opposition against the bleak and uncanny scene of the present home.

In general terms, this "marvelous scene" conjured up in nostalgic yearning may epitomize the mythical prototype of a childhood home embedded in the world of the   human unconscious; in particular, this remembered picture characterizes a pre-modern agricultural idyll that is vanishing and forever lost in modern China. However, the narrator refuses to allow himself to sink into his nostalgic flashbacks and intoxicate himself in the mirage of the "marvelous scene" in his childhood. He remembers it so as to dismember it, because his experience of the home in real time clearly shows that the idyllic home is just a fantasy, a simulacrum, and an illusion, which he has to abandon since the object of his return is to say farewell to his old home. The appearance of Runtu in real time is fatal in that it not only shatters the narrator's pastoral dream of the past home but also helps him split the fantasized home from the one in reality, ultimately leading to his complete break from his old home.

Since Runtu is the hero or the "little hero," as the narrator used to call him adorably, whose spectacular *mise-en-scene* engenders the "marvelous scene" in the picture of the narrator's flashbacks, he embodies all that is good, beautiful and pleasant of the narrator's old home. Actually Runtu is the personification of the narrator's old home ("Runtu" literally means "Intercalary Earth," i.e., the fate of belonging to earth, land or soil, according to the operation of the five prime elements). The narrator has had a strong emotional or psychological fixation on this charismatic figure for over thirty years after he had left his old home. In other words, because of his irresistible emotional attachment to Runtu, the narrator, as a new intellectual working in the city, has been so obsessed with his old home that he has not been able to release himself from it, even though he repeatedly claims that he will bid it farewell forever. Yet the old home haunts him like a specter or an apparition that always catches and tortures him:

> The old home I remembered was not in the least like this. My old home had been much better. But if you asked me to recall its peculiar charm or describe its beauty, I had no clear impression, no words to depict it. And it seemed as if it might have been there in such a way. Then I rationalized the matter to myself, saying: Home was always like this... (476)

As the narrator reencounters the adult Runtu, the spell that binds him to his old home is immediately shattered. For the current Runtu before the narrator is a middle-aged peasant with deep wrinkles, wearing worn-out clothes, standing there speechless like a stone statue or a wooden puppet—"it was not the Runtu I remembered" (481).

The degeneration of the adult Runtu exactly corresponds with the catastrophic degradation of the narrator's old home. Seeing the deformed Runtu, the narrator comes to the point of realization that there is actually nothing left in his old home worthy of emotional attachment and nostalgic yearning. Thus the appearance of Runtu in the narrator's present home leads decisively to abandonment of his dream of the idyllic home. This then gives rise to rejection of the current home, since it is no longer the hearth of happiness but a place of suffering, no longer the source of life and power but a site of death, ignorance, darkness and superstition. Without hesitation or fear of being destroyed like his playmate Runtu, the narrator flees—"I was leaving the old house farther and farther behind; the hills and rivers of my old home were also receding gradually ever farther in the distance. But I had no sense of regret" (485). But where to go? For the home as remembered is merely an illusion, and the home as seen in the real time is desolate and uninhabitable. Where is the new home? The narrator muses on a boat in the river on his departure to an uncertain future.

With the negation of both the past idyllic home and the present bleak home, a future home is projected at the end of the story, a home as imagined in the narrator's dream: "Sinking into a dreamy state, a stretch of emerald green sand by the seashore before my eyes, and above a round golden moon hanging against a dark blue sky" (485). Such a "brave new world" cannot be called completely new, since it appears identical to the recurrent image of the narrator's childhood home. Yet if we look at this imaginary new home carefully, we see that the narrator has made a significant reconstruction of the innocent natural world in the past. That is, as Lu Tonglin insightfully points out, this imaginary future home is an empty natural world from which human beings are excluded; not only is Runtu being excluded, but also the narrator himself, the authorial persona, cannot have access to it. Lu Xun is very radical and self-critical here: radical in that the possibility of building a new home can only take place after this present miserable home is destroyed; self-critical in that no one, including an intellectual like himself, from the old home is qualified to live in this future home unless s/he undergoes a complete transformation, that is, a new subjectivity must be constituted for the inhabitant of this new home. That is why "beautiful nature," as Lu observes, " as a reconfiguration of hope at the end of the narrator's journey, refuses entrance to any inhabitant of the old world" (1995: 38).

The narrator's ultimate farewell to his old home—feudalistic, agricultural, cannibalistic, and paternalistic-- indeed signifies a determined will towards this future new home, even though "distant and elusive". But a question arises here: on the one hand, since Chinese peasantry epitomized by the adult Runtu is rejected for entering into this future new home because he is ignorant, superstitious, subservient, and impoverished, hence representing the sickness of the national characteristics of the silent China; on the other hand, even the Chinese intellectuals who claim themselves to enlighten the people and save China from being annihilated are also excluded from this future home, because of their alienation from Chinese society. According to Lu Xun's interrogation in his stories, Chinese intellectuals are often caught between the crowd and the victim, lacking intellectual insight to challenge the social authority as well as moral courage to speak to/for the social oppressed due to their position as privileged members of the elite class (Anderson : 88-9). [2]Who, then, will be the legitimate subject of this imaginary new home, namely, the ideal soul of the modern nation? In other words, who should constitute the new nation?

Imagine an ideal space as home for a nation must create its own national subject at the same time. Before the emergence of the post-home new world, the narrator had actually brought forth four modes of new life, which he believed are "never experienced" by his country folks. If we look carefully at the "four modes of new life" the narrator hopes will be realized in a future home, we find that the four wished-for modes of new life in the future China exactly reflect the ideals of the Enlightenment—freedom, equality, justice, rationality, *bonheur*, social harmony, artistic beauty, and the dignity of humanity—which give rise to the grand narrative of Western modernity (Habermas 1988; 1989). The first new life of "no barriers" between the members of the younger generation signifies equality free of class difference; the second one, "no restless toiling," conveys happiness or *bonheur*; the third one, "not toiling to the point of stupefaction," expresses the idea of freedom or beauty of life, and the fourth one, "no dissipation," indicates a life of dignity or harmony. It is obvious that the narrator, who is the spokesperson of the author, strongly insists that these ideals of modernity are the foundation as well as the *telos* of a future new home for China. Only those who embrace or strive for these ideals are qualified to be the new dwellers of this new home. Since these ideals of new life are far from being realized, and the subjectivity for the future new home is not yet to be constituted, in this sense, the future home as imagined only exists as an utopian image or a constellation that looks down to us "from a deep blue sky" while projecting a beautiful dream for motivating the search for the road that leads to its ultimate fulfillment.

Lu Xun's exilic homecoming thus reflects his determined will to completely sever the umbilical cord that binds him to his natural past, a subversive turn away from his old home—a microcosm of the silent China symptomatic of darkness, death, backwardness, humiliation, oppression, exploitation, and disillusionment. It also represents a symbolic journey of a critical modern Chinese intellectual who digs into "his own world" and regresses into "the depth of his soul" for self-interrogation and self-rejuvenation (Wang 1993: 123). This anti-heroic act of returning to the old home and ultimately fleeing from its "dark hole" is one of the most powerful discourses that runs through the post-May Fourth literature, as witnessed in popular works such as Ba Jin's *Family* (1932), Cao Yu's *The Wilderness* (1937), and *A Trip to the South* (1942). With the dissolution of the old home and a farewell to the primal origin that no longer shelters and nurtures, a new place as home has to be imagined or invented. In Lu Xun's "*Guxiang*," the narrator's turn away from his old home shows his anti-mimetic disavowal of his natural origin on the one hand, while, on the other hand, the place imagined as a new home for a future China reminiscent of his childhood home indicates his inseparable affinity with that origin. In this light, the post-home fantasy exemplifies the ambivalent condition of modernity: the mimetic homeward/anti-mimetic home-splitting, nostalgia/utopian ideal of *Heimat*, which in a deeper sense characterizes the national anxiety and dream, and particularly the Chinese intellectuals' "obsession with China," that is, What is the ideal space as new home for the future China?

III. Shen Congwen: Specular Horizon and Myth of Home Identity

Lu Xun's anti-home narrative, while mainly inspired by his ideological critique of a sick China and its national characteristics, was a response to the post-home condition of spatial dislocation and temporal disruption which is fundamental to the national symptom of nostalgia and crisis of identity. He immediately dismisses the iconic fantasy of a beautiful rural home after witnessing its disfiguration brought about by the drastic progress of modernity, and he carries out a complete break away from this wretched idyll. However, the rural home/land is perceived as radically different by Shen Congwen (1902-1988) whose literary imagination is initiated precisely by Lu Xun's *Xiangtu* fictions.[3] Hailed as "the most important creator of the myth of the homeland in modern Chinese fiction" (Wang 1993:19) and the creator of "the first identity myth" ever associated with a home region (Jeffrey 1987: 7), Shen Congwen rediscovers in his hometown area—*Xiangxi* (West Hunan)—not a Lu Xun-esque rural misery but a rural idyll instead, a mythical land forgotten by time and history, and a border country which the Chinese, the Miao and the Tujia minorities inhabit together. Shen's reconfiguration of his homeland of West Hunan as a rural utopia stands in sharp contrast to the negative images of a silent China, a sick China, a poisoned China, and a sorrowful China that dominate the traumatic mentality of the intelligentsia in an era of cultural and political tumult. The legendary West Hunan which Shen recovers through his literary inscriptions has emerged in modern China as what David Lowenthal terms "key symbolic landscapes"—"landscapes that perennially catch the attention of mankind and seem to stand for, reflect or incorporate, the meaning and purpose of life itself" (1979: 41).

Diametrically opposed to Lu Xun's rural home of poverty, distress, and desolation, Shen's homeland of West Hunan is perceived as a land of amplitude, plenitude and happiness, a place of love and repose—briefly a legendary *Taohuayuan* (Peach Blossom Spring). Located geographically at the marginal hinterland of China, West Hunan is presented in Shen's works not as an image of a remembered place but as an organic place relatively unspoiled by modern urban culture—the country folk are healthy, industrious, good-natured, honest, and always in harmony with nature; the rural scenery and landscape are beautiful, peaceful, and picturesque surrounded by crystal-clear streams and green mountains; the land and fields are bountiful and productive, and tended by cheerful laborers; the air in the countryside is fresh and clean; and the rural life is restful, delightful, and familial, characterized by piety, sobriety and domestic affection.

This jolly picture of Merry West Hunan, perhaps the "marvelous scene" Lu Xun might have lost, is recuperated by Shen Congwen in his homeland. By dramatizing the moral superiority of the country folk and by glorifying the healthy state of his home country, Shen intends to introduce a different mode of life, one he has depicted as "a form of life which is fine, healthy, natural and in harmony with nature" as opposed to the decadent, chaotic, and parasitic urban world downstream (Shen 1936 in 1992: 33). Such an idyllic utopia is showcased in the masterpiece of his 1934 *xiangtu* fiction, *The Border Town* (Biancheng) in which a lyrical creation of a mythical kingdom bounded by cozy rural scenes, beautiful rivers, well-ordered cottages, fruitful arable fields, and the good country folk has not only turned West Hunan into an eloquent "chronotope"—a Bakhtinian term for a physical junction of time and space in the course of history— provoking the image of "rural China, peasantry, homeland, memory of the past, and nostalgia" (Wang 1992: 280), that is, the semiotic capital of *xiangtu* China; it also reinscribes a fantasy landscape that transcends social reality in the spatial unconscious of the national subjectivity in search of a new home for the nation.

Beyond doubt Shen's reconfiguration of his home region as a rural utopia expresses what an educated intellectual wishes to see or believe about the rural country and the rural people in modern society. When encountering the tension between what he sees as the past, present, future of his homeland, Shen's position is elusive. In other words, Shen's glorification of the countryside as a rural idyll obviously hides a certain harsh social reality. As Leo Lee has pointed out, Shen is pained by the obvious incompatibility between two life-styles—the carefree ways of his native people and the erosively changing modern world, so that two voices are always heard in his works: "that of an adulating narrator intertwined with that of a sober commentator" (Lee 1985: 297). Yet the voice of what the narrator wishes to see in his homeland always dominates that of what the self-conscious commentator observes, that is, the emotional attachment dominates the rational detachment. As a result, what is inscribed in Shen's writings is always myth over reality, fantasy over factuality, absent over present, and mystery over history.

At stake is the narrative strategy Shen adopts to reconstitute what he actually sees and to negotiate the tension between what is witnessed and what is expected. To reveal how the narrative strategy helps the author to reconfigure the myth of a utopian homeland, we need to examine two travelogues produced as a result of Shen's homecoming journey, *Random Sketches on a Trip to Hunan* (1934) and *West Hunan* (1938). What interests me most is not what Shen has presented of his view of his homeland, but how such a myth of home identity is created. Thus, I consider the dream landscape of West Hunan as a particular way of seeing focusing on the visual registers— eye, sight, viewing position, point of perspective and spectatorial (un)- consciousness, which I call "specular nostalgia", that is, the visual reconfiguration of a native homeland or a rural idyll as constituted through visual imaginary. The reason I choose, among Shen's other well-known stories, these two travelogues, is that they register a native son's dynamic reactions to the dramatic changes of his hometown when he returns, as a solitary intellectual traveler, from the outside.

Random Sketches is a volume of eleven excursive essays written by Shen during his return journey, after an absence of seventeen years, to his hometown of West Hunan to visit his dying mother in early 1934.[4] Before leaving Beijing, he promises his newly married bride that he will make daily notes about what he sees and what happens on the way, and send them back to her immediately. The two months' trip produces sixty letters of which only eleven are selected for this collection. In order to ease his wife's worry about the tense situation of a civil war then breaking out in his home region, Shen tells of his experiences in more cozy terms. As he later recalls: "The village along the river looked quiet, but actually there was tension in the air, and any disaster might strike. Life was very insecure. To spare my wife in Beijing worry, I wrote her one or two letters every day, giving details of *all* that I saw and heard on the river, and *deliberately* writing in a *light-hearted* way" (1982: 8; italics mine). *West Hunan* is a collection of nine gazetteer-like essays which Shen, while in retreat in his hometown during the China-Japan War in 1938, writes to correct the deep-rooted prejudice outsiders might have about West Hunan, to alleviate the fears of the travelers in this "barbarous" land, to unravel the mystery that haunts the outsiders, and to promote the charms of his home region. *Random Sketches* dramatizes the events and life of the native people in West Hunan; *West Hunan* re-enchants the landscapes of West Hunan.

From the outset, Shen's writing has an implied ideal reader: his wife, one who stays at home, and the outsiders who represent the general public. Here two points of view are introduced in the travelogues: the point of view of the eyewitness who actually sees and that of the ideal/imaginary reader who expects or imagines. In other words, Shen's vision of his homeland always carries within itself a double identity, a third eye that wants and provokes at the same time. As a result, the homecoming eyewitness is always interrogated by the absent eye about what West Hunan was or should be or will be; hence Shen's voyage becomes a site of contention for negotiating different desires, curiosity, and interests. To his wife, what might be most desirable is a home of comfort, repose and familiarity, and for the national readers, a homeland of mystic charm, cheerful labor and fantastic romance devoid of superstitions and barbarism. Thus in *Random Sketches*, beginning with a sharp contrast to Lu Xun's bleak panoramic view of his old home in "*Guxiang*," what first unfolds before the readers is a view that, as Shen exclaims, "is endearing to the heart and pleasing the eyes, " a scene that "is indeed like a picture" (Shen 1934 in 1976: 2). The reader's eye is further led by the traveler-narrator into what he calls a "fascinating holy land" (18)—boats of different sizes drifting on the rivers, plentiful foliage and vegetation, beautiful riverside stilts, a dragon boating festival, bountiful local resources and produce, steep precipices, and spectacular natural formations of caves and rocks. Facing such a view, the author can't help exclaiming: "What a beautiful painting, what poetry!" (34). Obviously Shen frames this pictorial and poetic homeland so as to fulfill the fantasy of what the urban readers (his wife and the general public) would like to see, on the one hand, and to show the excitement of the home rediscovered by the return of a native son, on the other.

It might be too naïve to trust what the homecoming traveler-narrator has witnessed as the real situation of West Hunan. To the contrary, eye witnessing is not a neutral point of view but one invested with a strong ideological preference, which creates an illusionary relationship to reality. The eyewitness, as Davis Richards observes, is "not a naturalistic representation of 'reality,' not a simple recording of a neutral or colorless representation of an actuality devoid of preferences, decoration or authorial intentions," but an observer who must "negotiate between various meanings of the reality presented" (1994: 70). Since Shen's homeward return to West Hunan is both a literal and a literary tour, he is governed by a logic of "explore/explain," that is, of articulating what the observant tourist has witnessed en route into a narrative that is both intelligible and interesting to those outside West Hunan. To achieve this, the eyewitness has to weave the gaps, gray reality and unpleasant scenes into self-coherent scenarios, according to social expectations and aesthetic conventions such as principles of Chinese landscape paintings.

From the literal tour, which occurs in real time, readers can observe the changes affecting the West Hunan in which Shen's country folk—fishermen, boatmen, hunters, farmers, even prostitutes --are bitterly struggling for survival. His rural folk, due to "the civil war, drugs, famine, and disaster of floods, are moving towards gradual degeneration and annihilation; all good customs of their life are losing their primordial model under the tremendous pressures" (66). The decadent tendency, as Shen further observes, has almost destroyed "the honest and plain human integrity typical of a rural society, which has given rise to the practical, selfish, and vulgar attitude toward life instead in a pragmatic society in the last twenty years" (1942 in 1992: 17). Although the scars produced by the modernizing process in Shen's home region are made visible by his temporal tour, the author-narrator doesn't look at them with an investigative eye but looks *over* them to the spots of cultural and scenic interest. As Jeffrey aptly points out, when encountering unpleasant reality, Shen usually "tells of natural disasters but seldom depicts them" or merely lists them (1987: 166).

This "overlooking" of the rural scenes is governed by the the poetic imagination for an image, West Hunan is thus rediscovered in its purified form, that is, as a spectacle—an iconic image, devoid of social conflicts, that both overwhelms reality and transcends history and time. What interests Shen for his literary inscriptions is not what has disappeared but what has been left behind in his home region, some residuality that he can reconstitute as spatial enclosures which exist "outside history" as if "they were now as they had been a hundred years ago, and would be a hundred years from now" (1934 in 1976: 36). For example, in "Boatmen at the Chen River," Shen arrives in Pu Town, a port market which used to be prosperous but is now declining. As an eyewitness, Shen first describes how thriving this port town was thirty year ago, though now its deterioration can be seen everywhere. Without digging into the hard reality of the decline, the author makes a sudden shift of his focus to the picturesque scenes of the river viewed as a rural idyll by an imagined tourist:

> Yet, if a tourist travels here, he can still enjoy a view of exciting scenes in the port. He can see a wide pool downstream at the end of the market, and a shoal in the upstream of the river. Whenever at sunset, the sun sinks into the earth, and the dusk clouds in the sky are burnt to a dark purple by the remaining light of the sunset; a large number of cargoes move into the port from the upstream to the downstream. The boatmen anchor their boats near the shore. On the surface of the river covered with thin fog, songs that stimulate the pulling of the boats can be heard. What splendid and rare songs! (1934: 67)

Perceived as existing in a timeless world where the distinction between past and present is blurred—"The scene before me that day may have been exactly the same as that seen by Qu Yuan two thousand years ago" (70)—these spatial enclosures acquire a temporal *anteriority* existing before the destructive time of history.

Thus, to go upstream in the river is like a homecoming journey in quest of the lost origin, truth, and authenticity that nurtures history and culture. In fact, Shen, in *Random Sketches*, starts his tour from Taoyuan, a legendary place where Tao Qian's utopia "Peach Blossom Spring" is believed to be located. As a native of this region, Shen's homecoming trip parodies that of Tao Qian's fisherman in "Peach Blossom Spring" in rediscovering this mythical utopia, or, at least discovering a new entry to it (Wang 1992: 254-6). This new entry into the enclosed utopia, as Shen tries to reveal in his tour, is a new point of view that opens a route leading to the Peach Blossom Spring.

The point of view shown in Shen's homeward roaming, as many critics have observed, is that of traditional Chinese landscape painting, a Shen-esque signature that has been widely appreciated.[5] Yet I would go further to argue that what constitutes Shen's "structure of landscape painting" are the *hengjuan* (the "horizontal scroll") and the *lizhou* (the "vertical scroll"), two major formats of scroll painting in traditional Chinese art. A *hengjuan* is usually called *shoujuan* ("handscroll"). A Chinese handscroll, according to Wu Hung's observation, is not a single-framed painting but a multi-framed composition, a "vista-vision plus" format characterized by its particular way of painting, positions of viewing, and the architectural space it bears (Wu 1996). Due to the difficulty of the visual field that cannot cover its entire horizontal dimension, the painter usually paints a handscroll from right to left, exposing one arm's length at a time, thus a handscroll painting is composed of a series of frames, sub-frames, double screens and moving panels, creating a layered surface and space in which individual scenes are revealed. Such a composition demands a particular way of viewing. The viewer unrolls the painting section by section, frame by frame, from right to left, which actually duplicates the process of painting. After viewing, the spectator rolls the painting back to the beginning of the scroll, which works as a re-viewing process in a reverse order (a flashback experience). In contrast, a *lizhou* is a vertical hanging composition in which the scene is constructed by the fore-, middle-, and distant grounds, as well as lower- and higher- viewpoint. In this sense, the time that moves on the *shoujuan* is not a linear progress from the past toward the future, but a backward regression or retroaction, which is basically a form of visuality governed by a logic of "specular nostalgia" from the present to the past.

Due to the movement, speed, and enthusiasm of the viewer, the handscroll painting is manipulated by the register of time. To begin with, the roll/unroll viewing position creates an open-ended narrative, a "stop-and-go" way of reading the scroll. That is, the viewer can halt now and then to view/review some details of scenic interest, thus creating one scene of supreme significance. The viewing position is also distinguished by the vertical and horizontal directionality of the scroll composition: namely, the vertical columns separate individual scenes and punctuate the flow of pictorial images, hence creating a relatively independent spatial unit of picture. However, when the viewer unrolls the scroll on a horizontal plane, each independent unit is finally connected, and a panoramic overall viewing of the painted scenes is obtained.

In a handscroll, the motion of unrolling is governed by the question of "what's next?"—a sense of suspense that postpones the isolated scenes into a continuous pictorial plane, but also encourages the viewer to keep unrolling the painting, seeking to explore the deeper and deeper inside. A vertical scroll, on the other hand, is a spatial construct that asks the question of "what's in the distance?"—a desire that is projected to view the prospect beyond the limits of vision, and a visual impulse that is always directed toward the horizon. In this light, the architectonic space-time of the scroll painting defines two areas—one before it and the other behind it—always exhibiting and concealing at the same time, and always inviting the viewer to explore and contemplate what is hidden and unseen. In this double screen of architectonic space-time, one picture interprets and paraphrases the other, which gives rise to a meta-pictorial poetics, namely, multiple verbal-visual ways of seeing that (re)produce their own scenic interests.

From a sequential point of view, the excursive movement of Shen's homecoming tour along the river exactly corresponds to the composition of a horizontal handscroll painting. Each move and stop creates a separate unity of scene that is self-contained and directed toward itself, and is framed as if in a painting. This individual scene appears like a still life frozen in time to be viewed at a distance, something "out there," that is, immortalized. When the traveler moves from one place to another, these separate units of scenes are endowed with an identity of landmarks that crystallize a preconceived myth or origin, landmarks like ports, villages or *Zhai*, towers, pavilions, cliffs, open markets, boating race, and riverside stilts, which are re-viewed by Shen as "scenic capital" for his West Hunan. Moving continuously along the river leads to the intersection of one scene with another, thus connecting them into a fluent, well-unified scene of handscroll painting. In his "Five Army Officers and a Miner," Shen impresses us by creating such a picturesque landmark from a panoramic point of view:

> Chenqi County lies at the confluence of two rivers. The small stone county town overlooks the water at the foot of a cliff, situated at the mouth of a river so clear that its bed can be seen thirty feet below. Lovely boats of different designs from Hunan and Guizhou ply up and down the river year in year out. On Lime Peak, rain or fine, dark smoke or white smoke always floats above the limekilns. Most of the houses have black tiles and white walls, forming a charming pattern of compact tiles and rafters. Upstream, on the other side of the river and little town, is a triangular mound with a dry dock where boats are repaired or built. A little way downstream a black triangular cliff rises from the water, its base pounded by the swift-flowing Yuan River on the one side and on its other side washed by the Mayang River, so that the rock is intriguingly eroded. Halfway up the cliff stands magnificent Red Hill Temple, with countless buddhas large and small carved in relief on the rock all around it…. The Temple commands a view of the white sails of boats tacking upstream, and stands within earshot of the songs of the boatmen rowing downstream. Further downstream is the long pool A Catty of Silk, so called because legend has it that its source lies so deep

that a whole catty of silk thread has to be unraveled to reach to its bottom. Cliffs of many colors rise on both sides like screen. Day and night there are hundreds of fishing boats on the lake, their silent black cormorants floating near by to catch fish. Small vessels have share and share alike of hazards and beauty spots.

(1934 in Gladys 1982: 80-1)

Such is the typical Shen-esque "sweeping" point of view that creates a "vista-vision plus" idyllic picture as if in a horizontal handscroll painting, section by section, frame by frame, one scene over another scene, juxtaposed and superimposed, and is finally transformed into a unified space by the moving glance. Not to look at one particular scene but to look *over* it, the glance wanders over the view so as to bypass some unpleasant sites of social reality. In other words, the act of "random sketches" gathers and collects those scenes that only please the eyes of the spectator, hence a sketch of fantasy, yearning and nostalgia. Shen's own sketches of the scenery that he views along his path can testify to this mythical rediscovery of his homeland as a spectacle, a moment when his homeland as he wishes to see it becomes a substitute for what he has actually witnessed.

In seeking to guide outsiders to explore the mystic beauty of his home region, Shen's *West Hunan*, from a perspectival vantage point, is composed like the vertical hanging scroll *lizhou* in which the spatial depth of landscape is experienced. Starting from the port city Changde, tracing upward through the rivers of the Yuan, the Chen, and the You, and finally reaching the author's hometown—Fenghuang, the destination of the whole journey— he progressively re-views and surveys the cultural, historical and scenic spots of West Hunan. As luminous distance, fostering a phantasmagoric desire for the homeland, is the goal of the traveler, the perspective that leads the route is always directed vertically up into the horizon, moving towards the interior of the pictorial prospect.[6] It can be argued that what governs Shen's way of seeing along the path of wandering about his "Peach Blossom Spring" is the logic of the "prospective/perspective;" the eye that looks forward is always directed to the distant horizon by crossing the foreground (scenes that appear before his eyes) with a vantage point of a telescopic vision.

If the horizontal movement of a handscroll reveals temporal *anteriority*, something "out there" (such as home, origin, young China), the vertical view in *lizhou* anticipates the spatial transcendence, something "over there" (such as myth, future, nostalgia, modern nation). In Shen's own pictorial sketches during his tour, we can see that his eye is immediately snatched to the height, the mountain peak where a o vast and beautiful horizon can be panoramically viewed by directly crossing the foreground. In "The People of Yuanling" (1938), Shen— after warning the travelers not to forget the dangers if they desire to enjoy the beauty of the landscape which recalls "the splendid painting of the Song Imperial Academy," scenes like "winding streams, clear and shallow, flowing over fine sand between boulders"— immediately directs his eye to the distant mountain top from which a well-ordered idyllic world below is viewed as if it were already over there:

> The peaks vie in splendor, emerald green or deep blue, while in light rain or sunlight their colors defy any description. In the woods below the hills are cottages, as if deliberately set in the best possible positions, and over the brook skirting the woods is a long bridge wreathed in mist. You have only to reach out a hand to pick fragrant herbs and wild flowers. The place seems haunted by the mountain spirits and Lord of the Clouds in the Songs of the Chu.   (1938 in Gladys 1982: 88)

Here the view is seen from above, commanding the eye to reorganize a delightful idyll—cottages, groves, bridges, fragrant flowers, and myth—that is filtered and transcended, i.e., looking *over* the disturbing, confusing, and incoherent foreground. It seems that there is nothing in the middle ground to hinder the viewer from projecting to the open peaceful world that lies in the far-off distance.

Significantly, this anticipatory prospective transforms the backward-looking nostalgia into a forward-looking vision through which the home is reconstructed, and rediscovered, not by means of memory but by a projection of desire. By directing the eye to "what's over there?" behind/beyond the horizon, Shen recreates or reveals a phantasmagoric space of the visionary, the imaginary, and the spectacular. In another part of the same essay, we can see more clearly how Shen manipulates the logic of "prospective/perspective":

> All travelers to Yuanling, even if their curiosity is not satiated, can find compensation in the lovely landscape. The view from the south bank of the hill town on the north bank shows a network of tiles and rafters skirting the hills, with parts of the city wall visible in the higher places. With trees in between this is a striking sight, in no way vulgar. Looking south from the north bank at the riverside hills one sees bamboo groves, woods, temples, pagodas and cottages, all in the most

> appropriate position. Beyond these hills rise peaks like screens, with shifting mist and clouds, jade-green or sapphire-blue. People watching them at dawn or dusk feel convinced that deities are riding dragons over there. (Shen in Gladys: 95)

This ideally reproduced spatial enclosure framed by a pictorial eye is so harmonious that it looks as if it were an eternal moment in a landscape painting. The perspective that views this place from changing positions always revolves around this mythic homeland—bamboo groves, woods, temples, pagodas, cottages, and playful deities, all beautifully and orderly demarcated by boundaries from the outside world. In this light, Shen recreates an iconic image of an agriculturally plentiful native China, a young instead of an old China that already exists beyond the horizon of the Peach Blossom Spring, before its present degradation and decline. So Shen claims that the farther one enters into this bounded center, "the more spectacular the natural landscape will be, and the more indistinct human beings and nature will become" (1938 in 1992: 185). His hometown of Fenghuang is the last homeland of magical spirits and legends in China but might also be a beginning for a new China.

As we have seen above, Shen's homecoming tour, on the one hand, is a temporal retrieval that looks back nostalgically to the idyllic past for its residual origin, and on the other, a vertical projection of the desire that looks forward to the luminous horizon for a future home and a not-yet-present new nation. At this point, Shen's specular nostalgia converges with Lu Xun's futuristic vision of the ideal space as the home for a new nation. What really differentiates them is that Shen never believes nor sees that his native homeland, the native China, is completely lost, while Lu Xun announces firmly that his old home has already died. For Shen, a native homeland which holds the power for national reconstruction still exists, "over there and out there," in his West Hunan, but the issue for him is that an eye or a point of view must be called forth to rediscover, recover and reconstitute it. Through his pilgrimage to his home region, Shen reveals an idyllic utopian border country that seems far off from urban China but is actually a primal and native homeland from which a future China could be remolded. Ever since Shen Congwen's reinscription of his homeland into the cultural narrative of modern China, West Hunan has emerged as a national icon of idyllic landscape that continues to capture the imagiNATION of the Chinese.

Notes

1. As in the myth of return in Greek epic, return always signifies the hero's return from death, darkness and danger to light, life and happiness, as denoted in these Greek roots of " *noos*," "*nes*," "*neo*," or "*nostos*." A heroic homecoming is to return to such homely and familiar state while returning to a strange and unhomely state of existence is what I call anti-heroic homecoming. For the mythic root of "return" in Greek epic, see Douglas Frame's *The Myth of Return in Early Greek Epic* (1978).

2. The "moral cowardice" of the intellectual narrator in the story lies in his inability of breaking "the high invisible wall" set up between him and the adult Runtu and his avoidance of pointing a way out for the victim. The narrator never asks the question of "Can Runtu be saved?" or "what can I do for this social victim?" Despite his sympathy for his harsh situation, he cannot even speak to him, nor to speak for him. As an onlooker, the narrator is tongue-tied and speechless when confronting his suffering country folk face to face. What he is pondering in his mind after witnessing this catastrophe is to flee away from his cannibalistic and vampirist old home so that he can at least save himself from being destroyed like Runtu. To escape from his native home rather than to commit himself to transform its harsh reality, as some scholars of Lu Xun have already pointed out, actually attests to the complicity of the Chinese intellectual with the cannibalistic old society (Anderson 1990; Qian 1991). In Fan's words, the massive "victorious escapade" of modern Chinese intellectuals from their rural home exactly reflects the failure of the enlightenment project spearheaded by modern intellectuals. That is why Lu Xun intends to exclude the intellectual narrator from the future new home.

3. Shen recalls many times later the influence of Lu Xun's native-soil fictions on his writings. For example, in one case, he wrote: "With the inauguration of Lu Xun, fictions with subject matter dealing with the memories of the countryside are gaining popularity among the readers. This gives my early pieces strong courage and confidence" (1982, 11: 69). And he comments on Lu Xun's works as "mixed with beauty of a little bit decadence, a little bit satire, and a little bit fantasy" (1982, 11: 166), which "make people feel sad and deplorable, hence a objective depiction of all about China's small towns" (173).

4. Shen later admits that he is strongly inspired by Ivan Turgenev's *A Hunter's Sketches*. "By using the method Turgenev wrote his hunter's diary," Shen wrote, " I combine travelogues with prose and fictional

stories into one unity so as to foreground the people and things against the bright and beautiful geographical stories into one unity so as to foreground the people and things against the bright and beautiful geographical background, making everything bear the flavor of 'raw material'" (1942: 27).

5.   See Jeffrey C. Kinkley (1987); Lin Yu (1985); Hua-Ling Nieh (1972) and Wong Yoon Yah (1998). Particularly Wong Yoon Yah, by examining three aspects of Chinese landscape painting —panoramic perspective, composition of landscape and method of expression—has discerned what he terms "the structure of Chinese landscape painting" in Shen Congwen's depiction of his rural home region (1998: 109-12).

6.   John Barrell and Peter Bishop's method of analyzing the position and point of view in representation of landscape has helped my formulation of visual reading of Shen Congwen's works here. See Barrell (1972) and Bishop (1995).

Works Cited

Anderson, Marston. *The Limits of Realism: Chinese Fiction in the Revolutionary Period*. Berkeley: University of California Press, 1990.

Chen Pinyuan. *A History of the Twentieth-Century Chinese Fiction*. Vol. I. Beijing: Peking University Press, 1989.

Fang Boqun. *A New Approach to Lu Xun's Fictions*. Beijing: Renming wenxue chubanche, 1986.

Feuerwerker, Yi-tsi Mei. *Ideology, Power, Text: Self-Representation and the Peasant "Other" in Modern Chinese Literature*. Stanford: Stanford University Press, 1998.

Frame, Douglas. *The Myth of Return in Early Greek Epic*. New Haven: Yale University Press, 1978.

Hsia, C. T. *A History of Modern Chinese Fiction, 1917-1957*. New Haven/London: Yale University Press, 1961.

Hua-Ling Nieh. *Shen Ts'ung-wen*. New York: Twayne Publishers, 1972.

Jameson, Fredric. *The Geopolitical Aesthetic: Cinema and Space in the World System*. Bloomington/Indianapolis: Indiana University Press, 1995.

---. *Postmodernism Or, the Cultural Logic of Late Capitalism*. Durham: Duke University Press, 1991.

Kinkley, Jeffrey. *The Odyssey of Shen Congwen*. Stanford: Stanford University Press, 1987.

Lee, Leo Ou-fan. "The Solitary Traveler: Images of the Self in Modern Chinese Literature." In *Expressions of Self in Chinese Literature*. Ed. Robert Hegal and Richard Hessley. New York: Columbia University Press, 1985.

Lin, Yu. *From the Border Town to the World: A Study of Shen Congwen as a Literary Writer*. Beijing: Joint Publishing House, 1985.

Lu, Tonglin. *Misogyny, Cultural Nihilism and Oppositional Politics: Contemporary Chinese Experimental Fiction*. Stanford: Stanford University Press, 1995.

Lu, Xun. "My Old Home." First prt. 1921. Rpt. in *The Complete Works of Lu Xun*. Vol. I. Beijing: Renming wenyue chubanshe, 1981. English trans. in *The Complete Stories of Lu Xun*. Trans. Yang Xiangyi and Gladys Yang. Bloomington: Indiana   University Press, 1981.

Shen, Congwen. *Collections of Shen Congwen*. Vol. IX. Hong Kong: Joint Publishing House, 1982.

---. "Preface to *The Early Novels of Congwen*." First prt.1936. Rpt. Changsha: Yuelu shushe, 1992. 27-36.

---. *Random Sketches on a Trip to Hunan*. First prt.1934. Rpt. Hong Kong: Wei Tung Book, 1976.

---. *Recollections of West Hunan*. Trans. Gladys Yang. Beijing: Panda Books, 1982.

---. *The Border Town*. First prt. 1934. Trans.

---. *West Hunan* First prt. 1938. Rpt. Changsha: Yuelu shushe, 1992.

---. "Xinhuiyou chengdi NO.23—Yi shoushi de tuolen." In YiShiBo. Sept. 20, 1947. Cited in Lin Yu: *From the Border Town to the World: A Study of Shen Congwen a Literary Writer*. Beijing: Joint Publishers, 1985.

Shi, Tuo. "A Paradise Lost" First prt. 1937. Rpt. in *Selection of Shi Tuo's Prose*. Ed. Fan Peisong. Tinjing: Baihua wenyi chubanshe, 1992.

---. "Preface to *The Orchard Town*." Shanghai: Shanghai wenyi chubanshe, 1958.

Wang, David Der-wei. *Fictional Realism in Twentieth-Century China: Mao Dun, Lao She, Shen Congwen*. New York: Columbia University Press, 1992.

---, ed. *From May Fourth to June Fourth: Fiction and Film in Twentieth-Century China*. Cambridge, Mass.: Harvard University Press, 1993.

Wong, Yoon Yah. *A New Approach to Lu Xun*. Shanghai: Xueling chubanshe, 1993.

---. *A New Approach to the Fictions and Fictional Theories of Shen Congwen*. Taipei: Wenshizhe chubanshe, 1998.

Wu, Hung. *The Double Screen: Medium and Representation in Chinese Painting*. Chicago: The University of Chicago Press, 1996.

Xu, Jie. *Lectures on Lu Xun's Fictions*. Xian: Shanxi renming chubanshe, 1981.

Zhang, Yingjin. *The City in Modern Chinese Literature and Film: Configurations of Space, Time and Gender*. Stanford: Stanford University Press, 1996.

Asian Culture and Urbanism: Meanings and Experiences of the Evolving Built Environment

Ian Morley

This paper explores urban culture and globalization in Asia during the past twenty or so years. It examines how Asian cities have become the seats of the continent's economic rise, and the locales where cultural growth has been most explicitly manifest. Yet whilst much literature on Asian culture and cities has ventured to explain the development of the Asian metropolis and life within it through means of the manifestation of the global economic system, the complexity of Asia's culture and urbanism makes explaining the evolution, role, and function of cultural traits problematic. Rejecting the common argument that imported templates of Western economics and urban development are 'evidence' of Asia's cultural expansion this work instead contends that any explication of Asia's evolutionary culture must unravel the interplay of global *and* local forces within its cities. As such this work adopts a diachronic approach thereby appreciating the plurality of local urban-based factors alongside contemporary changes so as to explicate the form and meaning of the modern Asian city as expressed in contemporary architecture and urban design.

Introduction: The Form of Urban Environments and Culture

Urban development is shaped by a veritable plethora of different factors, and the nature of the built environment articulates the disposition and vitality of numerous dynamics operating within society. Accordingly, the physical form of cities reveals their history, and likewise illustrates contemporary economic, political, cultural, legal, and artistic questions. In this context to examine the environmental character of urban places allows for a means to detect and determine the urban environment as a cultural conduit that speaks of, perhaps most significantly, the question of modernity and the advancement of what is often identified as 'civilization.'

In taking into account the associations and meanings of urban environments to the development of civilization, two matters must be noted: the physical structure of the environment has to be understood to be an actual/built fact; buildings and spaces possess cultural symbolism. In this framework it is vital to recognize that buildings and urban spaces convey ideas and values people in a society hold. As such the design of urban environments expresses people's thoughts, ideas, and ideals. As Czepczynski

(2010: 1) has indicated, the design of the urban environment discloses how people conceptualize and signify themselves to the world. Consequently the urban environment bestows a means to view and understand people, and so grasp how they interact with the world around them. Simply put, the built environment acts as a window to observe the culture of a particular place (Hendrix, 2012: 208). Buildings thus are artistic instruments whose form represents people in particular societies; they also represent the world around those people, and they represent their relationship to it. Yet the association people have with their cities is both abstract and material: it is based on the physical/actual form of the built environment *and* symbolic elements contained within the cityscape. In this context the urban environment acquires a value far beyond the materials from which it is actually constructed from, i.e. bricks, stone, glass, etc.

Modernity and its Impacts: Localism and Globalism

The rise of modernity has profoundly affected the nature of cities, and the cultures found within them. This is especially pertinent when examining settlements in Southeast (SE) Asia and East (E) Asia. By way of example, during the past twenty or so years, cities in SE and E Asia have substantially extended their urban sprawls, increased their vertical scales, and have enlarged the variety of architectural forms found within them. As an outcome of this situation, Asian metropolises have taken an appearance different to what they hitherto had with, in this milieu, their recently constructed buildings being perceived to possess a lack of reference to local cultural heritage. In other words with the assumption that modernization as expressed in architecture pays little respect to local aesthetic traditions, the sense of place that once so uniquely defined one Asian city from the other is thought to be eroded and is replaced. Instead Asian cities as defined by glass-box skyscrapers, grand boulevards, opulent hotels, and high-end shopping centers (Evers and Korff, 2000: 2) are viewed to acquire a character evident in many other parts of the world (Bishop, Philips, and Yeo, 2003: 10). But whilst this scenario might be pessimistically interpreted as occurring at the detriment to local culture matters such as globalization, urbanization, and broad social changes during the past couple of decades have not necessarily weakened local cultures. More to the point they have allowed cities to implement new architectural articulations. To illustrate this point during the past twenty or so years Asia has challenged the skyscraper hegemony of the United States (US): a monopoly that began in the late-1800s in cities such as Chicago and New York. With Asia now the new home of the skyscraper, as this paper shall subsequently explain, the growing vertical definition of Asian cities must be seen as being fundamental to Asian nations' place in the 'modern global community'.

A number of authors, including Edmund Bacon (1976) and Alexander Cuthbert (2006), have noted that civilizations represent themselves in the design of their cities. With people characterizing themselves *in* and *through* design processes that shape the urban environments in which they live and work, to thus understand people and their cultures is to understand their cities, and vice versa. As design is a function of culture, and it is not just an artistic, quantitative or technical construction process (Kaspirin, 2011: 11), changes to the built form of cities and urban culture have a reciprocal relationship. In SE and E Asia during the past twenty years or so, cities have been in a process of transformation as a result of the migration of people from the countryside, changes in governmental attitudes towards urban land development, the emergence of master planning and mega-projects, plus economic developments such as the rise of the globalized economy. Many scholars, including Malcolm McKinnon (2011), have remarked upon globalization's impact on Asian settlements. To offer an example of its influence, it must be noted that Asian governments at the both municipal and national level have embraced the rhetoric of globalization and, significantly, have also acted upon it. In China, to offer an example, by 2005 more than 180 cities described themselves as 'international metropolises', i.e. places operating within the global economy (Atkinson, 2007: 31). Such is the proximity of globalization with the urbanizing of large cities in Asia that they are now the conduits through which flows of local, regional, national, and international capital and services occur. Notably, this economic reality has reshaped the face of Asia's cities although in urban design terms, as already mentioned, it is often associated with a loss of place, identity, and native character (Elsheshtawy, 2004: 6).

The emergence of globalization during the 1990s has led to two generic societal developments in Asia: political, economic, and social activity becoming world-wide in scope; intensification in the interaction and interconnectedness of societies and states. Whilst conceptually globalization is not new (World Bank, 2002: 16), the nature of contemporary globalization as it pertains to technology, finance, information dissemination, and decision making (Schwab, 2005: 27) has profoundly affected the nature of Asian societies. With its emphasis on knowledge and innovation for managing and controlling the 'modern economies' (Komninos, 2008: 8), globalization has instigated a reshaping and reorganization of various activities within cities so that they have become the engines of economic development *and* the centers of social transformation, political change, and cultural innovation (Knox, 2011: 15). At the same time, globalization has allowed citizens as well as the business community and politicians to be more conscious of the potential of international processes to develop local society. As a phenomenon engaging with economic, political, social, cultural, and urban environmental contexts, globalization has led to the manifestation of five factors that have shaped contemporary city designing (Olds: 2001: 29):

1. The restructuring of the international finance system.
2. The expansion of the property market.
3. The rise of transnational corporations.
4. New power relations, interactions, and symbolism.
5. The growth, and implementation, of master plans and mega-projects.

As Elsheshtawy (2004: 6) has noted the architectural image of the modern Asian city implies no reference to local culture or identity. However as Jane Jacobs has explicated globalization per se does not necessarily lead to a loss of identity or heritage. It rather reconstitutes and revalidates issues of place and locality. Therefore whilst urban development since the 1990s has been associated with an image that insinuates modernity forges cities of the same appearance, in actuality urbanism under globalization has been an architectural and spatial dynamic in which the distinct nature of local cultures ventures to intercede forces of global hegemony. So, in order to appreciate more completely the contemporary Asian metropolis, many of which describe themselves as being a symbiosis of tradition and modernity (Evers and Korff, 2000: 5), two important actions must be undertaken: identifying physical urban changes that have taken place *within* cities since the 1990s; recognizing that those identifiable changes are hybrids, a result of a fusing of traditions with modern ideas, i.e. the uniting of local with national and international energies. However, significantly, even though between about 1950 and the early-2000s the percentage of urban dwellers in SE and E Asian leapt from about 15% to 50% (United Nations, *World Urbanization Prospects*), the proportion of people who live in urban locales varies greatly from nation to nation, as table 1 demonstrates.

Country	Percentage of the Total Population Residing in Urban Places (in 2009)
Burma	33.6
Cambodia	20.1
China	47.0
Indonesia	44.3

Malaysia	72.2
The Philippines	48.9
Vietnam	30.4

Table 1. The percentage of people in selected SE and E Asian nations who are urban dwellers (source: United Nations, 2009).

With the rise of urban growth in SE and E Asia – a rise in scale and velocity - a number of impacts on the environment and culture have become apparent. These impacts have had both positive and negative effects on people, and how they live (UN Habitat, 2008: 90). Urbanization, if examined in a positive manner, has greatly aided the economic maturation of many nations. It has contributed to the reduction of long standing socioeconomic predicaments, e.g. poverty and slum housing. Moreover municipal and national governments in some countries, e.g. China and Vietnam, have utilized urbanization as being socially beneficial so as to tackle longstanding social problems. In broad terms, the impact of urban development in SE and E Asia may be listed as follows:

- A rise in the number of cities. This is a consequence of settlements growing in spatial and demographic size, *and* administrative changes. In China administrative rulings have permitted the number of cities to rise from less than 200 in 1978 to over 660 by 2000 (Yu, 2004: 211).
- The emergence of the megacity. With rapid population growth, some cities now have populations in excess of ten million people. Another significant point: with the arrival of migrants from provincial locales, there has been an increase in intra-urban heterogeneity.
- A shift in the status of cities, with some places labeling themselves as 'international cities' as a result of their engagement with the global economic system. Many Asian cities no longer view/define themselves within a national context.
- As cities have grown in demographic stature, so too has been their contribution to the national economy. Bangkok, to offer one example, now comprises about 40% of the economy of Thailand. The wealth of the urban-based economy has granted an increase in the incomes of the poorest, has led to the improvement in the diet of those once living below the poverty line, and the granting of more life opportunities. In the

words of McCulloch (2002: 6) the process of urban development in Asia has been accompanied by general increases in living standards that were once unimaginable.

- The redevelopment of central sites has led to the reorganization of land uses, the reconfiguration of urban space, and the rejection of traditional ways of building. With the application of modern urban planning ideas land uses have changed from multi to single function. Likewise buildings now tend to be built from materials such as steel, concrete, titanium, and glass rather than traditional masonry such as brick and stone.

Modernity: Continuity and Discontinuity in Guangzhou, Taipei and Kuala Lumpur

Cities are complicated entities. They are difficult to understand, and so challenging to explain. Comprehending cities (in Asia), where historic and contemporary local, regional, national and international influences are so often intertwined, is no easy matter. With regard to urban design and urban culture, however, two fundamental factors can quickly be grasped: 1) the growing importance of cities as sites of cultural and economic transformation, and 2) the physical form of cities that act as physical markers both of their nation's status of their economic and cultural position. As such metropolitan expansion has become integral to the Asian understanding of national development. The value of cities to societal progress is not to be underestimated. Urban growth and modern design, amongst other things, has been perceived to offer pragmatic advantages to societies with aspirations to better themselves. Urbanization thus lends a platform from which to aid the capture of globalized economic forces, fortify links with other economies – a prerequisite for economic 'take off' – and impart new opportunities for national image building. More succinctly put, cities have become centers of change *and* for promoting change. They have evolved into locales with distinct functions: to mobilize entrepreneurs, to organize labor, distribute finished products, and allow for financial service activity; to bring together decision-making machinery from public and private sectors; to generate knowledge capital, and innovation; to help elevate people's quality of life (Knox, 2011: 16). In other words, cities have been managed and developed to ensure economic, social, and cultural matters achieve their highest form, and in such an intellectual framework to encourage urbanization is to stimulate the evolution of society. In the contemporary world the viewpoint has arisen within Asian culture that to be civilized and modern essentially means to be city-centered. Urbanity is an allied impulse to forge a 'better' world, a place that contrasts with what has existed before. Hence cities are fundamental to *paradigmatic modernity*, the type of modernization that emphasizes differences between the present and the past (Skirbekk, 2011: 7).

In coming to terms with the evolutionary nature of urban places and culture in Asia, especially since the 1990s, economic matters cannot be overlooked. Economic transition has been a major element in the transformation of Asian society. For instance, the need to renew urban land – an acknowledgement of the unsuitability of old city districts for stimulating local economic growth and 'capturing' the globalized economy – has led throughout SE and E Asia to the state-approved demolition of city districts, and the creation of robust alliances between municipal governments and entrepreneurs (Parker, 2011: 106). As a consequence of the pulling down and rebuilding of urban districts, amongst other things, a new property market has been established. In this new market, the vertical size of new buildings greatly exceeds those that previously existed, the primary use of the land differs from what it once was: for instance, districts of houses become transformed into modern business quarters. Equally notable is how this transformation has established new office buildings and new luxury high-rise residential units as citadels of economic expansion and affluence, as well as functional and symbolic manifestations of the emergence of the modern/global city (Olds, 2001: 30). With luxury housing, for example, being too expensive for many people to buy—clearly, paradigmatic modernity works in the realms of including certain social groups at the cost of excluding others—and with property prices skyrocketing, a decline in many people's well-being arises. As such, many city governments have been forced to implement policies to ensure property bubbles do not form, e.g. in Shanghai, so that housing remains allegedly 'affordable' to the masses.

As much as negative situations can arise from economic and cultural change, it would be erroneous to label land development under globalization as being inherently negative. After all, a major part of the demolition and rebuilding of cities has been the establishment of new cultural institutions; in some cities, cultural development has been consciously used to promote the economic potential and social value of the settlement (Cochrane, 2007: 104), and been utilized too to improve the somewhat unsophisticated image of particular places. Cultural growth can thus grant a settlement a means to reimage itself through the creation of new landmark buildings and institutions that put the settlement at the forefront of domestic societal advancement on the one hand, and put the city on the world map on the other. To offer an example, Guangzhou in China once had a blue collar reputation and an image lacking visual elegance, yet has been 'uplifted' in the past ten or so years by municipal policies. As a result, not only have massive office towers been built, e.g. the CITIC Plaza (1283 feet high) and International Finance Center (1440 feet tall), but major civic edifices have also been constructed, e.g., Guangzhou Library, Children's Palace, Guangdong Museum, and Guangzhou Opera House. Major international expos and sporting events have also being held in the city. Collectively these buildings and events have attracted new capital to the city, and likewise regenerated the settlement into a place of great cultural significance, a situation aided by municipality promoting Guangzhou with what might be labeled *selective place information*.

Designed by the internationally renowned architect Zaha Hadid, the Opera House in Guangzhou (opened 2010, and costing approximately US$200 million) has been described as possessing a form that is "highly theatrical" (Glancy, 2011). Boosting the city's cultural ambiance, and likewise its status as an 'international city', Hadid's building explicitly expresses the value and role of cultural development to the process of creating the modern Asian metropolis. In this setting the amount of what might be labeled 'countable culture', evident for instance in the number of cultural facilities a city has as well as in the verticality of the skyline, visibly indicates local society's affluence, status, and alliance with modernity (Morley, 2009: 68). Hence the more 'modern culture' a city has that can be seen and so counted, and with it consumed by its citizens, the wealthier the city is, and the more modern the city is perceived to be. Likewise the more developed the local economy is within the globalised economic network, and the greater the contribution the city is recognized as making to the promotion of its nation's development. Thus modern architecture can valorize a city as a site for the production *and* consumption of 'modernity'.

Figure 1. Foreground: The Opera House, and (in the background) the 103-floor International Finance Center, Guangzhou (source: Ian Morley).

As gainful as economic determinism and cultural commodification may be, it has nonetheless led to numerous tensions. One such conflict in bringing the Asian city to its modernistic potential is the narrative of loss articulated by the destruction of people's homes: to create a modern city requires the razing/removal of the existing one. Consequently countless buildings throughout SE and E Asia have been destroyed. Communities have been displaced and architectural heritage also destroyed. There are reasons as to why demolition has been so prevalent, e.g. in cultural-political terms old buildings do not fit into the urban imagery the elites of Asian society want to forge (Hulshof and Roggeveen, 2011: 151), and aged buildings do not contribute to the modern/global economy in a way that new industrial estates and office buildings can. Against such a backdrop the redevelopment of sites and the adoption of the real estate development model with its aim for rapidity and profitability (Genard, 2008: 95) is deemed imperative to the construction of the 'modern city'.

With the building of high-rise buildings for housing and skyscrapers for multinational corporations the 'new city' visually displays no apparent reference to what it previously was. Whereas the 'old city' prominently displayed a sense of place based on the distinctiveness of its local buildings and local culture, the 'new city' in contrast offers an appearance, so it seems, with an international rather than a localized face. Notably in this visual framework built symbols, such as high-rise buildings and high-tech industrial estates, project the economic competitiveness and creativity of a given place. With its distinct visualization that contrasts to the 'old city,' the modern Asian city is perceived by many westerners as being physical evidence of Asia's aspiration to 'catch up' with the West. But, as this paper now shows, this greatly miscalculates Asian culture and the complexity of architectural and urban imagery. To begin with the development of Asian cities with its enhanced verticality is based upon forging a deliberate picture through the application of architecture: a picture that is relevant to Asian nations *and* the West. Furthermore the implementation of particular architectural forms helps turn Asian cities into recognizable economic brands. In this milieu the rising cityscape, with landmark high-rise buildings within it, i.e. buildings of great contemporary economic and cultural significance, become iconic. As shall now be shown with reference to Taipei one single building has come to define the city, and the national identity of Taiwan.

In the milieu of Asia's modernization, a tall building can acquire great symbolic value. In the case of the Taipei 101 Tower it is an edifice that reflects, highlights, and defines many of the contemporary social, cultural, political, and economic issues in Taiwan. Erected at a time when President Chen Shui-bian was endorsing the transformation of Taiwan into a modern nation with its own (non-Mainland Chinese) identity, the construction of the Taipei 101 Tower was integral to establishing a modern state of existence that was, by definition, also inherently Taiwanese.

Completed in 2004 to a height of 508 meters - a height that made the building the world's tallest at that time - and to a cost of more than US$1.5 billion, the Taipei 101 Tower (see figure 2) quickly became the most recognizable landmark in Taipei. Composed as a piece of contextualist architecture—that is to say, the new edifice was designed to relate to what already is or has been (Ibelings, 1998: 18)—Taipei 101 Tower was built not so that Taipei could economically or culturally 'catch up' with cities in the West, but rather so that it could take a lead over rival cities in SE and E Asia. Thus, by having an economic and cultural advantage over other cities in the region, and so by perceiving itself as superior to its competitors, Taipei would, it was thought, be seen and read as *the* economic metropolis on the Asian side of the Asia-Pacific Rim. As Kusno (2000) has revealed, comparison is often an engine to realize change. To grasp this matter in relation to Taipei attention must be put on the Xinyi district, an area developed as 'Taipei's Manhattan' (Chen, 2006: 150). In this part of the city architecture and urban design extended beyond its usual parameters in Taiwan: making city life more convenient, comfortable, healthy, and safe (Sun and Liu, 2005).

Figure 2. The Taipei 101 Tower (source: Ian Morley)

In appreciating the form and meaning of the Xinyi district, and the Taipei 101 Tower, it must not be neglected that in SE and E Asia the metropolis is a symbol of nationhood. To understand how and why this meaning has arisen it is worth noting the urban history of Asia. Before the 1990s, the development of cities in many SE and E Asian nations was tied to European colonization, and with the fall of colonial rule in the second half of the 1900s, the concept of a fresh start was symbolically very powerful to nations such as Burma, Cambodia, Indonesia, Malaysia, the Philippines, Singapore, and Vietnam. To physically and symbolically redefine the built form of cities, particularly capital cities so that they could exhibit the vigor of local society and the nature of native culture, was a potent tool in enforcing a post-colonial agenda, so that the domestic audience *and* the world at large could see 'progress'. Whilst Taiwan did not emerge from the shadow of colonialism in the late-1900s, it did nonetheless come out of another shadow: that of mainland China. The rise of nationalist politics by the 1990s led to the emergence of the view that Taiwan was a nation-state in its own right and in this milieu the Taipei 101 Tower would demonstrate the significance as Taipei in the Asia-Pacific economic network but moreover show that Taiwan, as a nation, had not only 'arrived' but was indeed, in economic terms, an Asian leader.

In design terms, the Taipei 101 Tower articulates elements of local culture. Utilizing the best of technology from Asia and the West, thereby establishing a technological dialogue between Western and Oriental culture, the Taipei 101 Tower was designed to directly speak to people living on the island of Taiwan. Reaching to a height that no building had ever before achieved the Taipei 101 Tower would visually articulate the ambition of Taiwan as an advanced society because, in the words of the building's architect, CY Lee, each country has its own language when it comes to architecture (Binder, 2008: 30). Notwithstanding the overall allusion of the Taipei 101 Tower to a piece of bamboo, which grants an ever-upward, strong, and flexible impression of the building, the adornment of distinctive artistic elements help produce a piece of architecture like no other, i.e. like *something that can only be made in Taiwan*. The outside of the building reveals this: metal sculptures of ruyis, dragons, and coins denoting luck, happiness, abundance, and success (for Taipei and Taiwan). As a building, to look at the Taipei 101 Tower is thus drenched in denotative features for Taiwanese people to read so that they can connect their traditions and societal modernization with the uniqueness of their society, and *their sense of place in the modern world*. In this sense *gradualistic modernity* (Skirbekk, 2011: 7) is implemented. At the same time, the Taipei 101 Tower is a building to look *out from*: the observation deck on the 88th floor enables local citizens to see their capital city and so their nation in a 'new way'. By doing this and so seeing the vast sprawl of Taipei Taiwan's economic significance and cultural advancement is insinuated. Furthermore due to the politics of Taiwan at the time the building was opened nationalistic messages are also received. For example, so that people could see Taiwan as both a modern *and* independent nation it was envisaged that the Taipei 101 Tower's observation deck would perform three roles: look down on Taipei's sprawl, thereby appreciating its scale as the capital city; see the Taipei Basin, an environment formed with rivers and mountains, which enables people to see the beauty, quality, and exceptionality of Taiwan's natural setting; look beyond Taipei's bounds so that physically and figuratively people could see that Taiwan is not as small a place as it might be imagined, and so an appreciation of Taiwan, its geology, cultural heritage, and ultimately its place in the world can be grasped. As such Taipei can rightfully take a seat in the modern world. In view of this Taipei becomes a place of *performance* too: a city providing services at the forefront of contemporary civilization in light of its relationship to people, corporations, and organizations in the global economy (Kaufmann, Léautier and Mastruzzo, 2006: 28-9).

Figure 3. Left: The observation deck of the Taipei 101 Tower, and (right) the view north-west from the aforementioned observation deck towards Yangmingshan (source: Ian Morley).

The mechanisms between architecture, modernity and globalization are not always immediately comprehensible. As the example of the Taipei 101 Tower has shown, and as Lu notes (2012: 62), architectural modernity directs and promotes nations' sense of self. Modern architecture thus is not only a symbol of modernity, but it is also a conduit to project nationhood and receive international recognition, and notwithstanding the perception in the West that Asian metropolises as an effect of modernity look the same vernacular building traditions are still an integral part of architectural agendas in SE and E Asia. Neo-traditionalism is popular because of governmental attitudes to preserve cultural heritage, encourage a sense of nationhood, and maintain 'native-ness'. The aesthetics of place – local, specific, rooted (Soon and Goh, 2003: 16) – have a strong voice and this can be seen not only in Taipei but, for instance, in Kuala Lumpur, Malaysia too. The Petronas Towers, the tallest buildings in the city, were designed in such a manner in order to convey a distinct Asian identity, and to articulate the Malay way of life as a consequence of the building's aesthetic, one emanating from the distinct national culture of Malaysia.

Designed by Cesar Pelli, and opened in 1998 to a height of 452 meters (1,483 feet), the Petronas Towers were central to the modernization of the Malaysian economy and the redefinition of the country's image away from (British) colonialism. The towers stand as a structural and symbolic statement of what Malaysia had achieved by the 1990s: that is, an advanced society engaging with a global economy. Through their huge scale, the super-tall towers stand as proclamations of the advancement of Malaysia, an antithesis to how Malay society once was and saw itself to be. Super-talls, designed with reference to local cultural traits, the Petronas Towers have a plan that references the eight-pointed star of Muslim faith, a clear citation of Malaysia's cultural heritage, and makes the statement that this society, irrespective of its past, demographic size, or economic image, has the technology, capital, motivation, and resolve, both literally and metaphorically, not just to join the giants of world commerce, but to lead them.

Figure 4. The Petronas Towers, Kuala Lumpur (source: Ian Morley).

The development of the world's tallest buildings, as previously indicated, has shifted since the 1990s from the US to SE and E Asia. There are many reasons for this. First, as many regions in Asia are economically expanding new office buildings are required for international businesses. Second, they have been utilized, as already discussed, to promote Asian nations at a global level, because super-tall buildings of 300 meters or more in height, can express not only economic development but other symbolic messages. Indeed, super-tall edifices are beacons of symbolism. As Höweler (2003: 8) remarks, the scale and visual prominence of skyscrapers mean that they, more than any other building type, have the capacity to capture the public imagination. Ultimately, the skyscraper, along with new cultural institutions and their sometimes irregularly-shaped elevations, define the image of the modern Asian metropolis. They exemplify both urbanity *and* modernity, and the presence of such building types in Asian cities intersects issues of finance, real estate, social aspirations, and cultural sensibilities. As architecture and urban design is the manifestation of social, economic, technical, and artistic developments in a society at a given time (Evers and Korff, 2000: 18), it is erroneous to label modernism in Asia as simply modernity deriving from Westernization and 'supercapitalism', an economic state dominated by transnational corporations that operate at the expense of community values and local cultures (Knox, 2011: 52). As this work has implied it is impossible to comprehend the nature of Asia's newest corporate and public edifices, and the evolution of the continent's metropolises, without appreciating their relationship with 'old' urban places, i.e. the history, culture, and aesthetics. Although the process of renewing Asian cities has led to much cultural heritage destruction the 'new Asian city' maintains a sense of heritage through its newly formed 'historicized environment', that is to say newly constructed architectural features that relate to the nation's past. This re-use of historic traditions and elements of culture should not be taken lightly because architectural heritage is a fundamental component of what the modern city is.

Conclusion: The Intersection of the Old and the New, the Local and the International

Ultimately, modern architecture has visually encapsulated the urban transformation of Asia in recent decades, and has acquired positive meaning as a spectacle of the modern and the transformation of societies to a 'better world'. Architecture's presence, by showing the contrast between the 'new city' and the 'old world' and its problems, bolsters the process of advertising advancement, and at the same time it expresses an identity, one that is read locally *and* internationally. While much has been said of city designing in Asia, architectural and urban imagery is, as this article has emphasized, a vital element in understanding the evolving nature of Asian cities and their cultures since the 1990s. Most significantly, whereas the past and cultural references to it have been labeled during the age of globalization as backward in the West – modernism emerging in and through the destruction and deconstruction of all foundations (Heller, 2011: 141), in many cities in Asia cultural heritage has been embraced as part of modernization and modernity. Informed by a distinct understanding of the modern, in the past twenty or so years Asian architecture reveals how the Western notion of global modernity as a concept rooted in a plurality is flawed. Modern buildings in Asia reveal features distinct to their societies, and with their strong sense of place they explicitly reveal in many instances how they can only be borne from the societies in which they are found. The circumstances in Taiwanese society, as a case in point, means the Taipei 101 Tower could not have been built in the manner it is in Singapore, London, or New York, and likewise the Petronas Towers could not have been constructed in Paris, Tokyo, Washington DC or Taipei.

The 2004 edition of UN Habitat's *State of the World Cities* states that to speak of globalization risks making a double error as the phrase suggests cities have never before experienced global trade, and insinuates that cities belong to a single urban culture (2005: 10). Indeed, as this work has highlighted, in relation to parts of SE Asia with regards to architectural practice borne under globalization no universal aesthetic exists, and whilst the West may have rejected traditional architectural traits such a situation is not necessarily obvious to see in Asia. Rather modern architectural thought in Asia reveals a different kind of knowledge/grasp of modernity, one which shows a sophisticated familiarity with the regional vernaculars and cultural histories. Significantly, this situation offers an epistemological challenge to the West's grasp of modernity, in that it produces buildings and cityscapes of a similar form, a state of affairs based on the assumption, for example, that globalization issues forth symbolic forces that are directed *outside-in*: that is to say, from outside a particular nation's bounds which, due to their strength, then erodes both local cultures and their artistic expressions. As this paper has emphasiszed, modernist urbanism in SE and E Asia can involve a dual process: the application of forces from outside-in and inside-out, which manufacture thereby a distinct design that is both sincere and sensitive to local history, traditions, and culture. This approach rejects the concept of globalization as one bringing forth a universal type of architecture/civilization, or as one that rejects any link to history and historic design traditions. It thus rejects too the notion of placelessness, because urbanism carried out in the context of globalization has permitted a new abstraction as to how Asian people see themselves, their cities, their nations, and their place in the contemporary world, as well as its pathway of 'progress'. What is also apparent is that architectural compositions in Asia have enacted in structural forms, perceptions, concepts, social relations, and cultural values: ones that in the West, for various reasons, have been subordinated to modernist ideology. The translation of conceptual matters into aesthetic devices in Asia have thus produced a two-way conveyance unseen in the West between the allegorical and the real, one in which reason, self-consciousness, and ultimately 'advancement' have been expressed in the architectural design of prominent buildings.

Writing Spaces: Travel, Global Cities and Landscapes
Editors: I-Chun Wang, Mary Theis, and Christopher Larkosh

Works Cited

Atkinson, Simon. "A Revised Framework for the Design of Chinese Cities." *Proceedings of the Third International Symposium on Urban Development and Land Policy in China*. Hangzhou: Lincoln Land Institute, 2007. 31-42.

Bacon, Edmund N. *The Design of Cities*. New York: Penguin Books, 1976.

Binder, Georges. *Taipei 101*. Mulgrave: The Images Publishing Group Limited, 2008.

Bishop, Ryan, Philips, John, and Yeo, Wei-Wei. "Perpetuating Cities: Excepting Globalization and the Southeast Asia Supplement", Eds. Bishop, Ryan, Philips, John, and Yeo, Wei-Wei. *Postcolonial Urbanism: Southeast Asian Cities and Global Processes*. New York: Routledge, 2003. 1-36.

Chen, Nancy. "New Configuration in Taipei." Eds. Wu, Fulong ed. *Globalization and the Chinese City*. Abingdon: Routledge, 2006. 147-64.

Cochrane, Allan. *Understanding Urban Policy*. Oxford: Blackwell, 2007.

Cuthbert, Alexander R. *The Form of Cities*. Oxford: Blackwell, 2006.

Czepczynski, Mariusz ."Representations and Images of Recent History." Eds. Kleims, Alfrun and Dmitrieva, Marina. *The Post-Socialist City*. Berlin: Jovis Verlag, 2010. 1-14.

Elsheshtawy, Yasser. "The Middle Easetrn City: Moving Beyond the Narrative of Loss.", Elsheshtawy, Yasser ed. *Planning Middle Eastern Cities*. New York: Routledge, 2004.

Evers, Hans-Dieter and Korff, Rudiger. *Southeast Asian Urbanism*. New York: St Martin's Press, 2000.

Genard, Jean-Louis. "Architecture and Reflexivity." Eds. Pflieger, Géraldine, Pattaroni, Luca, Jemelin, Christopher and Kaufmann, Vincent. *The Social Fabric of the Networked City*. Lausanne: EPFL Press, 2008. 89-107.

Glancy, Jonathan. "Move over Sydney: Zaha Hadid's Guangzhou Opera House." *The Guardian*, 28 February 2011. <http://www.guardian.co.uk/artanddesign/2011/feb/28/guangzhou-oper a-house-zaha-hadid>.

Goss, Jon. "Urbanization.". Eds. Leinbach, Thomas R. and Ulack, Richard eds. *Southeast Asia: Diversity and Development*. Upper Saddle River: Prentice Hall, 2000.

Held, David. "Democracy, the Nation-State and the Global System." *Economy and Society* 20 (1991): 138-72.

Heller, Agnes. *Aesthetics and Modernity*. Lanham: Lexington Books, 2011.

Writing Spaces: Travel, Global Cities and Landscapes
Editors: I-Chun Wang, Mary Theis, and Christopher Larkosh

Hendrix, John. "Architecture as the Psyche of a Culture." Eds. Emmons, Paul, Hendrix, John, and Lomholt, Jane. *The Cultural Role of Architecture*. Abingdon: Routledge, 2012. 208-16.

Höweler, Eric. *Skyscraper*. London: Thames & Hudson, 2003.

Hulshof, Michiel, and Roggeveen, Daan. *How the City Moved to Mr Sun*. Amsterdam: Sun Architecture Publishers, 2011.

Ibelings, Hans, *Supermodernism: Architecture in the Age of Globalization*. Rotterdam: NAi Publishers, 1998.

Jacobs, Jane, *Edge of Empire: Postcolonialism and the City*. London: Routledge, 1996.

Jones, Gavin W.. "Urbanization Trends in Asia: Conceptual and Definitional Challenges." Eds. Champion, Tony and Hugo, Graeme eds. *New Forms of Urbanization*. Aldershot: Ashgate, 2004. 113-31.

Kaspirin, Ron. *Urban Design: The Composition of Complexity*. New York: Routledge, 2011.

Kaufmann, Daniel, Léautier, Frannie, and Mastruzzo, Massimo eds. "Globalization and Urban Performance." Eds. Léautier, Frannie, *Cities in a Globalizing World*. Washington DC: The World Bank, 2006. 27-67.

Knox, Paul L.. *Cities and Design*. Abingdon: Routledge, 2011.

Komninos, Nicos. *Intelligent Cities and Globalization of Innovation Networks*. London: Routledge, 2008.

Kusno, Abidin. *Behind the Postcolonial: Architecture, Urban Space and Political Cultures in Indonesia*. London: Routledge, 2000.

Lu, Duanfang. "Entangled Histories of Modern Architecture." Eds. Lim, William S.W and Chang, Jiat-Hwee. *Non West Modernist Past*. Singapore: World Scientific Publishing, 2012, 59-68.

McCulloch, Rachel. "Globalization: Historical Perspective and Prospects." Eds. Lee, and Kyung Tae. *Globalization and the Asia Pacific Economy*. New York: Routledge, 2002. 6-24.

McKinnon, Malcolm. *Asian Cities: Globalization, Urbanization, and Nation-Building*. Singapore: NIAS Press, 2011.

Morley, Ian. "Abstracting the City." Eds. Hasmath, Reza and Hsu, Jennifer. *China in an Era of Transition*. New York: Palgrave Macmillan, 2009. 61-78.

Olds, Kris. *Globalization and Urban Change*. Oxford: Oxford University Press, 2001.

Parker, Simon. *Cities, Politics, and Power*. London: Routledge, 2011.

Palen, John J.. *The Urban World*. Boston: McGraw Hill, 2002.

Rosenau, James N. and Wildsmith, Diane. "Jakarta as a Site of Fragmegrative Tensions." Eds. Bishop, Ryan, Philips, John, and Yeo, Wei-Wei eds.

Postcolonial Urbanism: Southeast Asian Cities and Global Processes. New York: Routledge, 2003. 187-202.

Schwab, William A., *Deciphering the City.* Upper Saddle River, NJ: Pearson Education, 2005.

Skirbekk, Gunnar, *Multiple Modernities.* Hong Kong: Chinese University Press, 2011.

Sun, Tom T.H. and Liu, Paul K.C., "Urbanization in Taiwan in the New Millenium." Eds. Ness, Gayle and Talwar, Prem eds, *Asian Urbanization in the New Millennium.* Singapore: Times Publishing Limited, 2005. 429-58.

Soon, Tay Kheng and Goh, Robbie B.H.. "Reading the Southeast Asian City in the Context of Rapid Economic Growth." Eds. Goh, Robbie B.H. and Yeoh, Brenda S.A. *Theorizing the Southeast Asian City as Text.* Singapore: World Scientific, 2003. 13-27.

The United Nations. *World Urbanization Prospects: The 2001 Revision Data Table and Highlights.* New York: United Nations, 2002.

The United Nations. *World Urbanization Prospects: The 2009 Revision.* New York: United Nations, 2009. See http://esa.un.org/unpd/wup/index.htm <accessed January 29 2012>. UN Habitat, *State of the World's Cities 2004-5: Bridging the Urban Divide.* London: Earthscan, 2005.

UN Habitat. *State of the World's Cities 2010-11: Bridging the Urban Divide.* London: Earthscan, 2008.

Yu, Zhu. "Changing Urbanization Processes and In Situ Rural-Urban Transformation." Eds. Champion, Tony and Hugo, Graeme eds, *New Forms of Urbanization.* Aldershot: Ashgate, 2004. 207-28.

World Bank Policy Research Report. *Globalization, Growth, and Poverty.* New York: Oxford University Press, 2002.

Notes on Contributors

Editors

Wang, I-Chun

I-Chun Wang is Professor of English and former Dean of the College of Liberal Arts at National Sun Yat-sen University where she teaches Renaissance and twentieth century drama, and directs the Center for the Humanities. Her research interests include comparative literature, Chinese and Taiwan dramas and English Renaissance drama. She edited two special issues for Purdue University. Her publications have appeared in *Gendered Boundaries* (*Studies in Comparative Literature* 28), *Gender and Boundary, East Asian Cultural and Historical Perspectives, and Identity Politics.* Her full-length studies include *Disciplining Women: the Punishment of Female Transgressors in English Renaissance Drama* (1997) and *Empire and Ethnicity: Empire and Ethnic Imagination in Early Modern English Drama* (2011).

Theis, Mary

Mary E. Theis is Professor of French and Russian at Kutztown University of Pennsylvania in Kutztownm, Pennylvania. She earned her B.A. in Russian from the Univesity of Iowa and received her masters in Russian Literature and her doctorate in Comparative Literature from the University of Illinois at Urbana-Champaign.
A specialist in meta-utopian reflections in current utopian and dystopian literature, she has presented numberous conference papers and published comparative articles and a book, *Mothers and Masters in Contemporary Utopian and Dystopian Literature* (Peter Lang, 2009), on this subject. Currently, she is also doing a comparative study of French and francophone literatuer and drama and completing her intercultural communication, she teaches modern Russian, French, and francophone literature along with French and francophone film.

Larkosh, Christopher

Christopher Larkosh is Assistant Professor of Portuguese at the University of Massachusetts Dartmouth (USA). Among his areas of research are comparative literature, translation studies, gender/sexuality, and migration and diaspora studies, specifically in relation to the Portuguese late colonial experience in Asia. He is the editor of the collection entitled _Re-Engendering Translation: Transcultural Practice, Gender/Sexuality and the Politics of Alterity_ (St. Jerome, 2011), as well as the co-editor of a second volume on German-Brazilian interculturalities, _Kulturconfusão_ (forthcoming with DeGruyter, 2013).

Contributors

Barros-Grela, Eduardo

Dr. Barros-Grela is an Associate Professor in the Department of English at A Coruna University (Spain), where he teaches American Studies and Cultural Studies. He is a graduate of the State University of New York (MA and Ph.D.). In 2002-2003 he worked as a Funded Research Fellow at the Humanities Institute (New York) and then was hired as a Professor at California State University (2003-2007). His academic interests include cultural studies, posthuman aesthetics, *in*organic bodies and spaces, visual studies, and the dialectics of representation and performance. His publications include works on American Studies (*American Secrets. The Politics and Poetics of Secrecy in the Literature and Culture of the United States*), Film ("Heterotopia Meets Autopia: David Lynch's Aesthetics of Californian Spatialities"), Ecocriticism ("Imaginary Representations and Cultural Performances of Ecocriticism"), Cultural Studies ("Performances of Uncertainty in Spaces of Contingency: Aesthetic Confinement and Mechanisms of Silencing in Paul Auster, Haruki Murakami, and Park Chan-wook" and "Chicano Visualities: A Multicultural Rewriting of Californian Spatialities"), and Literature ("Dystopian Scenarios in Heterotopic Spaces. Paul Auster's *Man in the Dark*").

Bobadilla-Pérez, María

Dr. Bobadilla-Pérez is an Assistant Professor in the Department of Specific Didactics at A Coruna University (Spain), where she teaches English Language teaching and literature. She received a Ph.D. in Languages and Literature at the State University of New York (2004) and has a Ph.D. in the same area from the Universidad Complutense of Madrid (2006). Her academic interests include gender studies, nineteenth century English literature, visual studies and ESL teaching methodologies. She has published on Gender and Literature studies (*Woman and Education in the Victorian Novel. The Governess as a Model in Jane Eyre*), Latino Literature *(Latino Literature in the United States. The Construction of Identity through Memory)*, and Critical Theory (*Postmodernism and its Consequences over Theoretical and Practical Feminism: Susan Bordo and Judith Butler).*

Borim, Dário
Dário Borim is Associate Professor and Chair of the Department of Portuguese at UMass Dartmouth. He is also translator, creative writer, concert producer, and radio programmer at WUMD. He holds a BA in languages from Universidade Federal de Minas Gerais, two MAs, in creative writing and Luso-Brazilian literature, and a Ph.D. in Hispanic and Luso-Brazilian literature and linguistics from University of Minnesota, Twin Cities. He teaches graduate and undergraduate courses in the Portuguese language, Luso-Brazilian literature, cinema, theater, and music.

Chen, Eric Chia-Hwan
Eric Chia-Hwan Chen is Assistant Professor in the Department of Children English Education, National Taipei University of Education, Taiwan. He received his PhD in Comparative Literature from University of Warwick, UK, with a thesis entitled *Images of the Other, Images of the Self: Reciprocal Representations of the British and the Chinese from the 1750s to the 1840s* in 2007. His research interest include imagology of comparative literature, stereotypes of the British and the Chinese in *Punch*, and the images of the British in the Chinese Opium Wars literature.

Chetty, Rajendra
Rajendra Chetty is professor and head of the department of research in the Faculty of Education and Social Sciences at the Cape Peninsula University of Technology. His research interests are commonwealth literature, literacy and race and class issues in education. He currently serves as the President of the English Academy of Southern Africa. He co-edited *The Diaspora Writes Back* (2005), *Transnationalisms and Diasporas* (2010) and *Trauma and Resistance: Post 1994 South African Writing* (2010). His most recent publication is *The Vintage Book of South African Indian Writing* (2010).

Writing Spaces: Travel, Global Cities and Landscapes
Editors: I-Chun Wang, Mary Theis, and Christopher Larkosh

Kim, Won-Chung

Won-Chung Kim is a professor of English Literature at Sungkyunkwan University in Seoul, South Korea. He received his Ph.D. from the University of Iowa, and has published articles on American ecopoets including Gary Snyder, Wendell Berry, Robinson Jeffers, A.R. Ammons, and W.S. Merwin in journals such as *ISLE* (*Interdisciplinary Studies of Literature and Environment*), *Comparative American Studies*, *Foreign Literature Studies*, and *Journal of English Language and Literature*. He has co-edited with Simon Estok *East Asian Ecocriticisms: A Critical Reader* (Palgrave Macmillan). Kim has also translated ten books of Korean poetry into English, including *Cracking the Shell: Three Korean Ecopoets* and *Herat's Agony: Selected Poems of Chiha Kim*, and John Muir's *My First Summer in the Sierra* and H.D. Thoreau's *Natural History Essays* into Korean. As a founding member of ASLE-Korea, Kim has served as the organization's president.

Koçak, Ateşci Betül

Betül Ateşci Koçak was born in Istanbul in 1984. She got her *BA in American Culture and Literature at Istanbul University* in 2006. She worked as an English Language Teacher for various languages courses in Turkey and Spain. She did her *MA in Advanced English Studies: Languages and Cultures in Contact at Salamanca University* in 2010. She is still a PhD student at the same university with her thesis 'Post 9/11 Fiction'.

Lee, Melissa

Melissa Lee lectures at the Chinese University of Hong Kong on American and Diaspora literature. She is the author of *Disenfranchised from America* (UPA 2009), She has published numerous articles on Early Modern as well as Diaspora literature. Lee is also a public art curator that has worked on several art projects in Hong Kong, New Zealand and Canada.

Mi, Jiayan

Jiayan Mi is an Associate Professor of Comparative Literature, Film and Critical Theory in the departments of English and Wold Languages & Cultures at The College of New Jersey. He is the author of *Self-Fashioning and Reflexive Modernity in Modern Chinese Poetry, 1919-1949* (2004) and co-editor with Sheldon Lu of *Chinese Ecocinema in the Age of Environmental Challenge*

(2010). He is currently completing a book project, tentatively titled *Heteroscape: Topography and Contested Navigation in Modern Chinese Literature, Art and Film*. He has published articles in Chinese and English on comparative literature, visual and cinematic culture, globalization and cultural consumption, and East-West postcolonial and gender politics.

Morley, Ian

Ian Morley is based in the Chinese University of Hong Kong's Department of History. His research centers upon the design of settlements in the modern era. He has participated in television documentaries on the Taipei 101 Tower for *The Discovery Channel* and *Voom!*, as well as been interviewed by *The Wall Street Journal Asia*, *The Los Angeles Times* and *La Stampa* about colonial architecture in Burma. He is the Book Review Editor for *Urban Morphology: Journal of the International Seminar on Urban Form*, and an editorial board member of the journal *Planning Perspectives*.

Rawson, Claude

Claude Rawson is the author of several books on Swift, Fielding and other eighteenth-century authors, and of numerous articles and reviews both in specialist journals and in the Times Literary Supplement, *New York Times* Book Review and London Review of Books. He is General Editor of the *Cambridge History of Literary Criticism*, the Cambridge Edition of *the Works of Jonathan Swift, the Blackwell Critical Biographies* and *the Unwin Critical Library*. From 1989 to 2001 he served as General Editor and Chairman of the Yale Boswell Editions. He was an Editor of the *Modern Language Review* and *Yearbook of English Studies* from 1974 to 1988.

Rawson is a Fellow of the American Academy of Arts and Sciences, and serves on the Educational Advisory Board of the John Simon Guggenheim Memorial Foundation. He is an Honorary Professor of the University of Warwick, where he once served at chairman of the Department of English and Comparative Literary Studies. He is a former President of the British Society for Eighteenth-Century Studies. He was the Clifford Lecturer for 1992 (American Society for Eighteenth-Century Studies), and Bateson Lecturer for 1999 (University of Oxford). He has lectured widely in Europe, the Americas, Australasia and the Far East.

Writing Spaces: Travel, Global Cities and Landscapes
Editors: I-Chun Wang, Mary Theis, and Christopher Larkosh

Shao, Yu-chuan
Yu-chuan Shao teaches contemporary literature and cultural studies at National Taiwan Normal University. Her recent publications include "Istanbul in Melancholy: Culture Fetishism and Postcolonial Trauma in Orhan Pamuk's *The White Castle*" (2012) and "Cosmopolitanism in Tienxin Zhu's *Ancient Capital (Gudu)*" (2010). Currently, she is working on the issues concerning visual culture and the limit of identity politics.

Yokota-Murakami, Takayuki
Associate professor. The Graduate School of Language and Culture. Osaka University. PhD in comparative literature, Princeton University. Research interests range from modern Japanese and Russian literature, history of sexuality, translation, and literary theories, to contemporary Japanese popular culture (esp. manga). Publication includes *Don Juan East/West: On the Problematics of Comparative Literature* (SUNY P, 1998), "The Creation of 'A Lady': Gender and Sexual Politics in the Earliest Japanese Translations of Walter Scott and Charlotte Brontë" (in *Re-engendering Translation: Transcultural Practice, Gender/Sexuality adn the Politics of Alterity,* ed. by Christopher Larkosh [Manchester, UK: St. Jerome, 2011]), etc.

Index